2009–2010 YEARBOOK

The Education Center, Inc.
Greensboro, North Carolina

The Mailbox® 2009–2010 Kindergarten Yearbook

Managing Editor, *The Mailbox* Magazine: Sharon M. Tresino

Editorial Team: Becky S. Andrews, Diane Badden, Jennifer Bragg, Kimberley Bruck, Karen A. Brudnak, Kimberly Brugger-Murphy, Pam Crane, Lynn Drolet, Amy Erickson, Sarah Foreman, Pierce Foster, Margaret Freed (COVER ARTIST), Tazmen Hansen, Marsha Heim, Lori Z. Henry, Krystle Short Jones, Debra Liverman, Kitty Lowrance, Jennifer Nunn, Tina Petersen, Gary Phillips (COVER ARTIST), Mark Rainey, Greg D. Rieves, Kelly Robertson, Hope Rodgers, Rebecca Saunders, Hope Taylor Spencer, Donna K. Teal, Rachael Traylor, Zane Williard

ISBN10 1-56234-956-2
ISBN13 978-1-56234-956-1
ISSN 1088-5552

Printed in the United States of America.

The Education Center, Inc.
P.O. Box 9753
Greensboro, NC 27429-0753

Look for *The Mailbox*® 2010–2011 Kindergarten Yearbook in the summer of 2011. The Education Center, Inc., is the publisher of *The Mailbox*®, *Teacher's Helper*®, and *Learning*® magazines, as well as other fine products. Look for these wherever quality teacher materials are sold, call 1-800-714-7991, or visit www.themailbox.com.

RRDWI061022353

Contents

Math Units

Seasonal Units

Arts & Crafts

Arts & crafts

On the Board

After these projects are complete, store them in a safe location. Then repeat the project at the end of the year and have students assess their progress.

Materials for one project:

9" x 12" brown paper   crayons
8½" x 11" white paper   green or black watercolors
apple cutout   paintbrush
                                                         glue

Steps:

1. Cut out the center of the brown paper to make a frame.
2. Use the crayons to draw a self-portrait on the white paper, making sure to press hard.
3. Paint the paper with the watercolors.
4. When the paint is dry, glue the frame atop the painted paper.
5. Write your name on the apple cutout and glue it to a corner of the frame.

Sue Fleischmann
Mary, Queen of Saints School
West Allis, WI

Geometric Bus

Have students sing "The Wheels on the Bus" as a follow-up to making these shapely projects.

Materials for one bus:

tagboard school bus tracer   two 1" orange triangles (headlights)
child's photo (no larger than 2")   two 2" black circles (wheels)
9" x 12" yellow construction paper   scissors
three 2" blue squares (windows)   two brads
1½" x 3" green rectangle (door)   glue

Steps:

1. Trace the school bus onto the yellow paper and cut it out.
2. Glue the windows, headlights, and door to the bus as shown.
3. Use brads to fasten the wheels to the bus.
4. Trim the photo and glue it to one of the bus windows.

Diane L. Tondreau-Flohr-Henderson
Kent City Elementary
Kent City, MI

"A-peel-ing" Apples

Have youngsters make these apples to give their fine-motor skills a workout.

Materials for one apple:

red construction paper apple cutout, programmed as shown
white construction paper apple cutout
brown and green construction paper scraps
glue
scissors
stapler

Steps:

1. On the white apple cutout, draw a picture of your favorite food made with apples.
2. Cut along the lines of the red apple.
3. Staple the red apple atop the white apple.
4. Cut a stem from the brown paper scraps and a leaf from the green paper scraps. Write your name on the leaf. Glue the cutouts to the apple.

Diane L. Tondreau-Flohr-Henderson
Kent City Elementary
Kent City, MI

Up, Up, and Away

Plan to complete these colorful projects over two days to allow time for drying between steps.

Materials for one project:

rubber spatula
nonmentholated shaving cream
tagboard hot-air balloon cutout
brown construction paper scrap
two equal-size lengths of yarn
different colors of tempera paint
paintbrush
scissors
tape

Steps:

1. Squirt a generous amount of shaving cream onto a covered surface.
2. Squeeze dollops of paint onto the shaving cream.
3. Use the paintbrush handle to swirl the colors together.
4. Pat the cutout on the colored shaving cream.
5. Lift the cutout and use the spatula to scrape off the excess shaving cream.
6. Cut a basket from the brown construction paper.
7. When the project is dry, tape one end of each yarn length to the back of the basket and the other ends to the back of the balloon.

adapted from an idea by Bernice Regenstein
Rochester, NY

Arts & crafts

Pumpkin Pal

To simplify the hand tracing required for this project, have students ask their classmates to help them trace their hands.

Materials for one pal:

9" x 12" black paper
9" x 12" white paper
two 2" x 12" purple paper strips (legs)
2" x 3" green paper strip (stem)

9" paper plate
orange paint
paintbrush
scissors
glue

Steps:

1. Paint the plate orange and set it aside to dry.
2. Trace your feet (with your shoes on) on the black paper and cut the tracings out. Glue each shoe cutout to one end of a paper strip leg.
3. Cut two eyes, a nose, and a mouth from the leftover black paper.
4. Trace your hands on the white paper and cut the tracings out.
5. Assemble the pal by gluing the legs, hands, facial features, and stem to the plate as shown.

Diane L. Tondreau-Flohr-Henderson
Kent City Elementary
Kent City, MI

A Shapely Scarecrow

This project doubles as a fun way to practice shape recognition and identification.

Materials for one scarecrow:

two 2" x 6" rectangles (legs)
two 1½" x 4" rectangles (arms)
4" square (body)
3" circle (head)

4" equilateral triangle (hat)
12" x 18" construction paper
crayons
glue

Steps:

1. Glue the body to the center of the construction paper.
2. Draw facial features on the head; then glue the head to the paper so that it touches the body.
3. Glue the hat to the paper, overlapping the head slightly.
4. Glue the legs and arms to the paper, overlapping the body slightly.
5. If desired, use crayons to draw additional features and background details.

Diane L. Tondreau-Flohr-Henderson

"Whoooo's" There?

Make this three-dimensional project after a read-aloud of *Owl Moon* **by Jane Yolen.**

Materials for one project:

plastic soda or water bottle cap
9" yellow paper circle
6" or 7" paper plate
orange and brown paper scraps
brown paint

2 sticky dots (eyes)
black marker
scissors
bottle of glue
paintbrush

Steps:

1. Paint the plate brown (owl).
2. When the paint is dry, cut a beak from the orange paper and glue it on the owl. Then attach the sticky dot eyes and draw pupils.
3. Tear feather shapes from the brown paper and glue them to the owl as shown.
4. Glue the plastic cap to the paper circle (moon) and then glue the owl atop the cap.

Cynthia Jamnik
Our Lady Queen of Peace School
Milwaukee, WI

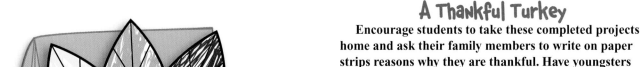

A Thankful Turkey

Encourage students to take these completed projects home and ask their family members to write on paper strips reasons why they are thankful. Have youngsters place the strips in the bags and then tuck the turkeys away for next year.

Materials for one turkey:
copy of the patterns on page 16
lunch-size brown paper bag
crayons
scissors
glue

Steps:

1. Color and cut out the patterns.
2. Place the bag on the work surface with the flap side down.
3. Glue the feathers to the bag and then glue the turkey head atop the feathers.
4. Open the bag so it stands up; then fold the top of the bag down.

Donna Follett, Kids Inn, Amherst, NH

Arts & Crafts

Big-Bellied Santa

Hang these jolly fellows on a bulletin board for a "ho-ho-holiday" display.

Materials for one Santa:

copy of page 17   scissors
red disposable plastic bowl   stapler
cotton balls   glue
crayons

Steps:

1. Color and cut out the patterns.
2. Place the bowl upside down and staple the patterns to the rim of the bowl as shown.
3. Stretch out a few cotton balls and glue them to the hat, face, mittens, and boots as shown.

Janice Shuman
Saint Brigid School
South Boston, MA

Mitten Wreath

Before they make these wreaths, have students use the mitten cutouts to practice patterning.

Materials for one wreath:

paper plate with the center cut out   glue
colorful mitten cutouts   hole puncher
scrap paper

Steps:

1. Glue mitten cutouts around the plate, overlapping them slightly.
2. Punch holes in the scrap paper.
3. Glue the resulting dots to the mittens for decoration.

Beth Kulczyk
Windom Elementary
Orchard Park, NY

Pleasing Penguin

Have each youngster write a message to a loved one on the back of her polar pal before giving it as a gift.

Materials for one penguin:

white paper heart (face)	black paint
2 black paper ovals (flippers)	paintbrush
3 yellow paper triangles (beak, feet)	glue
5 jumbo craft sticks	crayons
ribbon	scissors
index card	tape

Steps:

1. Paint the craft sticks.
2. When the paint is dry, make the penguin's body by gluing the craft sticks side by side to the index card.
3. Glue the beak to the face and draw two eyes.
4. Glue the face and flippers to the body as shown.
5. Cut notches in the feet so they look like webbed feet. Then glue the feet to the body.
6. Use tape to attach a ribbon hanger.

Michele Atlas
Eagle Point Elementary
Weston, FL

A Peaceful Dove

Honor Martin Luther King Jr. with this double-sided project that gives students practice folding and cutting.

Materials for one dove:

large white paper circle	glue
2 equal-size yellow paper triangles (beak)	crayons
	hole puncher
scissors	yarn

Steps:

1. Fold the circle in half, open it, and cut on the fold line.
2. Cut a few slits in one end of a semicircle (body) to look like tail feathers
3. Glue a beak and draw an eye on each side of the body.
4. Fold the other semicircle in half, open it, and cut on the fold line to make two wings.
5. Make a tab on each wing by folding down one of the straight edges. Glue one tab to each side of the body.
6. Hole-punch the top of the project. Thread a yarn length through the hole and tie its ends to make a hanger.

Amy Rodriguez
Public School 212
Brooklyn, NY

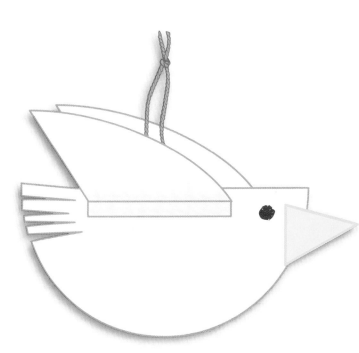

Arts & Crafts

Bag of Hearts

This project can be a heartfelt Valentine's Day gift for a parent or other special loved one.

Materials for one project:

construction paper copy of the poem on page 18
white paper lunch bag
five 4" colorful paper hearts
scrap paper

assorted craft supplies, such as glitter, stickers, and ribbon pieces
crayon or marker
scissors
glue

Steps:

1. Cut out the poem and glue it to one side of the bag.
2. Use the scrap paper and craft supplies to decorate the bag.
3. Write "I love you!" and other messages on each heart.
4. Place the hearts in the bag and fold down the top of the bag.

Sue Fleischmann, Mary, Queen of Saints School, West Allis, WI

On each heart inside
You will see
A special message
Just from me!

I love you!

Puppy Love

Made entirely from hearts, this puppy can be used as a valentine or in an eye-catching display.

Materials for one puppy:

2 large hearts (face and ears)
3 small hearts (eyes and nose)
glue
crayons
scissors

Wendy Jumper
Lewisburg Elementary
Olive Branch, MS

Steps:

1. Fold one of the large hearts in half and open it. Cut on the fold line to make two ears.
2. Glue the ears, eyes, and nose to the face, as shown.
3. Use crayons to draw a mouth, pupils, and other desired details.

Pot of Gold

As a follow-up to making this project, have students respond to the writing prompt "If I had a pot of gold…"

Materials for one pot of gold:
copy of the pot pattern from page 18   crayons
puffed corn cereal pieces   scissors
9" x 12" green construction paper   glue

Steps:
1. Color the pot and cut it out.
2. Glue the pot near the bottom of the green paper.
3. Glue the cereal pieces (gold nuggets) above the pot.

Jodi Darter
Cabool Elementary
Cabool, MO

A Big Cupcake!

Invite each youngster to make one of these tasty-looking treats in honor of his birthday.

Materials for one cupcake:
mixture of equal parts shaving   colorful paper scraps
  cream and glue (icing)   scissors
4" x 6" paper rectangle   crayons
9" x 12" construction paper   glue
small red paper circle (cherry)

Steps:
1. Trim the rectangle to resemble a cupcake liner and add desired details.
2. Glue the liner onto the construction paper.
3. Fingerpaint icing above the liner, as shown.
4. While the icing is still wet, cut the paper scraps into small pieces and gently press the resulting sprinkles and the cherry into the icing.

Arts & Crafts

A Bunny and a Basket

This simple-to-make bunny makes a great paper topper for a unique spring display!

Materials for one bunny:
copy of a basket pattern from page 19
two 2" x 5" pink paper ovals
two 3" x 9" white paper rectangles
6" white paper circle
8" white paper circle
pink pom-pom
scissors
glue
crayons

Steps:
1. Glue a pink oval to each of the white rectangles. Trim one end of each rectangle so the rectangles look like bunny ears.
2. Fold the 6-inch circle in half. Then unfold it and cut on the crease to make two bunny shoulders.
3. Glue the ears and the shoulders to the 8-inch circle (head) as shown.
4. Glue the pom-pom (nose) to the bunny's face.
5. Color and cut out the basket pattern and glue it to one of the bunny's shoulders.
6. Draw eyes, a mouth, and other desired details.

Sue Fleischmann
Mary, Queen of Saints School
West Allis, WI

Ladybug Card

Have each student give this card to a loved one as a special Mother's Day gift.

Materials for one card:
copy of a message card from page 19
two 6" red paper circles
3" black paper circle
black ink pad
brad
scissors
glue

Steps:
1. Use the ink pad to make fingerprints (spots) on one of the red circles.
2. When the ink is dry, fold the spotted circle in half. Then unfold it and cut on the crease.
3. Glue the black circle (head) to the other red circle as shown.
4. Sign your name on the message card. Then glue it to the center of the intact red circle.
5. Use the brad to attach the two cut halves (wings) to the intact circle.

Debbie Hill
Stone Elementary
Crossville, TN

Arts & Crafts

A Big Bug

This project doubles as a fun way to practice patterning!

Materials for one bug:

construction paper copy of the
    patterns on page 20
eight 3" construction paper circles
    (four in each of two colors)

crayons
scissors
glue

Steps:

1. To make the body, slightly overlap the circles in an *AB* pattern. Glue the circles together.
2. Color and cut out the patterns.
3. Glue the antennae cutouts to the head; then glue the head and wings to the body as shown.

Sue Fleischmann
Sussex, WI

Editor's Tip:
To have students practice *AAB* or *ABB* patterning, adjust the number of each of the colored circles.

A "Hand-y" Windsock

Hang these finished projects for a patriotic display.

Materials for one windsock:

white construction paper
red, white, and blue crepe paper streamers
shallow containers of red and blue paint

stapler
yarn
tape

Steps:

1. Dip the palm of one hand in a paint color. Make handprints on the paper. Repeat with the other paint color.
2. When the paint is dry, turn the paper over and tape lengths of crepe paper streamers along the bottom edge of the paper.
3. Roll the paper (handprint side out) into a cylinder, slightly overlapping the edges; then staple it closed.
4. To make a hanger, tape the ends of a length of yarn to opposite sides of the inside of the cylinder.

Nick Fountain
Goddard School
Skippack, PA

Turkey Head and Feather Patterns
Use with "A Thankful Turkey" on page 9.

TEC42045

TEC42046

Poem Patterns
Use with "Bag of Hearts" on page 12.

On each heart inside
You will see
A special message
Just from me!

TEC42047

TEC42047

¡ǝɯ ɯoɹɟ ʇsnſ
ǝƃɐssǝɯ lɐᴉɔǝds ∀
ǝǝs llᴉʍ no⅄
ǝpᴉsuᴉ ʇɹɐǝɥ ɥɔɐǝ uO

Pot Pattern
Use with "Pot of Gold" on page 13.

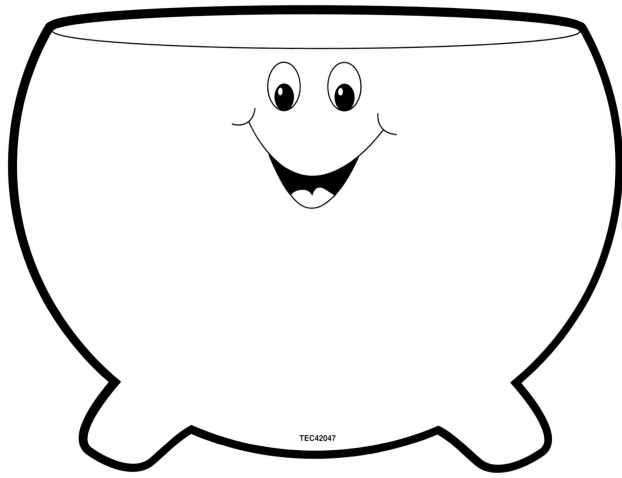

TEC42047

TEC42048

TEC42048

I spotted the best mom in the world— YOU!

I spotted the best mom in the world— YOU!

©The Mailbox® • TEC42048 • April/May 2010

©The Mailbox® • TEC42048 • April/May 2010

Bug Patterns

Use with "A Big Bug" on page 15.

TEC42049

THE BOOK CORNER

The Book Corner

Lunch

By Denise Fleming

No doubt youngsters will be eager to share what the hungry little mouse in this story might eat for dinner! In advance, cut out an enlarged gray copy of the mouse pattern on page 31 and attach the mouse to a sheet of chart paper. After a reading of the story, ask youngsters what the mouse might choose to eat for dinner. When a child suggests a food, have him name the color of the food and use a crayon to make a corresponding splotch on the mouse. Then label the youngster's food. Continue until each child has had a chance to share.
Identifying colors, dictating information

Shirley Gillette
Dorothy Stinson School
Safford, AZ

Denise Fleming

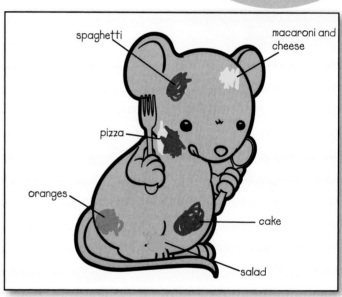

spaghetti

macaroni and cheese

pizza

oranges

cake

salad

The Kissing Hand

Written by Audrey Penn
Illustrated by Ruth E. Harper
and Nancy M. Leak

To prepare for this center activity, cut out ten enlarged copies of the raccoon pattern on page 31. Number the racoons from 1 to 10. Then place them at a center along with 55 Hershey's Kisses chocolate candies. (A 12-ounce bag contains about 72 pieces.) After reading the book aloud, have each child take a turn visiting the center and ordering the raccoons from one to ten. Next, have her place the appropriate number of kisses on each raccoon. After checking her work, give her a chocolate kiss for a special treat.
Identifying numbers, making sets

Lee Meehan
Miss Lee Ann's Inc.
Cranston, RI

The Kissing Hand
by AUDREY PENN

Illustrations by Ruth E. Harper and Nancy M. Leak

Child & Family Press

The Book Corner

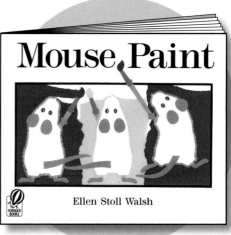

Mouse Paint

Written and illustrated by Ellen Stoll Walsh

Pairs of youngsters mix primary colors—and make friends—with this fun follow-up to the read-aloud! In advance, prepare shallow pans containing primary colors of paint. Help students recall that the mice had to mix two different colors to make green, purple, and orange. Then encourage each child in a pair to press his hand in a different color of paint. Have each pair make handprints on a sheet of paper programmed as shown. Next, prompt each child to rub his paint-covered hand against his partner's and make handprints that reveal the secondary color!

Jennifer Aubrey
North Dover Elementary
Dover, DE

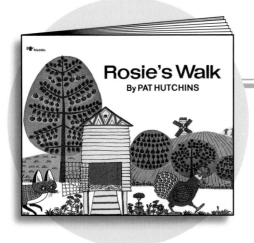

Rosie's Walk

Written and illustrated by Pat Hutchins

To reinforce positional words, take youngsters on a walk similar to Rosie's! As you lead youngsters on a walk throughout the school, take pictures as they travel through, around, over, and beside various rooms and objects. Have each child glue one of the photos to a separate sheet of paper labeled with the appropriate text. Then bind the pages in order behind a cover titled "The Kindergartners' Walk." Read aloud the resulting class book and then place it in your independent reading center.

Tawnie Bligh
Sea Gate Elementary
Naples, FL

The kindergartners went for a walk

across the playground.

around the flag pole.

past the office.

Pumpkin Day!
Written and illustrated by Nancy Elizabeth Wallace

With this whole-group activity, youngsters share what they learned about pumpkins during this informative read-aloud. Place a plastic pumpkin-shaped container on the floor. Then place white yarn (pulp) and craft foam seeds nearby. Prompt a child to share information she learned from the read-aloud. Then encourage her to choose a piece of pulp or a seed and place it in the pumpkin. Repeat the process with each remaining child. Then have youngsters note how the inside of the pumpkin is filled with yarn pulp and seeds, just like the diagram in the story.

I Know an Old Lady Who Swallowed a Pie
Written by Alison Jackson
Illustrated by Judith Byron Schachner

Youngsters feed their own little old lady with this environmental print activity! For each child, staple two red construction paper circles to make a flap. Then program the top circle as shown. Prompt each child to lift the flap and then cut and glue samples of food-related environmental print to the circle. Encourage her to add head, arm, and leg cutouts to the project in addition to any other desired details. Then help her read the text and identify the environmental print. That's one hungry lady!

The Book Corner

Literacy Ideas for Teachers®

Pattern Fish

Written by Trudy Harris
Illustrated by Anne Canevari Green

With this activity, youngsters make patterned fish similar to those in this colorful book! After a read-aloud of the story, place a few large fish cutouts at a center along with a supply of pattern blocks. Encourage each center visitor to place blocks on a fish to make a pattern. Then help him write his fish's pattern on a paper strip. If desired, take photos of the fish and display them on a wall with their written patterns. *Patterns*

Diane Billman
McKitrick Elementary
Lutz, FL

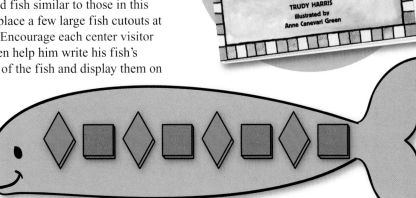

Diamond, square.

Old Black Fly

By Jim Aylesworth

Where is the old black fly buzzing? Why, on a variety of letters of course! Write letters on your board. Then read the story aloud. Next, tell youngsters that you see the old black fly sitting on a letter that makes a particular sound. Quietly give a flyswatter to a child; encourage him to find the letter that makes that sound and swat it. Erase the letter and exclaim that the fly got away. Repeat the activity until all the letters have been erased. *Initial consonant sounds*

Angie Kutzer
Garrett Elementary
Mebane, NC

Dream Snow
By Eric Carle

Students practice writing numerals with this adorable class book that's reminiscent of the story! After the read-aloud, have each child draw an animal on a 9" x 12" sheet of construction paper. Then have him place a transparency (or a piece of waxed paper) over his picture and brush it with a mixture of white paint and glue so the animal is concealed. When the paint is dry, stack the papers and transparencies between construction paper covers and bind them together. Then glue a copy of the prompt shown (without the number) on the back of the front cover and each paper except the last one. As you read the resulting story aloud, invite youngsters to complete the prompts, increasing the numbers in order through the story. *Writing numerals*

Andrea Lovejoy, Ben Franklin School, Milwaukee, WI

Then the snowflakes gently covered
8 with a white blanket.

My Crayons Talk
Written by Patricia Hubbard
Illustrated by G. Brian Karas

After reading the story aloud, ask youngsters to list other ways crayons talk. For example, crayons can be used to make signs, write letters, and illustrate stories. Write youngsters' ideas on a large sheet of paper titled "Our Crayons Talk." Then place the paper at a center and encourage youngsters to draw pictures on it. After each child has had an opportunity to add a picture, post the paper in your classroom. *Making a list*

Jo Ann O'Brien
Lilja Elementary
Natick, MA

Our Crayons Talk

Crayons can be used to
- illustrate stories
- color pictures in coloring books
- write notes
- decorate posters
- write your name

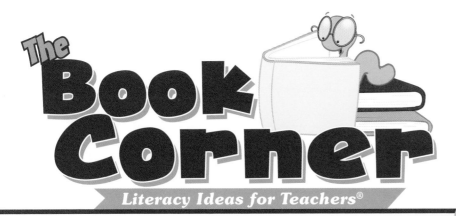

The Book Corner
Literacy Ideas for Teachers®

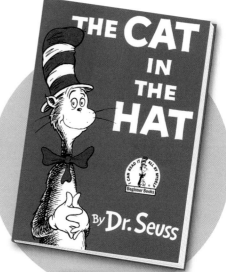

The Cat in the Hat
By Dr. Seuss

On a cold, wet day, Sally and her brother have nothing to do—that is, until the Cat in the Hat arrives. The mischievous feline conjures up all kinds of zany ways to pass the time, making it a day the twosome will never forget!

Youngsters practice early addition skills with this Cat in the Hat–themed booklet. To make a booklet for each child, staple four blank pages behind a hat-shaped cover. Have each child color red stripes on the cover. Then direct her to cut out the strips on a copy of page 32. Have her glue the title strip to the cover and each remaining strip to a different page. Prompt her to draw a picture to represent each addition sentence and then write the correct number in each blank. Finally, help her read her booklet aloud.

Ann Hestand, Watsonville, CA

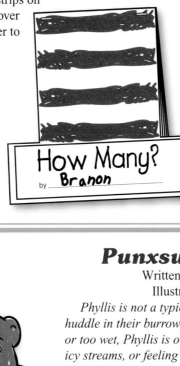

How Many?
by Branon

Tim has 1 cat.
Kim has 2 cats.
They have 3 cats in all.

Punxsutawney Phyllis
Written by Susanna Leonard Hill
Illustrated by Jeffrey Ebbeler

Phyllis is not a typical groundhog. While other groundhogs huddle in their burrows when the weather is too hot, too cold, or too wet, Phyllis is outside picking blackberries, wading in icy streams, or feeling the mud between her toes. Others laugh at her dream to be the next Punxsutawney Phil. After all, that position is reserved for boys. But on Groundhog Day, Phyllis's keen observation skills prove that she just might be the best groundhog for the job!

After a reading of the story, have youngsters make their own versions of Phyllis popping out of her burrow! Have each child brush glue on a paper cup and then place brown tissue paper over the glue. When the glue is dry, help her cut a slit in the bottom of the cup and insert a simple groundhog stick puppet (pattern on page 32) into the cup. Encourage youngsters to use the puppet to retell parts of the story.

Amy Rodriguez, Public School 212, Brooklyn, NY

Dear Tooth Fairy

Written by Pamela Duncan Edwards
Illustrated by Marie-Louise Fitzpatrick

Claire is six years old and still doesn't have a wobbly tooth. She's worried, so she writes letters to the tooth fairy. Interspersed with tips from the tooth fairy, the correspondence conveys Claire's excitement as she anticipates losing her first tooth.

With this idea, your youngsters can correspond with the tooth fairy just like the girl in the story. Encourage youngsters to dictate a letter to the tooth fairy as you write their words on an oversize tooth cutout. When the children leave for the day, compose a reply from the tooth fairy. Decorate the letter with glitter and then attach it to the tooth. If desired, place a special gift from the tooth fairy nearby, such as little tooth stickers. When students arrive for the day, read the letter aloud and present the gift.

Dear Tooth Fairy,

We hope that you bring us money when we lose our teeth. Some of us put our teeth in boxes. Kayla has a pillow that she puts her teeth in. Thank you for giving us money.

Miss B's Class

Dear Class,

The Tooth Fairy

Froggy's First Kiss

Written by Jonathan London
Illustrated by Frank Remkiewicz

Froggy is smitten with the new girl in class, Frogilina. His insides are all wiggly, and he can't take his eyes off her. They share smiles on the playground and treats at lunch. But when Frogilina gives Froggy a surprise kiss, he's not sure what to do!

Frogilina gives Froggy a different treat every day at lunch. What would your youngsters give Froggy for a treat? After a read-aloud of the story, review the treats Frogilina gives Froggy. Then have each child draw and label a different treat he believes Froggy will enjoy. Place all the treats in a lunchbox. Then gather students and reveal each new treat. During subsequent readings of the story, replace the treat names with youngsters' new treat ideas.

cupcake

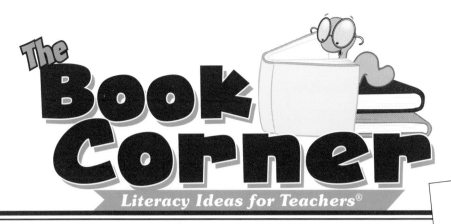

The Very Hungry Caterpillar
Written and illustrated by Eric Carle

Join a ravenous caterpillar as he eats his way through the days of the week. By Saturday he has eaten so much that he has a stomachache. But the caterpillar knows what to do. He eats a leaf; spins a chrysalis; and, more than two weeks later, emerges as a beautiful butterfly!

Your students will just adore this fun story innovation. After a read-aloud of the book, prompt each youngster to use the edge of an unwrapped crayon to color a paper plate green. Then have him draw and label on the plate a food item he particularly enjoys. During a second reading of the story, substitute the items the caterpillar ate on Saturday with the items your youngsters have chosen, displaying and reading the plates in turn. Then complete the read-aloud. If desired, post the plates on a wall with a plate decorated to resemble the caterpillar's head.

Molly Guinane, Sherwood Park Elementary
Fayetteville, NC

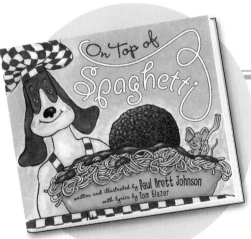

On Top of Spaghetti
By Paul Brett Johnson
With lyrics by Tom Glazer

What happens to a meatball after somebody sneezes? It's sent on a journey until it is smacked out of a ballpark and grows into a meatball-and-tomato-sauce tree!

Choose from the ideas below to pair this adorable book with a variety of skills!

- **Creating a story innovation:** Toss a crumpled sheet of brown tissue paper (meatball) to a child. Write a sentence on a sheet of chart paper telling who you tossed it to. Then have the child toss the meatball to a desired person or location. Have her dictate a sentence describing where it went. Prompt another child to pick up the meatball and repeat the process.

- **Writing:** For each child, label each page of a circle-shaped booklet with a different story element. Have each youngster write to describe each element and then draw matching pictures. Finally, have her color a plate red and then glue yarn and pom-poms (spaghetti and meatballs) to it. Bind the plate atop the booklet to make a taste-tempting cover.

- **Comparing sets:** Provide a bowl of brown pom-poms (meatballs), a spoon, and two plates of white yarn (spaghetti) for this partner activity. Each youngster takes a plate. Then she puts a spoonful of meatballs on her plate. After the youngsters count their meatballs, they compare amounts.

Hannah Teague, Ida Elementary, Ida, MI

The Book Corner
Literacy Ideas for Teachers®

Animals should definitely not wear clothing.
Written by Judi Barrett
and drawn by Ron Barrett

Animals Should Definitely <u>Not</u> Wear Clothing
Written by Judi Barrett
Illustrated by Ron Barrett

Why shouldn't animals wear clothing? Well, it could "be disastrous for a porcupine" and "make life hard for a hen." This book's easy-to-read text and silly illustrations will leave your students giggling as they discover these and other reasons why clothing is not a good fit for animals.

With this creative-writing activity, youngsters realize that animals should definitely not wear clothing! After the read-aloud, give each child a sheet of paper programmed with the prompt shown. Encourage each youngster to complete the prompt. Then have her draw a picture to match the words. Bind youngsters' finished work to make a class book and place the book in your independent reading center.

Kelsea Wright, Seal Elementary, Douglass, KS

An <u>alligator</u> should not wear <u>sandals</u> because <u>they would keep falling off its feet.</u>

Whopper Cake
Written by Karma Wilson
Illustrated by Will Hillenbrand

Happy birthday, Grandma! To celebrate, Granddad prepares to bake a whopper of a cake in this mouthwatering tall tale. In the end, the only thing bigger than this cake is Grandma's heart—and Granddad's mess!

Youngsters practice math skills when they create a cake recipe just as outlandish as Grandpa's recipe in this entertaining story! Number a set of cards from 40 to 60 and place them in a bag. Tell students that you are interested in making a cake that's even bigger than the whopper cake! Have youngsters decide on a name for the cake. Write the name on a sheet of chart paper. Then ask how many sticks of butter should go into the cake. Invite a child to draw a number from the bag and identify it. Then help her write the number and ingredient beneath the title. Continue in the same way with other common cake ingredients.

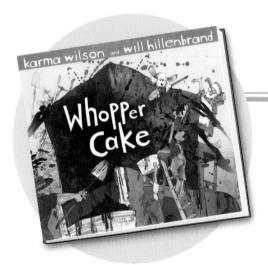

Super-Duper Giant Cake
56 sticks of butter
49 pounds of sugar
44 bags of flour
58 eggs
50 boxes of cocoa
59 bottles of vanilla
47 boxes of baking soda

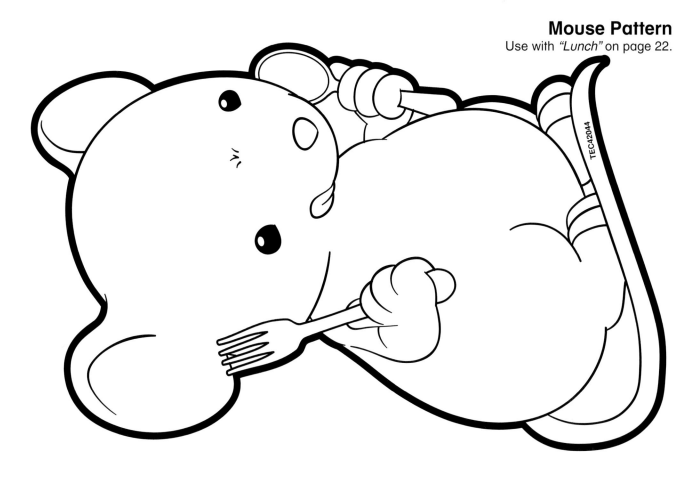

TEC42044

Raccoon Pattern
Use with *"The Kissing Hand"* on page 22.

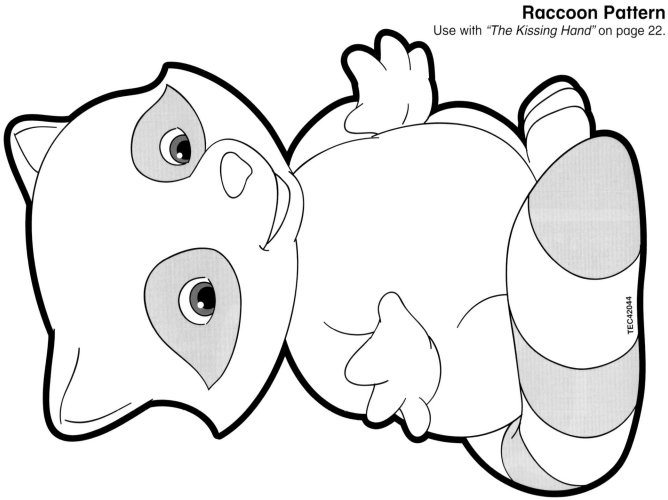

TEC42044

How Many?

by _____

Tim has 1 cat.

Kim has 2 cats.

They have _____ cats in all.

Sam has 2 hats.

Pam has 2 hats.

They have _____ hats in all.

Ken has 2 bats.

Jen has 3 bats.

They have _____ bats in all.

Mom has 1 mat.

Tom has 1 mat.

They have _____ mats in all.

Groundhog Pattern
Use with *"Punxsutawney Phyllis"* on page 27.

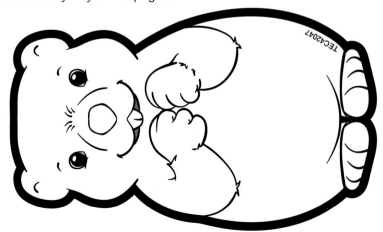

TEC42047

BUILDING MATH SKILLS

Building Math Skills

Decorated Dates

Calendar skills

Prior to the beginning of each month, cut a supply of cards sized to fit the date spaces of your classroom calendar. Then label each card with a date. Give a card dated with a school day to each student and have him write his name on the card and then decorate it. Attach each card to its space on the calendar. Each day at calendar time, invite the student whose card is displayed to be the calendar helper for the day. Have him announce the month, date, and year. Then invite him to help perform various calendar tasks.

Jessica Keller
Columbia Academy
Columbia, MD

Clap and Count

Number recognition, counting

To prepare, number separate large cards from 1 to 10. Invite a student to stand with her back to her classmates; then tape a card to her back. Next, guide the seated students to silently read the number and then clap in unison that number of times. Direct the standing student to count the number of claps and state the answer. Remove the card from her back and encourage her to check her answer. Continue with the remaining cards.

Ellen Moser
South Kortright Central School
South Kortright, NY

clap
clap
clap

Three!

3

Shape Up

Making and identifying shapes

For this hands-on activity, give each student a pipe cleaner. Instruct each youngster to bend his pipe cleaner to form a circle. Then have him unbend his pipe cleaner and make other shapes. After students have practiced making several shapes, divide the class into pairs. Instruct one partner to make a shape; then have the other partner name the shape. Continue for several rounds, encouraging students to switch roles each time.

Jennifer Foutch
Leisure Park Elementary
Broken Arrow, OK

Building Math Skills

What's the Rule?

Sorting

In advance, ask each child to bring a few plastic lids from home. To begin, gather students in a circle and then place the lids in the center. Sort the lids by one attribute and ask students to name the sorting rule. Then invite students to suggest other ways to sort. Enlist students' help in sorting the lids using one of the suggestions. Continue sorting as time allows.

Lucia Kemp Henry
Fallon, NV

Orderly Moves

Number order

Prepare a set of cards for half of your class by writing each number in sequence on a separate card. Then make an identical set for the other half of your class. Have each half of the class stand in a designated area; distribute a card set to the members of each group. Invite the groups to hop, skip, or jump around their areas. After a few moments, say, "Order, order!" as a signal for the members of each group to quickly arrange themselves in order. After checking each group's order, have students switch cards and play again.

Bonne Fuller, Dotlen Academy, Pottstown, PA

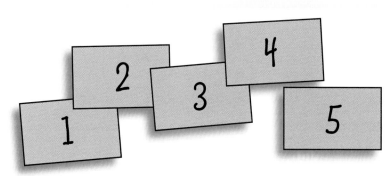

Shapely Creations

Shape recognition, counting, math vocabulary

In advance, cut a large supply of colorful paper shapes in various sizes. On a sheet of paper have a child glue desired shapes to create a picture. Then have him complete a copy of a recording sheet from page 42 and attach it to his shape picture. Encourage each child to describe his picture using shape names, positional words, and other math vocabulary, such as *more* and *less*.

Amy Rodriguez
Public School 212
Brooklyn, NY

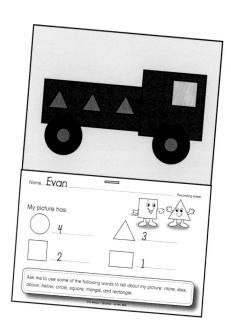

Building Math Skills

Just Jivin'

Counting by fives

Have youngsters do the "Five Jive" to integrate skip-counting and movement. Invite students to stand and hold their hands up in the air with palms facing out. Demonstrate a hand motion, such as moving your hand in circles. Then lead youngsters in counting by fives to 100 as they perform the motion, alternating hands with each number said. Repeat the activity using a different hand motion.

Jodi Darter, Cabool Elementary, Cabool, MO

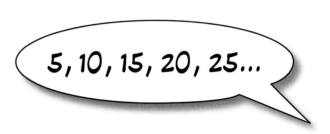

5, 10, 15, 20, 25...

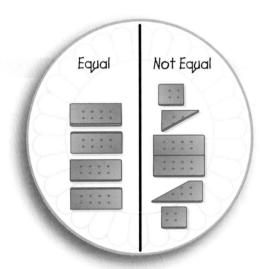

Equal   Not Equal

Math-Time Snack

Equal and unequal parts

Give each child two whole graham crackers and a paper plate labeled as shown. Instruct her to break one of the crackers on the division lines, creating four equal pieces. Then have her break the other cracker at random. Invite her to put each piece on the correct side of the plate. Then ask her to explain the placement of the pieces before eating her crackers.

Jodi Darter

Weather Calculations

Gathering data, adding

Prepare several copies of the weather cards from page 44 for use with a magnetic whiteboard. Arrange one set of the cards in a column near the side of the board and store the other cards nearby. Each school day of the month, invite youngsters to observe the weather. Draw a tally mark beside each card that matches their observations. On the last day of the month, have students total each set of tally marks. Then choose two weather types and write an addition problem using the numbers of tally marks. Use the other sets of cards as counters to help youngsters solve the problem. Continue with other weather combinations. To extend the activity, have students graph the results of the month's weather observations.

Rena Swyers, Placentino Elementary, Holliston, MA

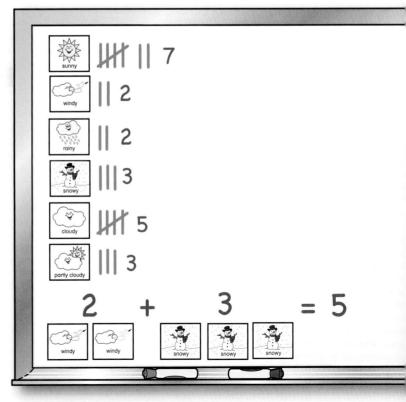

Building Math Skills

Ladybug's Spots

Odd and even numbers

Give each child a copy of the ladybug on page 46 and several black pom-poms (or black paper circles). Write a number on the board. Then direct each child to place the matching number of pom-poms on her ladybug, alternating between each wing. Explain that if each pom-pom has a partner on the other wing, the number is even. If one pom-pom does not have a partner, the number is odd. Have her compare the groups of pom-poms to determine whether the number is odd or even. Then have youngsters remove the pom-poms and repeat the activity with a different number.

Allison Griswold
Carelot Children's Center
East Lyme, CT

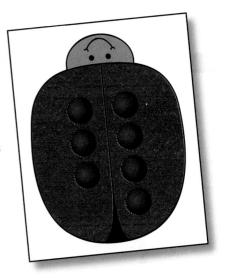

Leaping Lily Pads

Modeling subtraction

Youngsters pretend to be frogs with this whole-group activity. To prepare, attach green yarn to the floor in the shape of a large lily pad. Invite a desired number of students (frogs) to crouch on the lily pad. Tell a subtraction story, such as "Five frogs are on a lily pad. Three jump off. How many frogs are on the lily pad now?" Then lead a corresponding number of frogs in jumping off the pad to determine the answer. Invite the seated students to explain how the frogs solved the story problem. Continue until each child has a turn to be a frog. **To extend the activity,** write on the board the subtraction problem that matches the story.

Kathy Ginn, Jeffersonville Elementary, Jeffersonville, OH

Hanging Around

Problem solving

Monkeying around is the key to this small-group activity. Gather a magnetic hook, a large die, and six monkeys from a Barrel of Monkeys game. Place the hook on a magnetic surface. Hang some of the monkeys on the hook and place the other monkeys nearby. Invite a child to roll the die and count the number of dots. Ask another child to add or remove monkeys to match the number on the die. Then invite him to explain his problem-solving strategy. Continue until each child has had a turn to work with the monkeys.

Michelle Johns
Shrewsbury Elementary
Shrewsbury, PA

Editor's Tip:
Use links in place of the monkey game pieces.

There were three monkeys. I needed four, so I added one more!

Building Math Skills

Chicken Coops

Addition combinations

Little chicks and a hungry wolf lead to lots of barnyard math fun! Have students sit around two yarn circles (chicken coops). Then set out six large yellow pom-poms (chicks) and tell youngsters that the chicks need to go into the chicken coops to hide from a hungry wolf. Ask student volunteers to help put the chicks in one or both coops. Write the corresponding addition combination on chart paper. Then remove the chicks and play again to represent a different combination. Continue as described until you record all the possible combinations for six. If desired, repeat this activity with a different number of chicks.

Mary Lou Rodriguez
Primary Plus Elementary
San Jose, CA

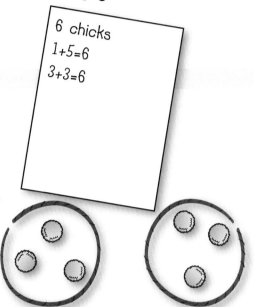

6 chicks
1+5=6
3+3=6

Ladybug's Questions

Data collection and analysis

Use this cute ladybug to gather information about your students. Laminate a jumbo ladybug cutout without spots and post it in a student-accessible location. Use a white crayon or paint pen to personalize a black paper circle (spot) for each child. If desired, laminate the spots for durability. Label a blank card with a question and use Sticky-Tac adhesive to attach the card to the ladybug. Then invite each child to answer the question by attaching his spot on the appropriate wing. Lead the class in counting the spots on each wing and comparing the numbers. To reuse the ladybug, simply remove the spots and post a different question.

Debbie Hill
Stone Elementary
Crossville, TN

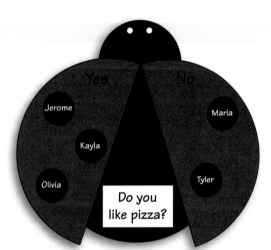

Invisible Numbers

Counting by twos

On the board, write the numbers needed to count by twos to 30. Have students name each number as you point to it. Then erase a few numbers and tell youngsters that those numbers are now invisible. Instruct youngsters to say the numbers again as you point to them, making sure to point to the invisible ones too. Repeat this process until all the numbers are invisible.

Diane Billman and Karen Fullilove
McKitrick Elementary
Lutz, FL

2   6 8   12 14 16   20 22 24

Editor's Tip:
Use this idea to reinforce other skills, such as counting by fives or tens to 100 and naming the alphabet.

Building Math Skills

Pepperoni Pizzas

Story problems

For this small-group activity, give each child a paper circle (pizza), ten red counters (pepperoni slices), and a copy of the recording sheet on page 48. Announce in story-problem style directions for making a pizza. For example, say, "Put two pepperoni slices on the pizza and then add four more pepperoni slices. How many pepperoni slices are on the pizza in all?" Have each child place the corresponding number of pepperoni slices on his pizza. Then, on his recording sheet, have him draw a pizza to match the one he made and write the matching number sentence below. Continue until the recording sheet is complete.

Michelle Claire, Solomon Elementary, Wahiawa, HI

A Hands-On Clock

Time

Reinforce telling time with this supersize prop. Gather number cards from 1 to 12, two large arrow cutouts of differing lengths, and a plastic hoop. Place the gathered materials on the floor and invite students to sit around them. Enlist youngsters' help in positioning the number cards and arrows inside the hoop to make a clock. Then name a time and have a volunteer move the arrows to show that time. Continue using different times.

Kristin Saunders
Grove Hill Elementary
Shenandoah, VA

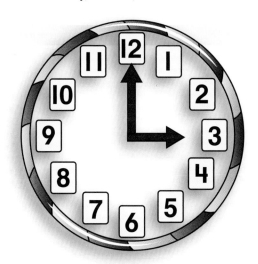

Making Sandwiches

Graphing

What type of sandwich do your youngsters prefer? Find out with this tasty graph. For each of three to five sandwich choices, gather two white paper strips (slices of bread) and write the sandwich choice on one of the slices. Place the labeled slices on a graph and set the remaining slices aside. Have each child color a personalized white paper rectangle to match the filling of her sandwich choice. Then invite her to place it above the appropriate bread slice on the graph. To complete each sandwich, place one of the remaining bread slices at the top of each column. Lead youngsters in counting the filling pieces inside each sandwich and comparing the numbers.

adapted from an idea by Marie E. Cecchini
West Dundee, IL

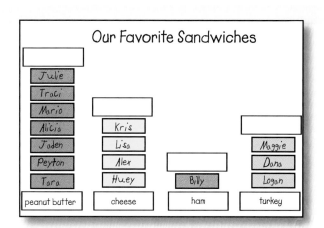

Order Up

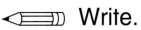
 Count.

 Write.

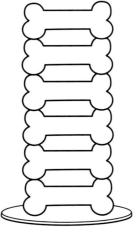

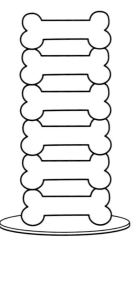

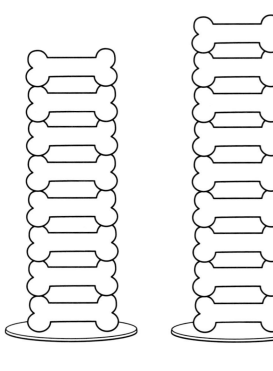

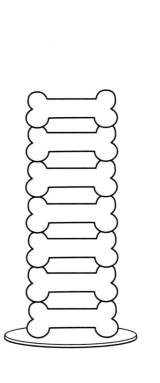

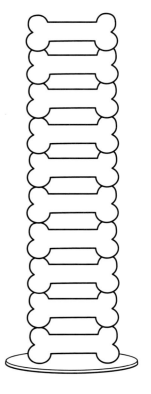

Apple Picking

Cut. Sort.

Glue to match.

Big Apples

Small Apples

Name ____________________ Recording sheet

My picture has:

 ____

 ____

 ____

 ____

Ask me to use some of the following words to tell about my picture: *more, less, above, below, circle, square, triangle,* and *rectangle.*

Name ____________________ Recording sheet

My picture has:

 ____

 ____

 ____

 ____

Ask me to use some of the following words to tell about my picture: *more, less, above, below, circle, square, triangle,* and *rectangle.*

©The Mailbox® • TEC42045 • Oct./Nov. 2009

 Note to the teacher: Use with "Shapely Creations" on page 35.

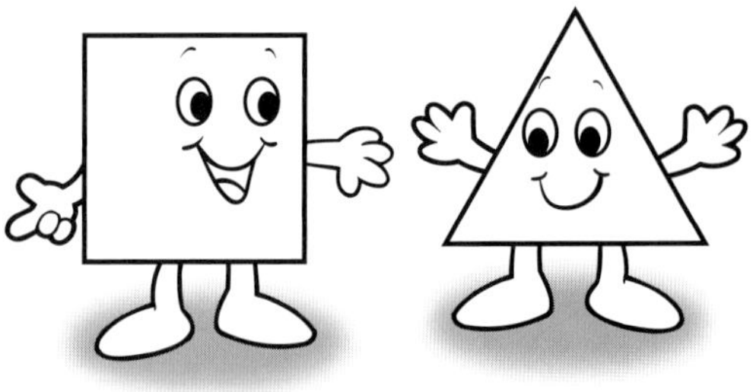

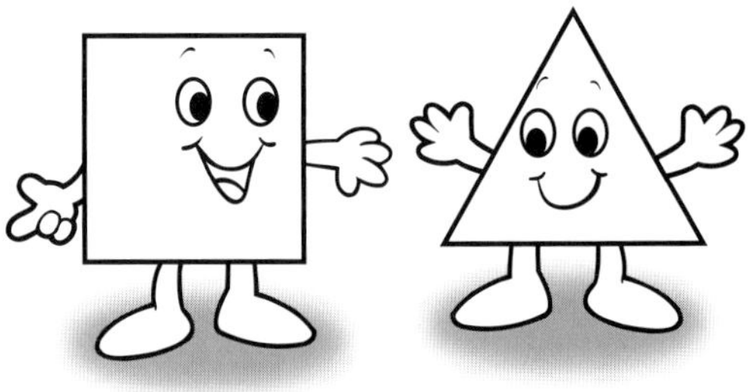

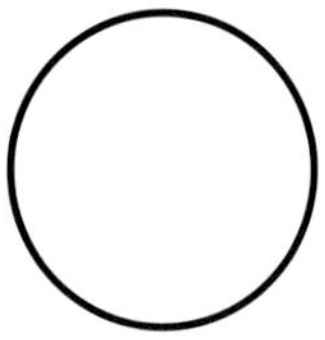

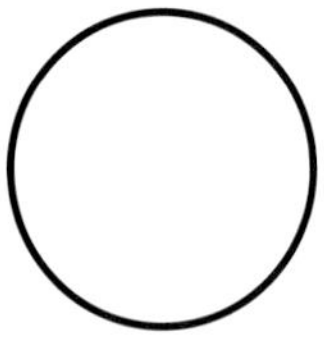

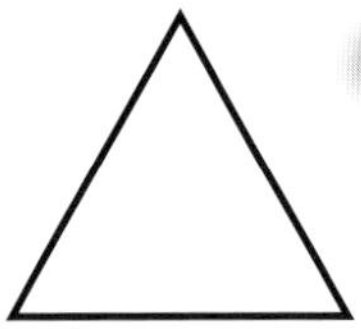

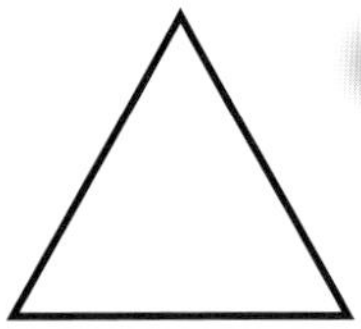

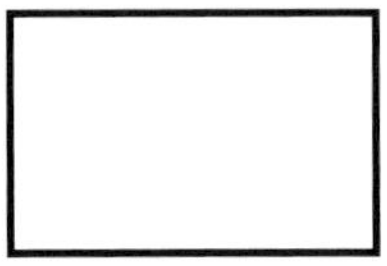

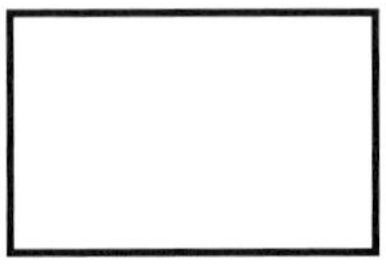

On the Farm

 Count.

 Color to make a graph.

Farm Animals

 Write how many.

 Circle.

 _____

Which has the **most?**

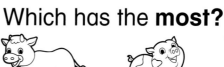

 _____

_____

Which has the **least?**

Weather Cards

Use with "Weather Calculations" on page 36.

sunny

TEC42046

windy

TEC42046

rainy

TEC42046

snowy

TEC42046

cloudy

TEC42046

partly cloudy

TEC42046

Make a Splash!

 Write the missing numbers.
Use the number bank.

Number Bank

3	4	6	8
10	12	13	14
15	16	18	19

7, _____, 9

11, _____, 13, _____, _____, 16

2, _____, _____, 5, _____, 7

8, 9, _____, 11, 12, _____

15, _____, 17, _____, _____, 20

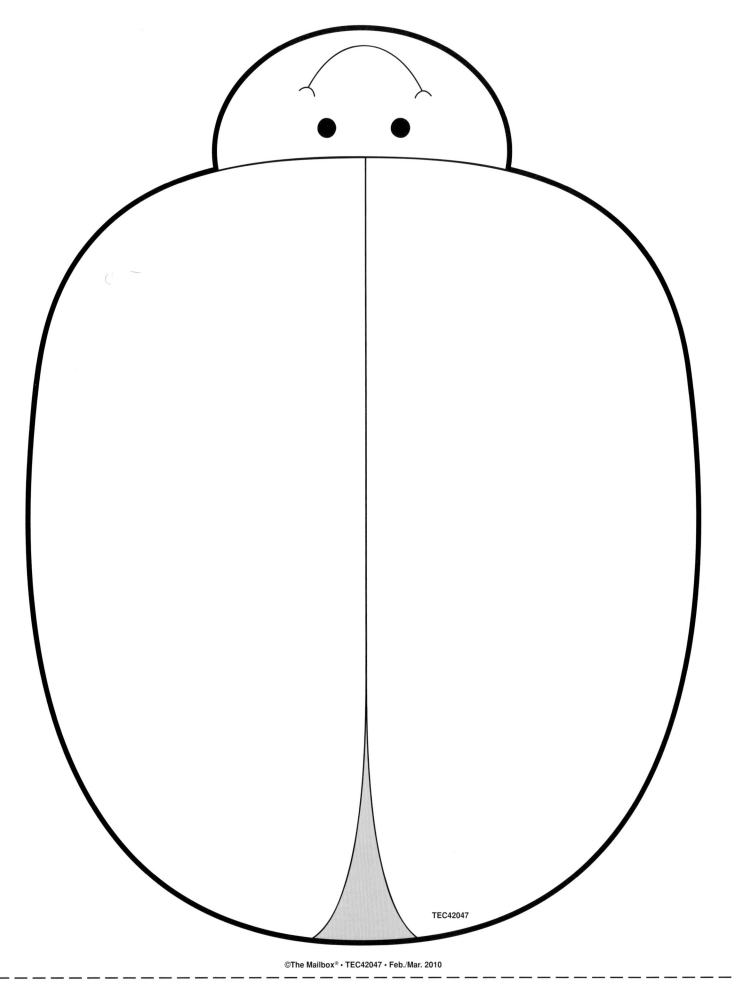

TEC42047

Note to the teacher: Use with "Ladybug's Spots" on page 37.

Buzzing to the Beat

Cut.

Add.

Use the counters to help you.

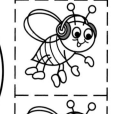

3 + 1 = _____   1 + 4 = _____

2 + 3 = _____   4 + 2 = _____

5 + 2 = _____   4 + 4 = _____

0 + 7 = _____   1 + 8 = _____

7 + 2 = _____   4 + 6 = _____

Pepperoni Pizzas

✏️ Draw.
   Add.
✏️ Write.

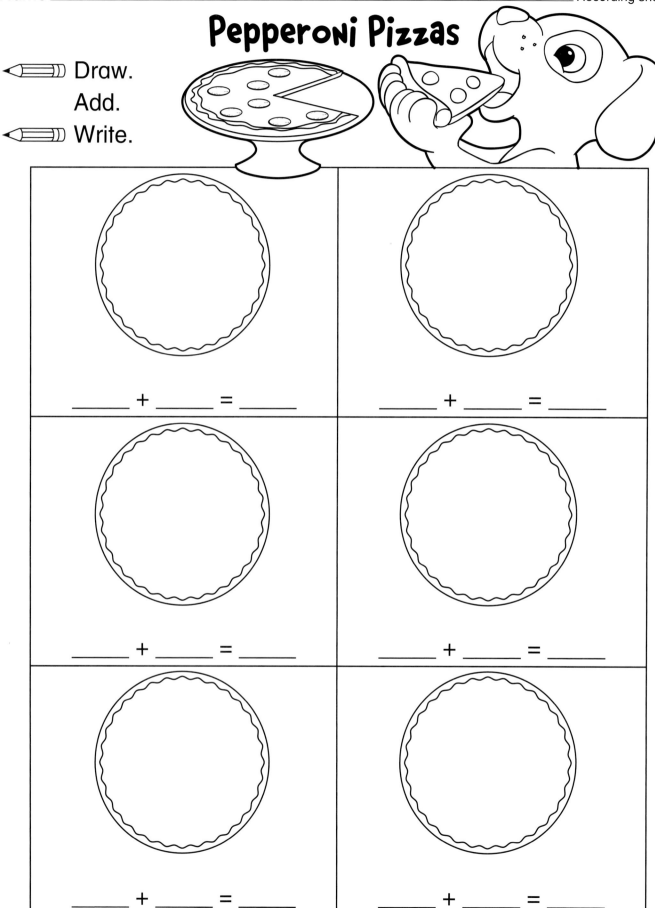

_____ + _____ = _____

_____ + _____ = _____

_____ + _____ = _____

_____ + _____ = _____

_____ + _____ = _____

_____ + _____ = _____

Note to the teacher: Use with "Pepperoni Pizzas" on page 39.

Hungry for Apples

START

FINISH

Partner game: Use with the directions on page 51.

Fast on the Farm

Start on this side.

You pick!

#1 Goose

#1 Pig

#1 Lamb

©The Mailbox® • TEC42044 • Aug./Sept. 2009

50 THE MAILBOX   **Partner game:** Use with the directions on page 51.

Hungry for Apples

Skill: Counting

What You Need
gameboard
number cube (Mask the 6.) 5 3
20 two-color counters

How to play:

1. Play with a partner. Decide who will use each color on the counters.

2. Toss the cube, in turn.

3. If you roll a number, name it. Put that many counters on the board.
   If you do not roll a number, count how many blank spaces are left.

4. Play until you reach FINISH.

©The Mailbox® • TEC42044 • Aug./Sept. 2009

Fast on the Farm

Skill: Plane figures

What You Need
2 gameboards
paper clip
pencil
crayons

How to play:

1. Play with a partner.

2. Spin, in turn.

3. If the spinner lands on a shape, name it. Color the first matching shape.
   If the spinner lands on "You pick!" color any shape.

4. Play until one player colors all the shapes in one row. The matching animal wins!

©The Mailbox® • TEC42044 • Aug./Sept. 2009

Note to the teacher: Use with the gameboards on pages 49 and 50. To make "Hungry for Apples" a longer game, mask both the 5 and 6 on the number cube.

Name _____

Monkey Business

FINISH

Circle, circle, triangle.

You pick!

START

Partner game: Use with the directions on page 54. **For a shorter game,** make one copy of this page. Draw the next three shapes in the pattern and then make student copies.

Blast Off!

A

B

Monkey Business

Skill: Patterning

What You Need

2 gameboards
paper clip
pencil

How to play:

1. Play with a partner.

2. Say the shape pattern.

3. When it is your turn, spin the spinner. If the spinner lands on the next shape in the pattern or "You pick!" draw the correct shape in the first empty box. If the spinner does not land on those things, your turn is over.

4. Play until you reach FINISH.

©The Mailbox® • TEC42045 • Oct./Nov. 2009

Blast Off!

Skill: Comparing sets

What You Need

gameboard
7 counters
number die
12 Unifix cubes

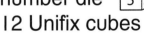

How to play:

1. Play with a partner. Put the counters on the circles. Decide who will be Players A and B.

2. When it is your turn, roll the die and say the number. Make a tower with that many cubes. Lay it on your side of the board.

3. Compare your tower with your partner's. The player whose tower has more cubes takes a counter. If the towers have the same number of cubes, no one takes a counter.

4. Play until there are no counters on the rocket.

©The Mailbox® • TEC42045 • Oct./Nov. 2009

Note to the teacher: Use with "Monkey Business" on page 52 and "Blast Off!" on page 53.

Name _____

Number order

In the Clouds

Buddy's Balloon Rides

1 2

4

6

8 9

11 12

14 15

16

18

20

3 10 17

19 5

7 13

Partner Game Use with the directions on page 57.

Name _____

Bank on It!

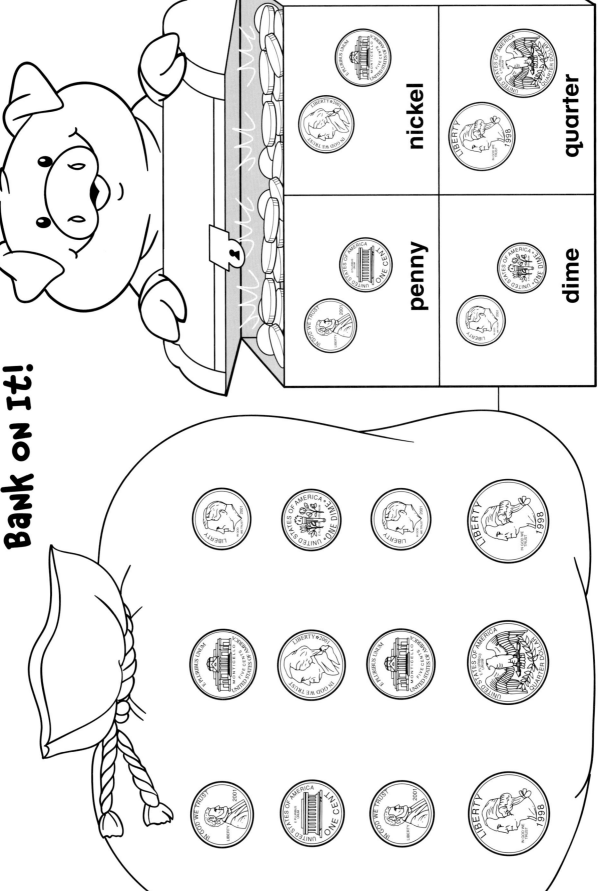

| nickel | penny |
| quarter | dime |

Partner Game Use with the directions on page 57.

In the Clouds

Skill: Number order

How to play:

1. Play with a partner.

2. Take turns spinning.
   - If you spin a number, name it and write it on the correct cloud. (If the cloud already has the number, your turn is over.)
   - If you spin 😊, pick a cloud. Write the correct number on it.

3. The first player to write all the missing numbers wins.

Buddy's Balloon Rides

Bank on It!

Skill: Coin identification

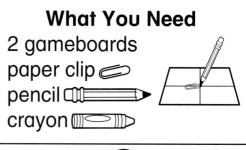

How to play:

1. Play with a partner.

2. When it's your turn, spin and name the coin.

3. Color a matching coin. (If there are no matching coins left to color, your turn is over.)

4. The first player to color all the coins wins.

Note to the teacher: Use with "In the Clouds" on page 55 and "Bank on It!" on page 56.

Diving for Coins

0¢	10¢
1¢	5¢

©The Mailbox® • TEC42047 • Feb./Mar. 2010

Partner Game Use with the directions on page 60.

Bert's Berry Pie

Partner Game Use with the directions on page 60.

Diving for Coins

Skill: Coin values

How to play:

1. Play with a partner.

2. When it is your turn, spin and name the amount.

3. Color a matching coin. If there is no matching coin, your turn is over.

4. Play until one player colors all his or her coins.

What You Need
2 gameboards
paper clip
pencil
2 crayons

Bert's Berry Pie

Skill: Addition to 6

What You Need
2 gameboards
2 game markers
die
2 crayons

How to play:

1. Play with a partner. Put your marker on a star.

2. When it is your turn, roll the die and move your marker.

3. Read the problem. Say the sum. Color a matching box on the pie.

4. The first player to color all the boxes in one row wins.

Note to the teacher: Use with "Diving for Coins" on page 58 and "Bert's Berry Pie" on page 59.

Lunchtime!

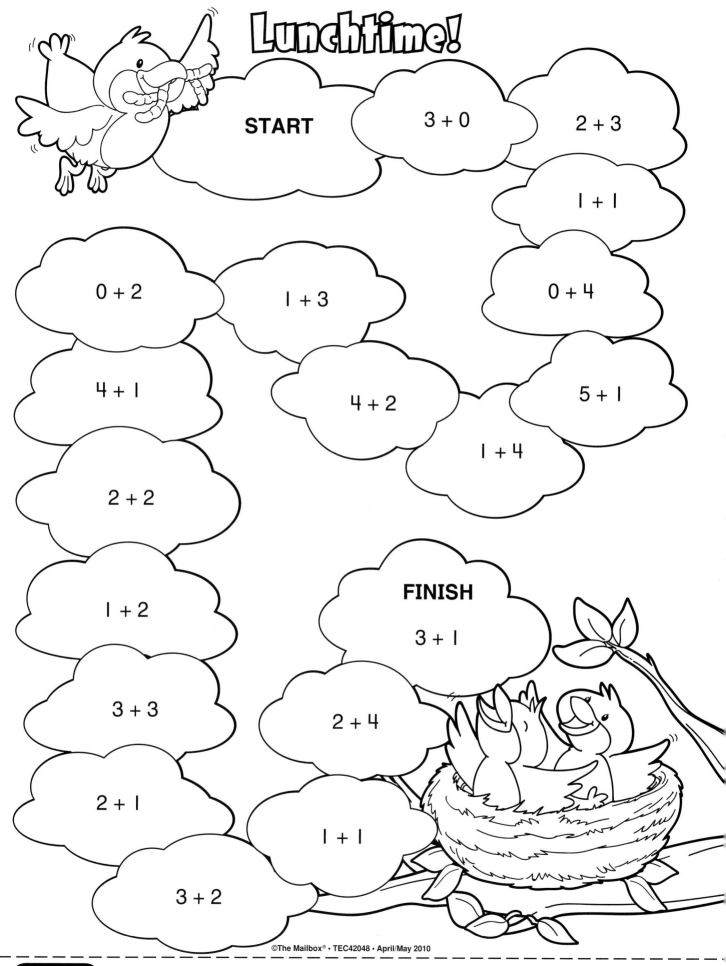

START

3 + 0

2 + 3

1 + 1

0 + 2

1 + 3

0 + 4

4 + 1

4 + 2

5 + 1

2 + 2

1 + 4

1 + 2

FINISH

3 + 1

3 + 3

2 + 4

2 + 1

1 + 1

3 + 2

Kitty Snacks

⊂x⊃ ⊂x⊃ ⊂x⊃ 3 fish 1 fewer is _____.	⊂x⊃ ⊂x⊃ ⊂x⊃ ⊂x⊃ 4 fish 2 fewer is _____.	⊂x⊃ ⊂x⊃ ⊂x⊃ ⊂x⊃ ⊂x⊃ 5 fish 1 fewer is _____.
⊂x⊃ ⊂x⊃ ⊂x⊃ 3 fish 2 fewer is _____.	⊂x⊃ ⊂x⊃ ⊂x⊃ ⊂x⊃ 4 fish 1 fewer is _____.	⊂x⊃ ⊂x⊃ ⊂x⊃ ⊂x⊃ ⊂x⊃ 5 fish 2 fewer is _____.
⊂x⊃ ⊂x⊃ ⊂x⊃ 3 fish 1 fewer is _____.	⊂x⊃ ⊂x⊃ ⊂x⊃ ⊂x⊃ 4 fish 2 fewer is _____.	⊂x⊃ ⊂x⊃ ⊂x⊃ ⊂x⊃ ⊂x⊃ 5 fish 1 fewer is _____.

You Pick!

4 fish

3 fish

5 fish

Lunchtime!

Skill: Addition to 6

How to play:

1. Play with a partner. Put the game markers on START.

2. When it is your turn, toss the cube. If you do not roll a number, your turn is over.

3. If you roll a number, name it. Move your marker to the first problem that has the sum you rolled. If there is not a problem with this sum, your turn is over.

4. Play until both players reach FINISH.

What You Need
gameboard
2 game markers
number cube
(Mask the 1.)

©The Mailbox® • TEC42048 • April/May 2010

Kitty Snacks

Skill: Subtraction to 5

How to play:

1. Play with a partner. When it is your turn, spin the spinner.

2. Find and circle a matching set of fish snacks. If all the matching sets are circled, your turn is over. If you spin "You Pick!" find and circle any set of fish snacks that is not circled.

3. Read. Cross out fish to make fewer. Count. Write your answer.

4. Play until one player has filled each answer blank.

What You Need
2 gameboards
paper clip
pencil

©The Mailbox® • TEC42048 • April/May 2010

Note to the teacher: Use with "Lunchtime!" on page 61 and "Kitty Snacks" on page 62.

THE MAILBOX **63**

Time for Tennis!

6:00	3:00	9:00	5:00
8:00	7:00	1:00	10:00
2:00	11:00	12:00	4:00

©The Mailbox® • TEC42049 • June/July 2010

64   THE MAILBOX   **Partner Game**   Use with the directions on page 66.

Name _____

Ring the Bell!

Player A

28	9
15	3
19	30
22	10

Player B

10	15
9	28
30	3
19	22

FINISH

A | B
A | B
A | B
A | B
A | B
A | B
A | B
A | B
A | B
A | B

START

Time for Tennis!

Skill: Time to the hour

What You Need
2 gameboards
24 round counters
crayons

How to play:

1. Play with a partner.

2. Put a counter on each clock.

3. When it is your turn, point to a time on the net. Say the time.

4. Remove a counter. If the time on the clock matches the time you said, color its space on the net. If the time on the clock is not a match, put the counter back.

5. Play until all the spaces on one player's net are colored.

©The Mailbox® • TEC42049 • June/July 2010

Ring the Bell!

Skill: Comparing numbers to 30

What You Need
gameboard
2 paper clips
2 pencils
2 crayons

How to play:

1. Play with a partner. Decide who will be Players A and B.

2. Choose a crayon. Find START on the gameboard.

3. To take a turn, each player spins.

4. The player with the greater number colors one gameboard space. (If the numbers are the same, the turn is over.)

5. The first player to reach FINISH colors the bell!

©The Mailbox® • TEC42049 • June/July 2010

Note to the teacher: Use with the gameboards on pages 64 and 65.

BUILDING READING SKILLS

Building Reading Skills

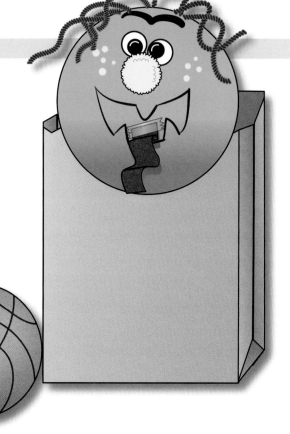

Alphabet Monster
Letter-sound association

Use craft materials to transform a box, bag, or other container into a friendly monster. Then gather items that all begin with the same sound and place them in the monster. To begin, tell youngsters that the hungry monster ate some items that all start with the same letter. Then show each item as students name it, stressing the beginning sound. Next, ask youngsters to determine the letter that all the items begin with. **For an added challenge,** ask students to name different items the monster might have eaten if it had visited their homes.

Barbara Dell
Old Dominion University
Norfolk, VA

Walk That Turtle!
Concepts of print

Use this cute pointer for reading from charts or big books. To prepare, use pipe cleaners to make a turtle shape like the one shown. Add paper eyes and then glue the turtle to a craft stick so that it is facing right. As you read aloud from a chart or big book, "walk" the turtle as you read from left to right. To focus on individual words, use the open shell to frame words. Then invite students to take turns using the turtle to read aloud to the class.

Starin Lewis
Phoenix, AZ

ABCs Around Us

Beginning letters, environmental print

For each letter of the alphabet, take a photograph of a familiar place or object in the community that begins with the letter's sound. Then have each youngster glue a photo to a sheet of paper and identify the beginning letter. Next, help him write a sentence for his letter as shown. (Invite early finishers to complete a second page for the extra letters.) Bind the pages in order to make a ready-to-read class book.

Kari Murray
Lincoln Elementary
West Allis, WI

Airport starts with A.

High Five!

High-frequency words

Post a large handprint cutout on your classroom door. Attach a high-frequency word card on the palm of the hand. As students are entering or exiting the room, have each child read the word as the password to proceed. If the child reads correctly, encourage him to give the paper hand a high five! To practice different words, simply change the password.

Kim Camelotto
Lansdowne Elementary
Baltimore, MD

Is.

is

An Animal Hunt

Rhyming

Cut out copies of the animal cards on page 80 to have one card per student. While the children are out of the classroom, place the cards around the room. To play, lead youngsters in singing the first two lines of the song shown, repeating the lines as needed, while each player hunts for an animal card. Have each child sit in your group-time area after she finds a card. Then invite each youngster, in turn, to complete the unfinished phrase in the fourth line of the song by naming the animal on her card for the first blank and using a phrase that rhymes with it in the second blank. **To extend the activity,** have her illustrate her rhyme.

(sung to the tune of "A-hunting We Will Go")

A-hunting we will go, a-hunting we will go,
Heigh-ho, the dairy-o, a-hunting we will go!
A-hunting we will go, a-hunting we will go,
We'll catch a [fox] and put it [in a box],
And then we'll let it go!

Kim Criswell, Wilson, KS

Building Reading Skills

Our Favorite Snacks

Environmental print, predictable text

In advance, ask each child to bring to school a wrapper or name label from a favorite snack. To make a class book, help each child write the name of her snack on a sentence starter like the one shown. Tape the completed sentence near the top of a gallon-size resealable plastic bag and seal the snack wrapper in the bag. Hole-punch the resulting plastic pages and bind them between construction paper covers. Encourage youngsters to read the book independently or with a partner.

Susan DeRiso
Barrington, RI

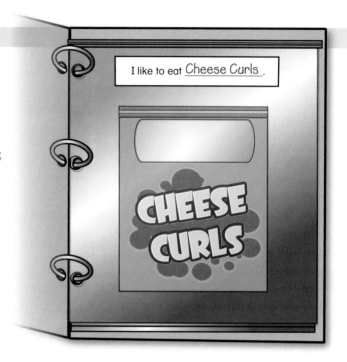

I like to eat Cheese Curls .

CHEESE CURLS

Solve the Mystery

Letter-sound association

Conceal a tagboard letter cutout between the halves of a folded sheet of white paper and tape the paper to a hard surface. To begin, say different words that begin with the hidden letter's sound. When a student correctly names the letter, invite him to do a crayon rubbing to reveal it. **For an added challenge,** name different words that end with the letter's sound.

Marie E. Cecchini
West Dundee, IL

Editor's Tip:
Bulletin board letters work great with this idea!

Choo! Choo!

Rhyming

Students name rhyming words to be part of this pretend train. Instruct small groups of students to stand in different classroom areas (train stations). Next, pretend you are a train engine and "chug" to the first station. Name a word. As each child names a real or nonsense rhyming word, have him get in line behind you and pretend to be a train car. When the train station is empty, lead the train to the next stop and name a different word for a new set of rhymes. Continue at each train station until all your students are part of the train!

Heather Nichols, KiDoodles Learning Center, Holden, MA

What's the Letter?

Letter-sound association

Students will refrain from calling out answers with this clever idea. Place in a bag objects that feature the same beginning sound. To begin, remove one object from the bag and name it. If a child thinks she knows the beginning letter, she cups her hands and pretends to blow into a balloon. Continue until the bag is empty and the imaginary balloon is nearly full. Then invite all students to "pop" their balloons before naming the featured letter.

Jessie Roberts, Mt. Bethel Elementary, Marietta, GA

Here's the Scoop!

High-frequency words

Use this sweet incentive to encourage students to learn word lists. Have each youngster glue an ice cream cone cutout to the front of a folder and have him store several ice cream scoop cutouts in the folder. Each time he demonstrates mastery of a word list, ask him to choose one of his scoops for you to initial. Then have him glue the scoop to his cone.

Julie Defelice, Shoal Creek Elementary, Conyers, GA

Building Reading Skills

Practice Makes "Purr-fect"

Word family: -at

Students are sure to enjoy reading the *-at* words on this adorable cat! Give each child a copy of the cat pattern and whisker strips on page 83. Lead youngsters in reading aloud the words on the whiskers. Next, have each child color his cat pattern and then cut out the cat and whiskers. Direct him to glue the whiskers to the cat, taking care not to overlap the words. Encourage each child to take his cat home to practice reading the *-at* words with a family member.

Amy Ingram
Rootstown Elementary
Rootstown, OH

Roll, Read, and Color

Color words

For this partner game, program each side of a cube with a different color word. Label a graph with the same color words and the numbers 1 to 10; then make a copy for each student pair. To begin, Player 1 rolls the die and reads the color word. Then she colors a box in the matching column on the graph. Next, Player 2 takes a turn in the same manner. Alternate play continues until one color reaches ten and is declared the winner! **For an easier version,** write each color word with a marker of the corresponding color or repeat color words on the cube.

Kelly Kramer
Rivercrest Elementary
Bartlett, TN

Editor's Tip:
To make an extra large cube, cover a cube-shaped tissue box with paper and then label the sides.

Trace and Write

Letter formation

To prepare, write at the top of a sheet of paper the uppercase and lowercase letter pair you would like to feature. Next, draw and label a simple outline of an object whose name begins with the featured letter. Then give each child a copy of the page. A student traces the letters at the top of the page, practices writing the letters inside the outline, and reads the word. To reinforce letter-sound association also, have her point to each letter she wrote and quietly say the letter's sound.

Amanda Bangert
Trinity Lutheran School
Grand Island, NE

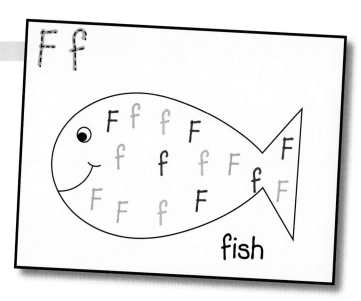

An Active Response

Letter-sound association

Looking for a way to add a little action to your phonics activities? Try this! Write a letter on the board and review its sounds. Guide youngsters to agree on an action associated with the letter, such as popping like popcorn for /p/, rowing a rowboat for /r/, or digging like a dog for /d/. Then say a word. If the word begins with the letter's sound, students perform the predetermined action; if not, they remain still. If desired, have youngsters say the letter's sound aloud while in motion.

Patricia Conner
St. Thomas More Academy
Buckeystown, MD

Train Connections

Beginning, middle, and end

Foster students' ability to identify different parts of a story with this visual aid. Cut out a copy of the train patterns from pages 83 and 84. After reading a story aloud, invite a child to hold the train engine and tell the beginning of the story. Next, have a different youngster hold the train car and tell the middle of the story. Then ask another student to hold the caboose and tell the end of the story. **For an added challenge,** provide several train car patterns to enhance a more detailed retelling of the tale.

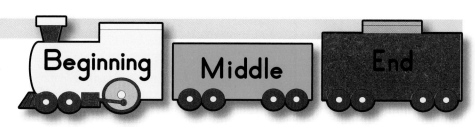

Jodi Darter, Cabool Elementary, Cabool, MO

Building Reading Skills

Gum Words

Phonics

Fold and tape a sheet of paper to make a pocket (gum wrapper) for each child. Give each youngster a gum wrapper and ten paper rectangles (sticks of gum). Have her write "gum" on her wrapper. Then choose an option below.

Initial consonant *g*: Lead students in naming words that begin with *g* as you write them on the board. Then have each child underline the *g* on her wrapper and copy a different word on each stick of gum.

Ending consonant *m*: Lead students in naming words that end with *m* as you write them on the board. Then have each child underline the *m* on her wrapper and copy a different word on each stick of gum.

Short *u*: Lead students in naming short *u* words as you write them on the board. Then have each child underline the *u* on her wrapper and copy a different word on each stick of gum.

After checking for accuracy, instruct each child to store her words in her wrapper. When time permits, encourage her to practice reading her words with a partner.

Denise L. Kettles
Milford Elementary
Marietta, GA

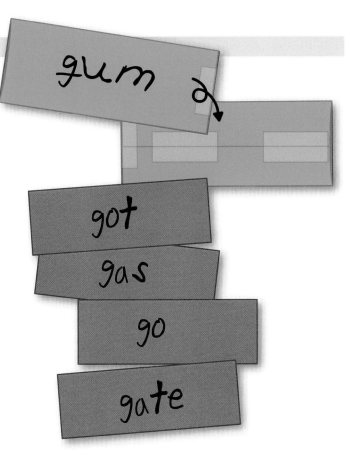

Tic-Tac-Bingo

Letter-sound association

Review initial consonants or blends with this small-group game! Cut out a copy of a selected card set from page 85 and write on the board the beginning letters or blends associated with the cards. Give each player a tic-tac-toe grid drawn on a paper plate. Have him copy a different letter or blend onto each space on his board.

To play, identify a winning combination, such as four corners, X, or T. Then display a card and have students name the picture and its beginning letter or blend. Each child with a matching letter or blend places a marker on the space. Play continues in this manner until a student has a winning board and announces, "Bingo!"

Katrina Conley
Bonham Elementary
Charleston, WV

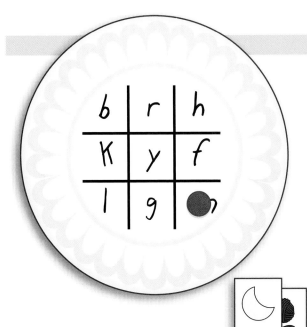

Confusing Letters

Letter knowledge

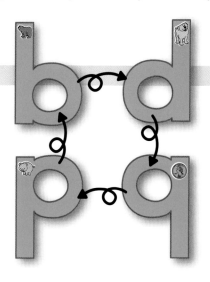

If your students mix up the letters *b, d, p,* and *q,* try this hands-on solution! For each child, place a picture sticker that begins with /b/ at the top of a lowercase letter *b* cutout. Then flip the letter to reveal a *d* and place a sticker that corresponds with /d/ at the top of that letter. Continue flipping and turning, as shown, for letters *p* and *q.* (If desired, point out that the letter *q* is often made with a tail.) Then encourage youngsters to use the sticker clues to remember the shape and sound of each letter.

Bernadette Bowen
Woodridge School
Cranston, RI

Splat!

High-frequency words

This reading review game is a quick time filler. Draw two side-by-side grids on a transparency. Program each grid with the same set of words you would like to review. Also gather two clean flyswatters.

To play, have a player from each of two teams stand on each side of the board holding a flyswatter. Then turn on the overhead projector to display the words on the board, and name a word. The first player to swat the correct word wins a point for the team. Have other players take turns swatting words as time permits or until one team has earned ten points.

Greta Delparte, Centennial Elementary, Bismarck, ND

Comprehension Critters

Reading strategies

Color and cut out a copy of the cards on page 86 and glue each one to a craft stick. Then use the resulting puppets to foster students' understanding of text. **To extend the activity,** give each youngster a personal puppet collection to use independently as a reminder of ways to support comprehension.

Picture clues: Hold up "Picturing Pig" to remind students to use the pictures to help develop the meaning of the story.
Context clues: Hold up "Noticing Newt" to ask youngsters whether something in the words helped them to understand unfamiliar words or the meaning of a passage.
Making connections: Hold up "Connection Cat" to pause and ask youngsters to make connections to the text.
Making predictions: Hold up "Guessing Goat" to ask youngsters what they think might happen next in the story or to ask how the story might end.
Making inferences: Hold up "Inference Inchworm" to guide youngsters to recognize the meaning of an inference used in a story.
Monitoring meaning: Hold up "Meaningful Mouse" to stop and ask students, "Does the story make sense?"

Khindra Kent, Crandall Elementary, Crandall, TX

Building Reading Skills

"Sound-sational" Caterpillar

Segmenting words into phonemes

For this hands-on activity, give each student five paper circles and have her decorate one circle to resemble a caterpillar's head. Then say a word that has one to four phonemes. Instruct each child to put a circle (caterpillar body part) behind the head for each sound she hears. Then have her slowly repeat the word, touching one body part per sound. To build a different caterpillar, have her move the body parts away from the head and then listen for a different word.

Katharine Petitt
Lutheran Home Child Care
Wauwatosa, WI

/F/–/i/–/sh/.

On the Hunt

Beginning sounds

To prepare for this scavenger hunt, cut out 30 flower cards (patterns on page 87); then color six flowers red and the remaining flowers yellow. Cut apart the first row of picture cards on page 87 and glue each card to a separate red flower. Then cut apart the remaining cards and glue each one to a yellow flower. Put the yellow flowers around the room.

To begin, arrange your youngsters in six groups and give each group one red flower. Encourage group members to look around the room for four yellow flowers that show pictures whose names have the same beginning sound as the one on the red flower. To review, have each group, in turn, name its flower collection.

Renee Koegler
Harkers Island Elementary
Harkers Island, NC

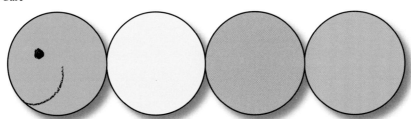

Read That Chip!

Students are sure to find lots of *-ip* words in this bag of potato chips. Cut out several ovals (chips). On each chip, write a different onset that forms a real word when paired with the rime *-ip*. Label a paper bag as shown and place the chips in the bag. To begin, invite a child to take a chip and make the onset's sound. Then have him clip the chip to the bag and lead the group in chanting the rhyme shown. After reading the word, he sets the chip aside. Continue with each remaining chip.

We got a chip-ip-ip-ip! This word says [/h/]-ip. [Hip]!

Crack!

Write high-frequency words on colorful egg cutouts. On another egg cutout, write the word *Crack!* Store the eggs in a bag. To play, invite youngsters, in turn, to pull out an egg and read the word. Play continues until *Crack!* is revealed. Then youngsters count the total number of words read, write the number on a sticky note, and place it on the bag. At a later time, have students play again to try to beat their best score! **For other times of the year,** use different seasonal cutouts and replace *Crack!* with words such as *Boo!* (October); *Gobble, gobble!* (November); *Ho, ho, ho!* (Christmas); and *Drip, drop!* (spring).

Maryann Stewart
Midwestern Intermediate Unit 4
Grove City, PA

A Spring Story

The repetitive text in this seasonal booklet is sure to develop fluency as well as other literacy skills! Give each child a copy of pages 88 and 89. Have her cut out and sequence the pages, stack them between construction paper covers, and staple the resulting booklet together. After youngsters write their names on their covers, lead the class in reading the story aloud. Then choose an option below for a word-related review.

Positional words: Guide youngsters to circle the positional word on each page. Then reread the story, calling attention to the location of each object in the text.
Rhyming words: Write the words *see* and *tree* on large cards. Invite youngsters to name other words that rhyme with *see* and *tree.* Then instruct youngsters to underline *see* and *tree* on each page.
High-frequency words: Choose a high-frequency word or two from the booklet and write it on the board. Then encourage each youngster to color the word with a yellow crayon each time it appears.

White cloud, white cloud, what do you see?

I see happy kids beside the tree.

5

Cathy Welwood, Woodbine School, Calgary, Alberta, Canada

Building Reading Skills

Words to Go!

Onsets and rimes

Looking for a way to add a little action to word family practice? Try this small-group game idea! Label a four-sectioned takeout drink holder with a rime of your choice. Then label each of the four sections with a different onset that forms a real word with the rime. To begin, invite a child to toss a pom-pom into the holder. Instruct him to blend the onset with the rime to form the word. Continue until all four words have been read. If desired, have youngsters write each word on a sheet of paper to form a word family. **For an added challenge,** set out two or more drink holders to review more than one word family at a time.

Heidi Kasle
E. Ethel Little School
North Reading, MA

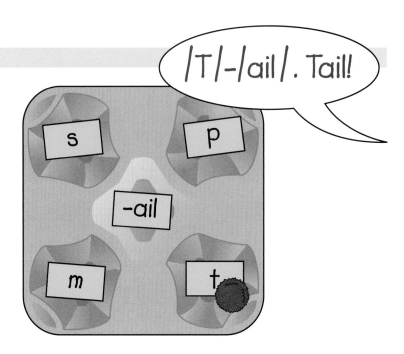

/T/-/ail/. Tail!

ABC Quilt

Beginning consonants and vowels

Write each letter of the alphabet on a grid that resembles a quilt. Color and cut out a copy of the picture cards on pages 90 and 91 and put them in a bag. Then invite a child to remove a card from the bag as you lead the remaining youngsters in the first verse of the song below. Next, have the child answer the question posed by naming the picture; then use the initial sound to lead youngsters in singing the second verse. To answer the final question, the child names the initial letter and tapes her card atop the matching letter on the quilt. Play continues for each remaining picture card.

(sung to the tune of "The More We Get Together")

Oh, can you name the picture, the picture, the picture?
Oh, can you name the picture you see on the card?

[/<u>d</u>/], [/<u>d</u>/], [/<u>d</u>/], [/<u>d</u>/], [/<u>d</u>/], [/<u>d</u>/],
[/<u>d</u>/], [/<u>d</u>/], [/<u>d</u>/], [/<u>d</u>/], [/<u>d</u>/], [/<u>d</u>/],
Now can you name the letter for this sound you hear?

adapted from an idea by Kathryn Davenport
Partin Elementary
Oviedo, FL

The Blender

Blending words

When students pretend to be blenders, the result is a decoded word! On a large strip of paper, use three different-colored markers to list several CVC words. Display the list; then point to a word and slowly say the sound of each letter. Have youngsters repeat the sounds with you. Then have each child slowly turn around in a circle, pretending to be a blender. After a few circles, prompt students to stop and announce the blended word. Repeat the activity with each word on the list.

adapted from an idea by Lisa Jarosh
St. Elizabeth Elementary
Pittsburgh, PA

Word Wall Chains

High-frequency words, vocabulary

This end-of-the-year review makes a perfect summer study tool! Feature a select group of words from your word wall that you would like to review. Have each student write each word on a separate paper strip. Then have her make a paper chain, keeping the words to the outside. After reviewing the words in class, send the chains home so students can practice with family members and friends.

Ashley Morrell
Armstrong Elementary
Sachse, TX

Step and Tell

Comprehension

Label each of three different-colored sheets with the word *beginning, middle,* or *end.* Before reading a story, tape the sheets to the floor. To model a retelling, gently step on each of the sheets as you retell the corresponding part of the story. Then, on another day, ask volunteers to help you retell each part of the story. Gradually lead youngsters, in turn, to step on each sheet and retell the story independently. **For a more detailed retelling,** increase the number of sheets labeled "Middle."

Gwenn Rives, Tequesta, FL

Animal Cards
Use with "An Animal Hunt" on page 69.

TEC42044

TEC42044

TEC42044

TEC42044

TEC42044

TEC42044

TEC42044

TEC42044

TEC42044

TEC42044

TEC42044

TEC42044

Matching uppercase and lowercase letters

Mouse's Cheese

✂ Cut.

Glue to match.

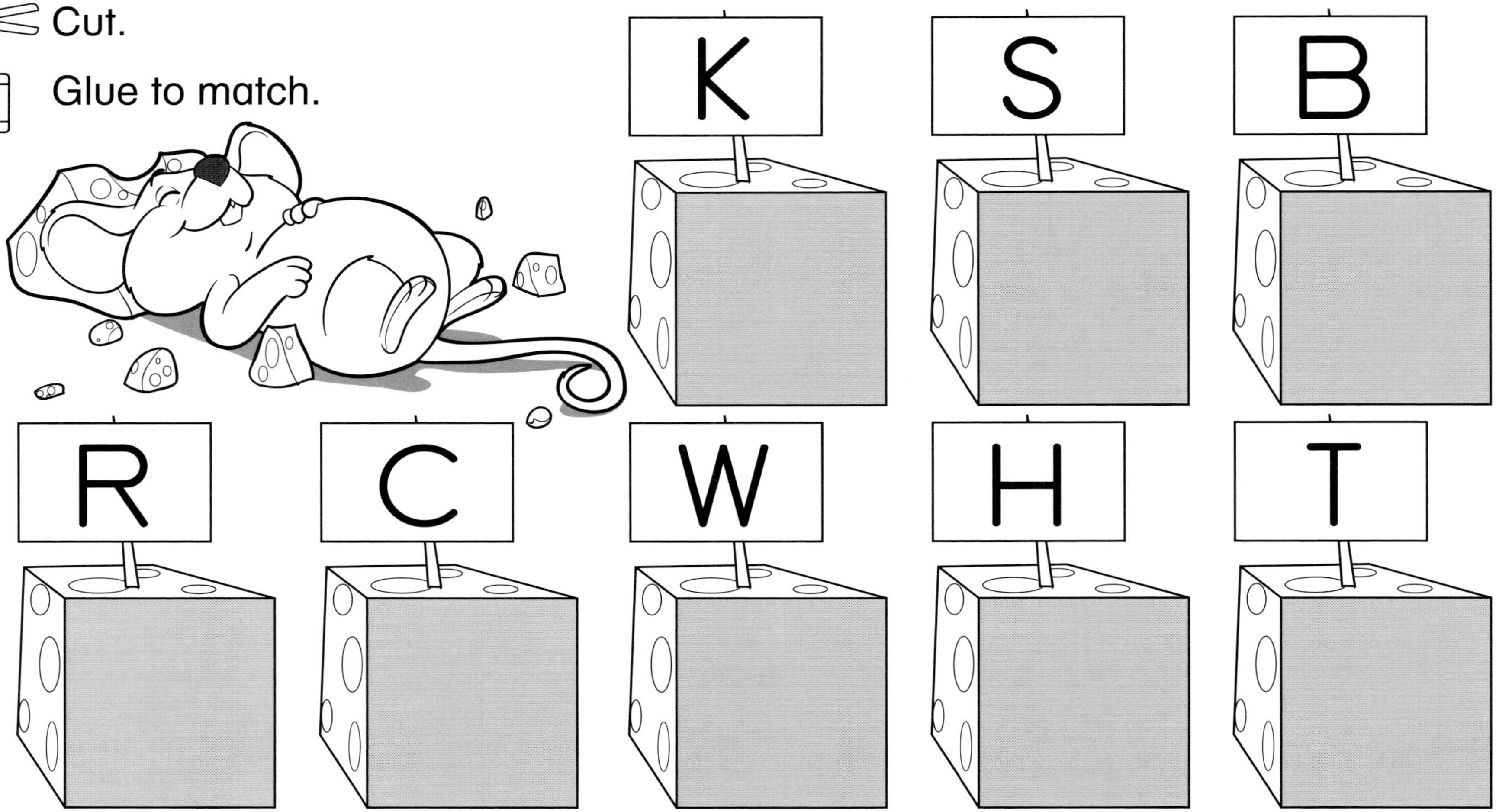

B

S

K

T

H

W

C

R

81

c h t s b r w k

Name _____

Barnyard Friends

Cut.

Glue to match.

Hh

Cc

Pp

©The Mailbox® • TEC42045 • Oct./Nov. 2009

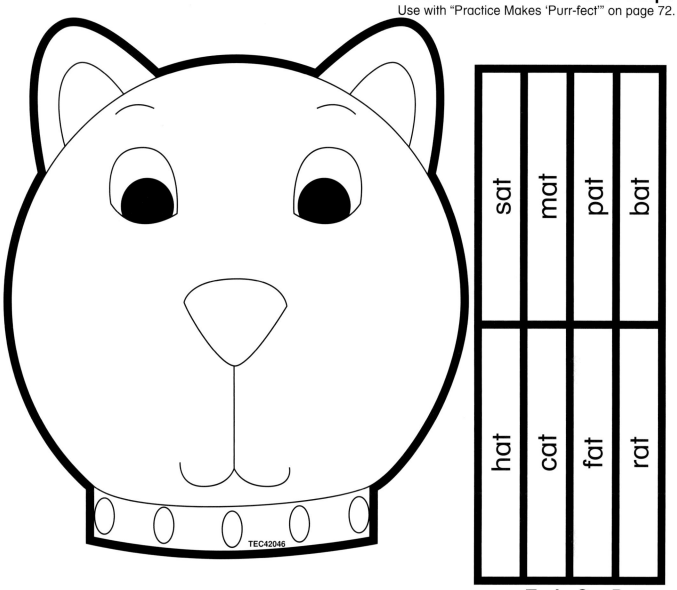

sat	hat
mat	cat
pat	fat
bat	rat

TEC42046

Train Car Pattern
Use with "Train Connections" on page 73.

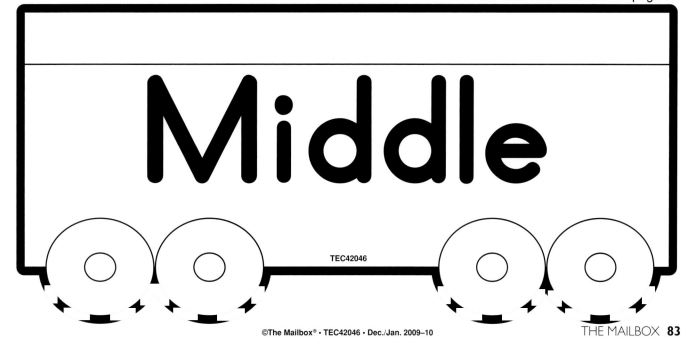

Middle

TEC42046

Train Engine and Caboose Patterns
Use with "Train Connections" on page 73.

Beginning

TEC42046

End

TEC42046

Initial Consonants

Initial Consonant Blends

Puppet Patterns
Use with "Comprehension Critters" on page 75.

TEC42048

TEC42048

TEC42048

Springtime Booklet Pages 1, 2, and 3

Use with "A Spring Story" on page 77.

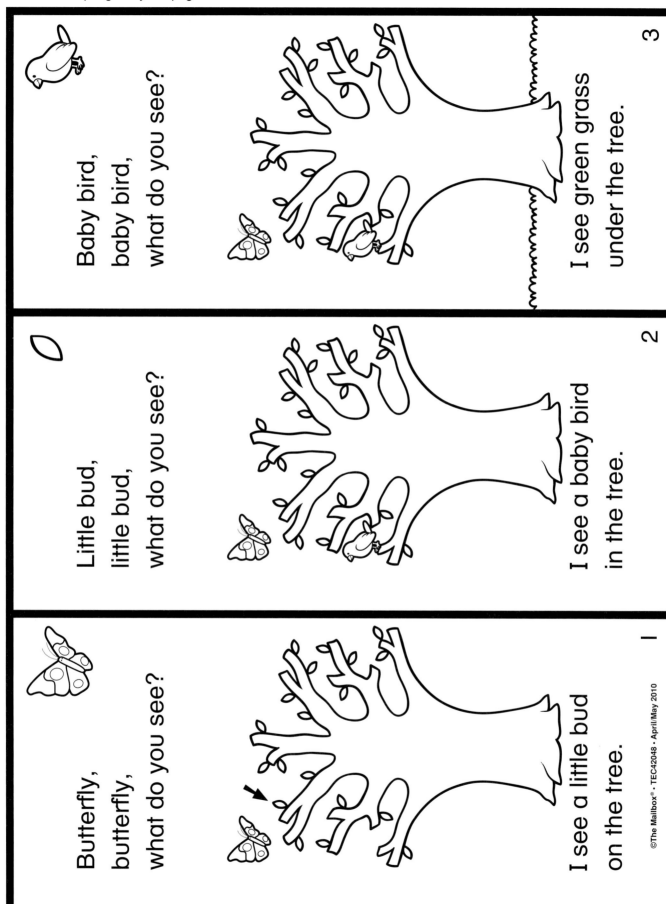

3

Baby bird,
baby bird,
what do you see?

I see green grass
under the tree.

2

Little bud,
little bud,
what do you see?

I see a baby bird
in the tree.

1

Butterfly,
butterfly,
what do you see?

I see a little bud
on the tree.

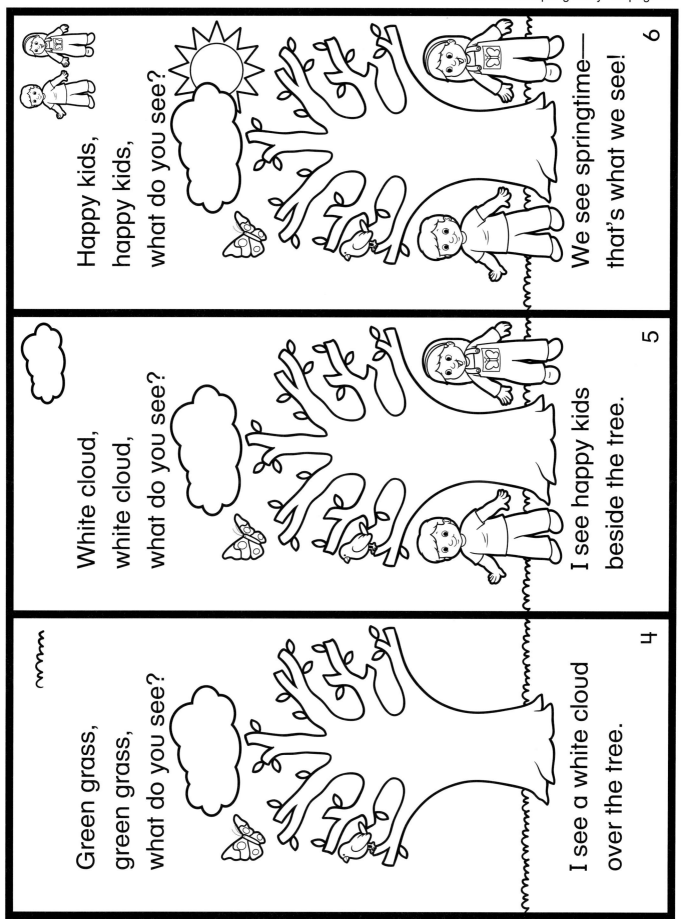

6

Happy kids, happy kids, what do you see?

We see springtime— that's what we see!

5

White cloud, white cloud, what do you see?

I see happy kids beside the tree.

4

Green grass, green grass, what do you see?

I see a white cloud over the tree.

A to *M* Picture Cards

Use with "ABC Quilt" on page 78.

TEC42049

Sorting Activity

Each child cuts out a copy of the sorting header and cards. He names the animal on each card and sorts the card according to the number of syllables in the name. To take the cards home for additional practice, he glues the header to the front of a legal-size envelope and stores the cards inside.

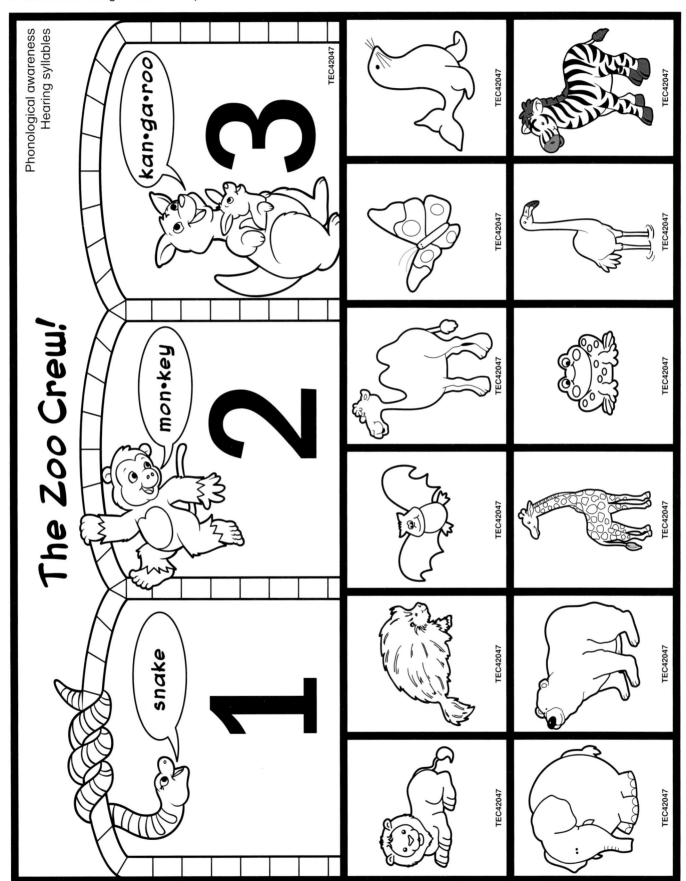

Each child cuts out a copy of the cards below and sorts them on a copy of page 94. For additional practice, he puts the cards in a resealable plastic bag; then he takes the cards and mat home. For assessment, he completes a copy of the activity below.

- -

Name _____

To the Hill!

Color the pictures with ĭ as in 🐷.

A Big Hill

Sorting Mat

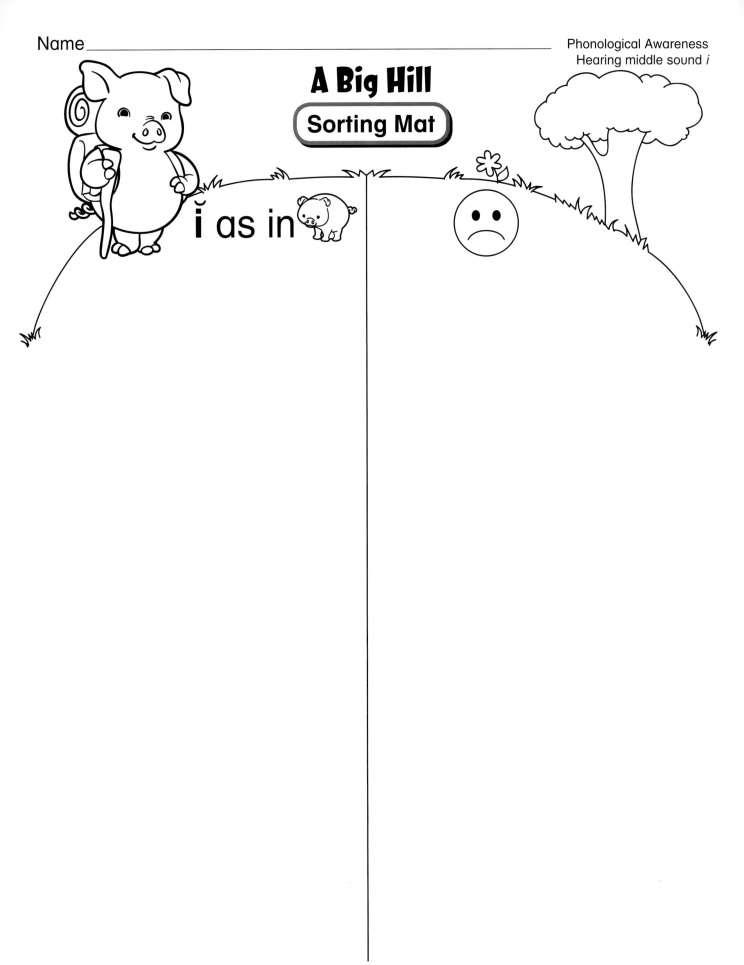

ĭ as in

Note to the teacher: Use with the sorting activity on page 93.

Have each child cut out a copy of the onset and rime cards and the word list below. Instruct her to form words with the cards, read the words, and then write them on paper. Invite her to take the cards and the word list home in an envelope for practice. If desired, follow up with the activity on page 96.

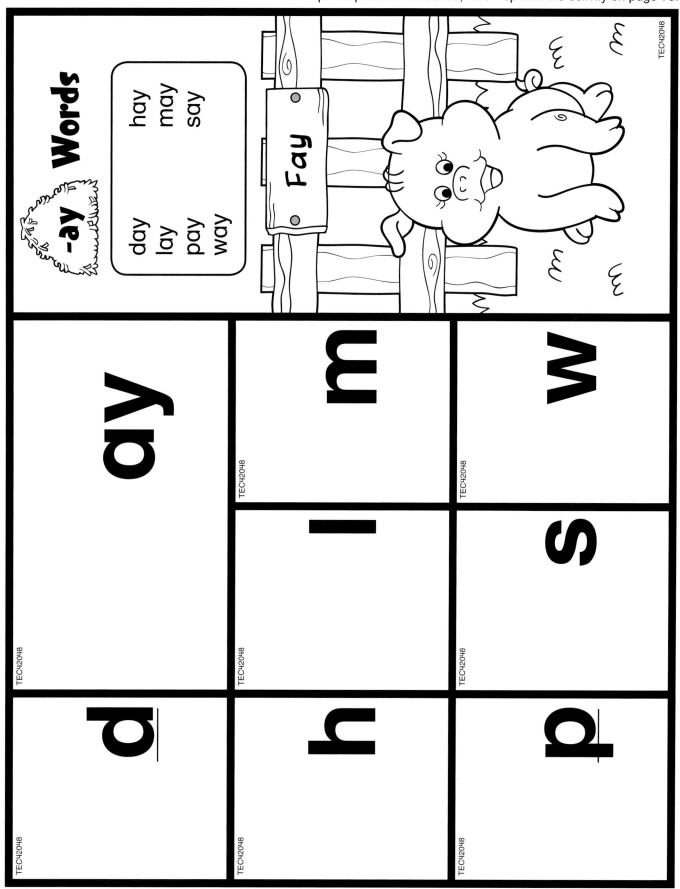

-ay Words

day	hay
lay	may
pay	say
way	

Fay

ay

m

w

l

d

h

s

p

t

A Day With Fay

 Cut.

Glue.

1. Look at my pig, ⬜ .

2. She likes to ⬜ in mud.

3. Fay likes ⬜ too.

4. Get out of the ⬜ , Fay!

| way | play | Fay | hay |

Have each child cut out a copy of the cards and word list below. Instruct her to form words with the cards, read the words, and then write them on a sheet of paper. Invite her to take the cards and word list home in an envelope for practice. If desired, follow up with the activity on page 98.

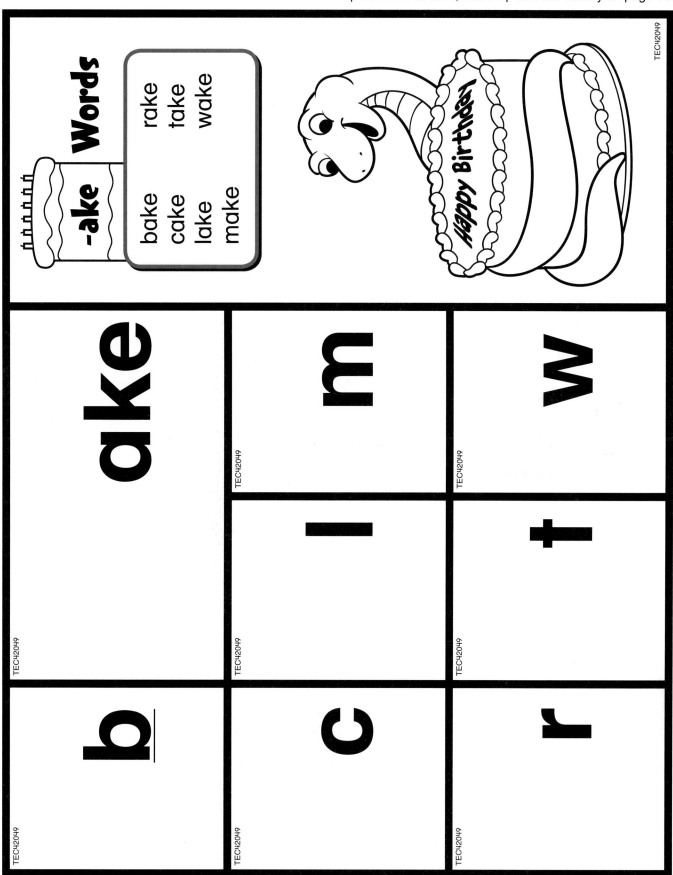

-ake **Words**

rake	bake
take	cake
wake	lake
	make

ake

m

w

l

t

b

c

r

TEC42049

A Birthday Cake

✏️ Write.

🖍️ Color the matching balloon.

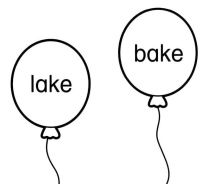

lake bake cake wake

1. Mr. Snake, _____ up!

2. It is time to _____ .

3. It is a _____ .

4. Let's go to the _____ .

CLASSROOM DISPLAYS

CLASSROOM DISPLAYS

Skit, Skat, Skoodle, Doot.

Flip, Flop, Flee!

Who Do You See in the Coconut Tree?

Who's in this cute coconut tree? Why, your youngsters are! After reading *Chicka Chicka Boom Boom* by Bill Martin Jr. and John Archambault, have each child help fringe-cut large leaf cutouts and attach a head shot photo of herself to a coconut cutout. Mount the leaves and coconuts above a paper trunk. Then have youngsters identify letter cutouts and add them to the display.

Beverly Rexrode, Franklin Elementary, Franklin, WV

Pop In and Meet the Class!

Popcorn

Display an oversize tagboard popcorn bucket. Then have each child draw a self-portrait on a personalized popcorn cutout. Wrap pipe cleaners around pencils, remove the pipe cleaners, and then hot-glue each pipe cleaner to the back of a popcorn cutout. Next, hot-glue the pipe cleaners on and around the bucket. If desired, add other popcorn cutouts to the display.

Stephanie Ebersole
Elmwood Elementary
Bloomdale, OH

Job Pockets

This unique display is sure to receive plenty of compliments! Cut pockets from pairs of jeans, keeping the pockets attached to the material. Then use puff fabric paint to label the pockets with different job names. Mount the pockets on a wall and add flower cutouts, if desired. To use the display, simply place a personalized jumbo craft stick in each pocket to assign a student to each job.

Karri Ann Hraban, St. Teresa School
Lincoln, NE

In advance, take a photo of each child and trim a circle around her head. Have each student color a copy of the rocket ship on page 106. Then have her glue her photo and tissue paper flames to her rocket as shown. Display the projects along with glittery star cutouts.

Felice Kestenbaum, Jericho, NY

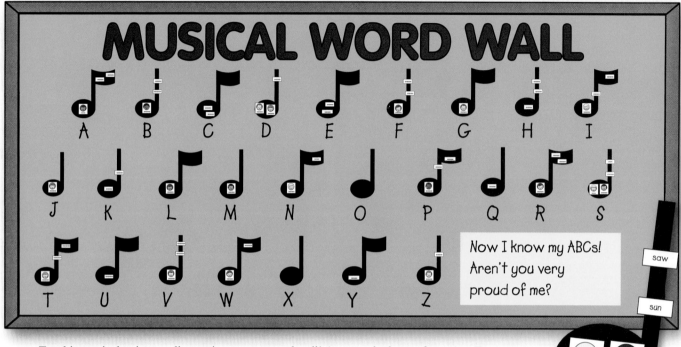

Try this musical twist to call attention to your word wall! Arrange the letters from *A* to *Z*, musical notes, and an alphabet song ending as shown. Label each student's photo with her name and attach it to the musical note by the first letter in her name. Feature different words throughout the year, posting each one on the note by its beginning letter.

Melissa Bonney, Drummond Elementary, Drummond, WI

Patch Match

Students match numbers to sets on this interactive display. Write different numbers on pumpkin stem cutouts. For each number, put the same number of sticker dots on a pumpkin cutout. Post the pumpkins on an easy-to-reach display embellished with green streamers (vines) so the display resembles a pumpkin patch. Mount the hook side of a Velcro fastener above each pumpkin and the loop side of a Velcro fastener on the back of each stem. A student counts the number of dots on each pumpkin and attaches the stem with the matching number.

Valerie Wood Smith, Morgantown, PA

Editor's Tip:
Don't have Velcro fasteners?
Use Sticky-Tac instead!

CLASSROOM DISPLAYS

To make this festive scene, have each child fingerpaint a bear cutout (pattern on page 107). After the paint is dry, instruct him to draw paw pads and facial details. Then have him glue on his bear winter clothing and accessories cut from construction paper scraps. Display the bears with a gift cutout and the title shown.

Shannon Martin, Provena Fortin Villa, Bourbonnais, IL

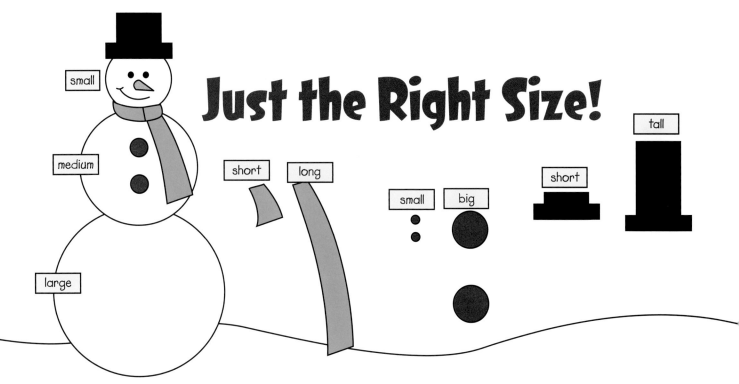

Use descriptive words to compare the sizes of objects on this adorable snowman! Post a snowman that features three different-size circles. Lead youngsters to compare the circle sizes and label them as shown. Next, offer snowman embellishments—such as scarves, buttons, and hats—in three different sizes for students to compare. Then display the items, placing the most appropriate one in each set on the snowman and labeling the remaining pieces.

Jana Sanderson, Rainbow School, Stockton, CA

CLASSROOM DISPLAYS

Looking for ways to foster friendships? Try this! Glue a photograph of each student on the inner circle of a separate muffin liner. Glue the muffin liners to a large heart cutout so it resembles a box of chocolates. Post the heart on a board with the title shown. Then ask youngsters to name different ways they can be kind to a friend. Record responses on individual heart cutouts and use them to embellish the display.

Andrea Roser, Livingston Manor Elementary, Livingston Manor, NY

This science-related display is perfect for Groundhog Day! Invite each youngster, in turn, to stand in front of a light source to see her shadow. Use a white crayon to trace her shadow on a sheet of black paper. Help each youngster cut along her shadow outline and then post the silhouettes on a display similar to the one shown.

Sharon Colgin, Hopkins Elementary, Richmond, VA

CLASSROOM DISPLAYS

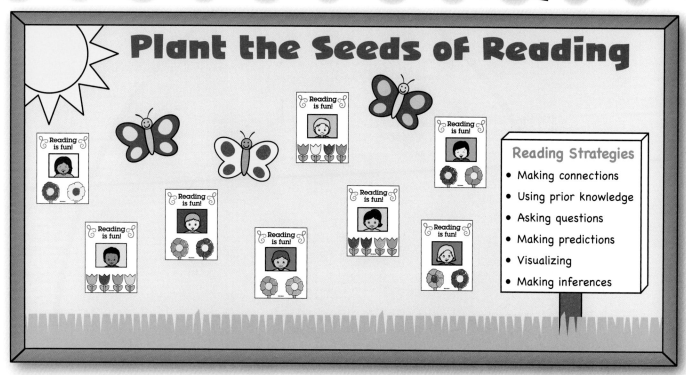

Plant the Seeds of Reading

Reading Strategies
- Making connections
- Using prior knowledge
- Asking questions
- Making predictions
- Visualizing
- Making inferences

This spring display is sure to encourage youngsters to use multiple reading strategies. Write different strategies on a sign cutout. For each student, glue a personal photograph to an individual copy of a seed packet pattern from page 108. Then have the student color his seed packet. Post the sign, the seed packets, and the title shown on a seasonal scene. Then use the display, as desired, to foster improved reading comprehension.

Joyce Carter, Ewing Elementary, Ewing, VA

Spring

Spring is pretty.

Spring is flowers.

Spring is warm.

Spring has sprung.

Our Kindergarten "Poet-tree"

Celebrate National Poetry Month in April with this handmade tree! Have youngsters cut out several handprints (leaves) from green construction paper. Display the leaves above a paper tree trunk to form the treetop. Then encourage each youngster to write a poem that describes a season, a favorite activity, or a special friend. Post the poems and title for a perfectly poetic finish.

Amy Lawrence, Neason Hill Elementary, Meadville, PA

Editor's Tip:
To save time, substitute leaf cutouts in place of the handprints.

Rocket Ship Pattern
Use with "Blast Off Into Kindergarten!" on page 101.

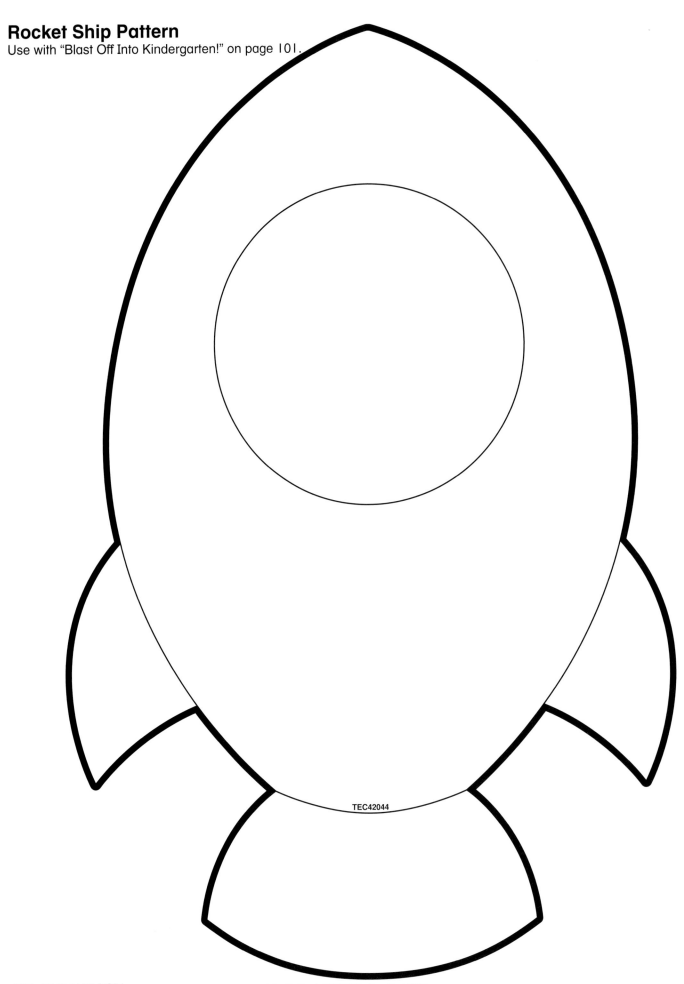

TEC42044

Bear Pattern
Use with "Have a 'Bear-y' Merry Holiday!" on page 103.

TEC42046

Seed Packet Patterns
Use with "Plant the Seeds of Reading" on page 105.

Reading is fun!

TEC42048

Reading is fun!

TEC42048

Reading is fun!

TEC42048

Reading is fun!

TEC42048

LEARNING CENTERS

Learning Centers

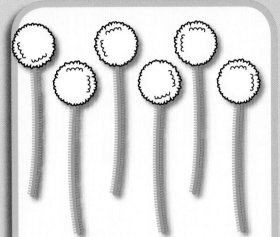

Dandelions in a Row
Math Center

Place in each of several resealable plastic bags equal numbers of green pipe cleaners (stems) and white pom-poms (dandelion heads). A student takes a bag and arranges the stems in a line. Next, she places a dandelion head atop each stem as she counts the number of dandelions. **For an added challenge,** she draws the dandelions on a sheet of paper and then writes the matching number. *One-to-one correspondence*

Marie E. Cecchini
West Dundee, IL

Stamp It!
Literacy Center

On a copy of page 118, stamp different uppercase letters in the first column. Then copy the page to make a class supply. Place the copies at a center along with lowercase alphabet stamps, a washable stamp pad, and pencils. In the second column of his paper a student stamps matching lowercase letters. Then, in the last column, he writes the letter pair. *Matching uppercase and lowercase letters*

Jennae Snow
Snow Preschool
St. George, UT

Cover It!
Math Center

For this partner game, use sticky dots to make two tagboard gameboards like the one shown. Set out the gameboards, a number cube, and a supply of counters. In turn, each player rolls the number cube and covers a matching number of dots on her gameboard. Play continues until one player has covered all the dots on her board. *Number recognition, counting*

Bonnie Lanterman
St. Charles, MO

Learning Centers

Pick a Letter
Literacy Center

For this partner activity, make two pumpkin gameboards like the one shown. Set out the gameboards and a plastic pumpkin-shaped pail containing two sets of letter manipulatives. To take a turn, a child removes a letter from the pail and names it. Then he places the letter on his gameboard. If he chooses a letter that is covered, he returns the letter to the pail and his turn is over. Play continues until all the letters on both gameboards are covered. **To reinforce uppercase-lowercase letter matching,** write lowercase letters on the gameboards and put uppercase letters in the pail. *Letter recognition*

Leonor Maya
George Washington School
Schiller Park, IL

Clip It
Math Center

Glue a foam animal shape to each clothespin in a supply. Put the clothespins in a shoebox and place the box at a center. Have each center visitor clip the clothespins along the box rim to make a pattern. If desired, direct her to copy each pattern she makes. **For an easier version,** set out pattern starter cards for students to copy. *Patterning*

Jodi Darter
Cabool Elementary
Cabool, MO

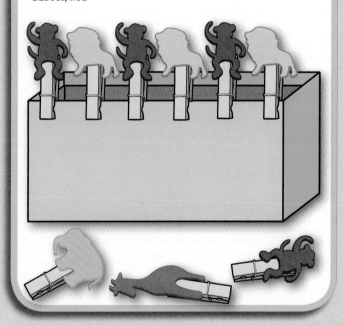

Frogs on Logs
Literacy Center

For a rhyming activity that youngsters can really hop into, prepare 18 frog cards (pattern on page 119) and six brown paper rectangles (logs). Cut apart the first row of picture cards on page 119 and glue each card to a separate log. Then cut apart the remaining cards and glue each one to a frog. Place the frogs and logs at a center. A student names the picture on each frog and puts it on the log with a matching rhyming picture. *Rhyming*

Brooke Shaw
Irmo Elementary
Columbia, SC

Learning Centers

Seasonal Measurement
Math Center

Design seasonal rulers with this simple idea. To make a ruler, affix a series of the same sticker or clip art to a tagboard strip. Use different stickers to make additional rulers. Place the rulers at a center along with assorted objects for measuring. Have each center visitor use a ruler to measure each object. If desired, direct her to draw each object on a sheet of paper and record its length. ***Nonstandard measurement***

Janice Shuman
Saint Brigid School
South Boston, MA

> ### Editor's Tip:
> For assessment, number the back of each ruler and have each child record the number on his paper. When you review a child's work, you'll know which ruler he used.

A Lovely Garden
Literacy Center

Program each of five pairs of clothespins (stems) with a vowel. Then color and cut apart a tagboard copy of the flower cards on page 120. Place the cards and the stems at a center. A student chooses a flower and names the picture. Then she clips a matching stem to the card and stands it up. After she finishes, she unclips the stems to ready the center for the next child. ***Beginning sounds***

Leanne Swinson
Newport, NC

Nighttime Nibbles
Math Center

For this matching activity, color a copy of the center mat on page 121. Color and cut out a copy of the center cards on page 122. Write the matching number on the back of each corn card to make the activity self-checking. To complete the activity, a student spreads out the cards faceup. She puts a number card on the mat. Then she puts the matching corn card faceup beside it. To check her work, she flips the corn card and looks for the matching number. She pairs the remaining cards in the same manner. ***Matching numbers to sets***

Catherine Broome-Kehm, Melbourne Beach, FL

Learning Centers

Cooking Up Words
Literacy Center

Program copies of the recipe cards from page 123 with different high-frequency words. Store the cards in a plastic recipe box. Place at a center the box, a pot of foam letters (including those needed to spell the words), a whiteboard and marker, and a large spoon. A child chooses a card and reads the word. She scoops out the matching letters and arranges them to spell the word. Then she writes the word on the board. After rereading the word, she returns the letters to the pot, erases the board, and continues with a different word. *Spelling, writing*

Clintona Richardson
Joseph C. Shaner Memorial Elementary
Mays Landing, NJ

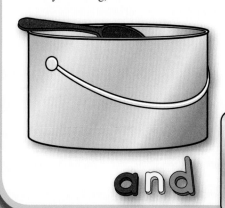

Coin Sort
Math Center

Place a supply of coin manipulatives in the middle section of a plastic sectioned tray such as a vegetable tray. Then label the remaining sections for each coin value. A child sorts the coins into the matching sections. **For an easier version,** label each section with a picture of a coin instead of the value. *Coin values, sorting*

Brandy Bowen
Iowa Elementary
Nampa, ID

From Here to There
Math Center

In advance, collect a supply of cardboard tubes from gift wrap and paper towels. Store each size of tube in a separate container. Use tape to mark two lines on the floor, and place the container and copies of the recording sheet from page 123 nearby. A youngster estimates how many tubes of one size he thinks it will take to reach from one line to the other. After writing his estimate on a recording sheet, he arranges a line of tubes between the two lines. He counts the tubes, writes the number on his recording sheet, and compares the number to his estimate. He returns the tubes to the basket and repeats the activity with the other size of tube. *Nonstandard measurement*

Lucia Kemp Henry, Fallon, NV

Learning Centers

Valentine Fun
Literacy or Math Center

Use valentines to review a variety of skills. Set out several boxes of valentines and choose one of the options below.

High-frequency words: Write a list of high-frequency words on a heart-shaped chart. Post the chart at a center and set out a supply of paper. A student reads each word; then she looks through the cards to find the words. She keeps a list of each word she finds.

Patterning: A child organizes the cards to make two or more different patterns.

Sorting: A student sorts the cards by a rule of her choice. Then she re-sorts the cards a different way.

Jodi Darter
Cabool Elementary
Cabool, MO

Editor's Tip:
Plan ahead for next year! Purchase cards right after Valentine's Day to get them at a fraction of the cost.

Picture Books
Literacy Center

For this sorting activity, cut apart a copy of the cards on page 124 and label three simple book-shaped cutouts as shown. Place the books and cards at a center. A child takes a card, reads the word, and places the card on the corresponding book. He continues until all the cards have been sorted. Then he reads the words in each word family. **For an easier version,** use two books and two sets of cards. *Word families*

Kimberli Carrier
Wise Owl School
Nashua, NH

Punched-Out Patterns
Math Center

Place at a center several shaped hole punchers, paper strips, colorful paper scraps, and glue. A child punches shapes from the paper scraps and then glues the shapes to a paper strip to form a pattern. After it is complete, she labels the pattern below the shapes. *Patterning*

Michelle Allen, Northwest Elementary, Ankeny, IA

Learning Centers

On the Green!

What You Do
Put a ▢ picture-side up.
Find the matching ▢.
▢ to check.

Pots of Gold
Math Center

For this partner game, prepare a set of cards showing addition problems to ten and another set of cards showing subtraction problems from ten. Also make a copy of a gameboard from page 125 for each child and set out 30 yellow counters (gold). Then choose one of the options below.

To provide addition practice, stack the addition cards face-down. Each child takes an addition card and uses counters to solve the problem on his gameboard's ten frame. The youngster with the larger sum places a counter atop a gold coin on his game-board. Each child returns his card to the bottom of the stack. Play continues until one student has five coins on his pot.

To provide subtraction practice, stack the subtraction cards face-down. Students play as directed above for addition. The youngster with the smaller difference puts his coin on the pot.

Tannis Rossi, West Brookfield Elementary, West Brookfield, MA

5 + 2 =   1 + 4 =

On the Green!
Literacy Center

Color a copy of the envelope label on page 126. Attach the label to the front of a manila clasp envelope. Color and cut out a copy of the cards on page 127. Write the matching initial consonant on the back of each picture card to make the activity self-checking. Put the cards in the envelope.

A student takes the cards and spreads them out, placing the picture cards picture-side up. She puts a picture card below the envelope and says the name of the picture. Then she finds the matching initial consonant card and places it beside the picture card. To check her work, she flips the picture card. She continues in this manner until all the cards are paired. *Initial consonants*

Catherine Broome-Kehm, Melbourne Beach, FL

A Colorful Food
Literacy Center

In advance, collect empty gelatin boxes featuring a variety of colors. Cut the front panel from each box and make a color-word card to match each panel. Make each panel self-checking by writing the corresponding color word on its back. Arrange the panels in a row and set the stack of word cards nearby. A child takes a word card, reads it, and places it below the matching panel. He continues with the remaining cards until he's satisfied with the cards' placement. Then he turns over each panel to check his work. *Color words*

Kate Lane, Frederick, MD

Grape   Strawberry   Lime   Orange   Lemon   Berry Blue

yellow   purple   red   blue

Learning Centers

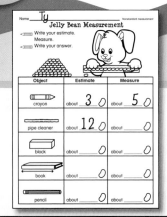

Jelly Bean Measurement
Math Center

Sweeten your kindergartners' nonstandard measurement skills with this mouthwatering ruler. To make one, arrange a line of 20 jelly beans on the sticky side of a strip of clear mailing tape. Then put another strip of tape over the jelly beans and seal the edges, trimming them if necessary. Place at a center the ruler, a class supply of the recording sheet on page 128, and the objects listed on the sheet. A child estimates the length of an object and writes his estimate on his recording sheet. Then he uses the ruler to measure the object and writes its actual length on his paper. After comparing the estimate to the actual length, he repeats the process with each of the remaining objects. **Nonstandard measurement**

Jennie Jensen, North Cedar Elementary, Lowden, IA

Poetry Highlights
Literacy Center

This simple idea reinforces a variety of skills. Place a transparency of a familiar poem on an overhead projector. Position the projector so the poem is displayed on a student-accessible portion of a whiteboard. Set pointers and markers near the board. Designate a skill—such as letter recognition, sight words, or punctuation—for students to practice. A child reads the poem and uses the pointers and markers to complete the activity. To ready the center for the next student, she simply erases the board. **Print awareness**

Kelsea Wright
Leonard Seal Elementary
Douglass, KS

"In My Garden"
See the green peas,
Small as you please.
See the orange carrot,
So big I can share it!
See the green bean,
Long and lean.

R P B M T

Small Gifts
Literacy Center

Label several small gift bags with different consonants. For each consonant, gather one or more small objects whose names begin with the consonant. Store the objects in a container; place the container and bags at a center. A child chooses an object, names it, and identifies the beginning letter. Then she puts the object in the matching bag. She continues with the remaining objects. **For a more advanced version,** provide objects whose names end with the consonants on the bags. **Initial consonants**

Michelle Taggart, Coverdell Elementary, St. Charles, MO

Learning Centers

River Hopping
Math Center

For a skip-counting activity that youngsters can hop into, use the patterns on page 129 to make ten alligator cutouts and ten log cutouts. Label each alligator with an odd number from 1 to 19 and label each log with an even number from 2 to 20. If desired, laminate the cutouts for durability. Place two parallel strips of painters' tape (or lengths of blue yarn) on the floor to make a river. A child arranges the cutouts in sequential order in the river. Then he hops from one end of the river to the other by only hopping on the logs. As he hops on each log, he reads the number written on it. *Counting by twos*

Kelly Young
Charleston School
Charleston, TN

Projected Writings
Literacy Center

In advance, prepare transparencies with sentences that youngsters can read, leaving space under each sentence for students to write. Staple a blank transparency atop each programmed transparency. Set up an overhead projector and place the transparencies and overhead markers nearby. A child turns on the overhead projector and places a transparency on it. Next, she traces and then copies the sentences on the transparency as she reads them. Then she looks at the projection to reread the sentences. She repeats the activity with different transparencies as time allows. **For an easier version,** write sight words on the transparencies. *Writing*

Sarah Payne
North Duplin Elementary
Mount Olive, NC

I like my friends.

I like my friends.

I see a big dog.

I see a big dog.

Race to Measure
Math Center

Set out a supply of similar-size toy cars along with assorted objects to measure. A child chooses an object and estimates its length in cars. She puts the object on a work surface and places cars in a line beside the object. Then she counts the cars and compares the actual length of the object to her prediction. She repeats the process with different objects. *Nonstandard measurement, estimating lengths*

Patrice Clynes
Plantsville Elementary
Plantsville, CT

Matching uppercase and lowercase letters

Stamp It!

Stamp.

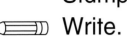 Write.

Note to the teacher: Use with "Stamp It!" on page 110.

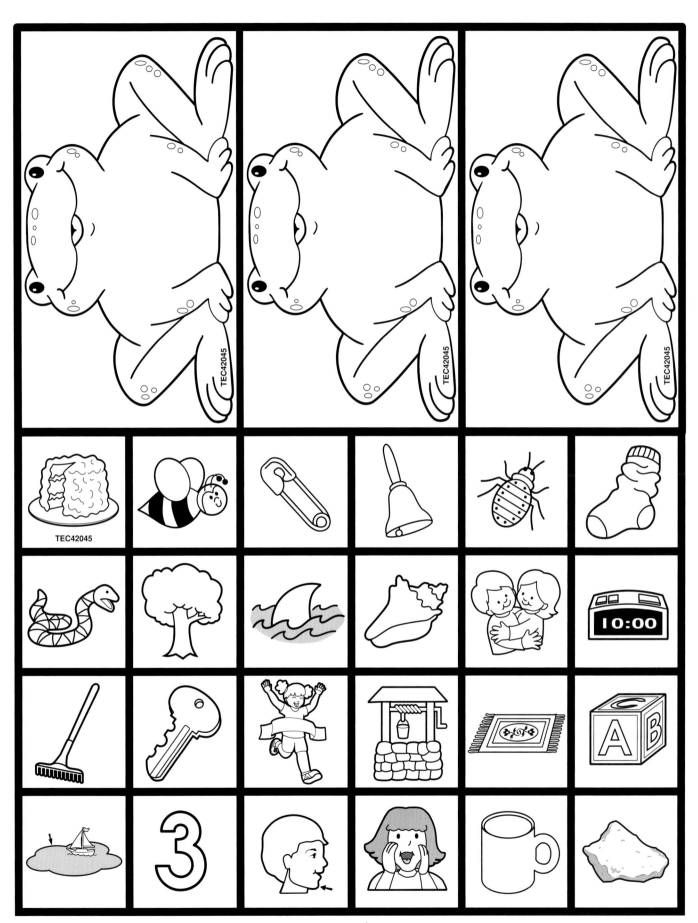

Flower Cards
Use with "A Lovely Garden" on page 112.

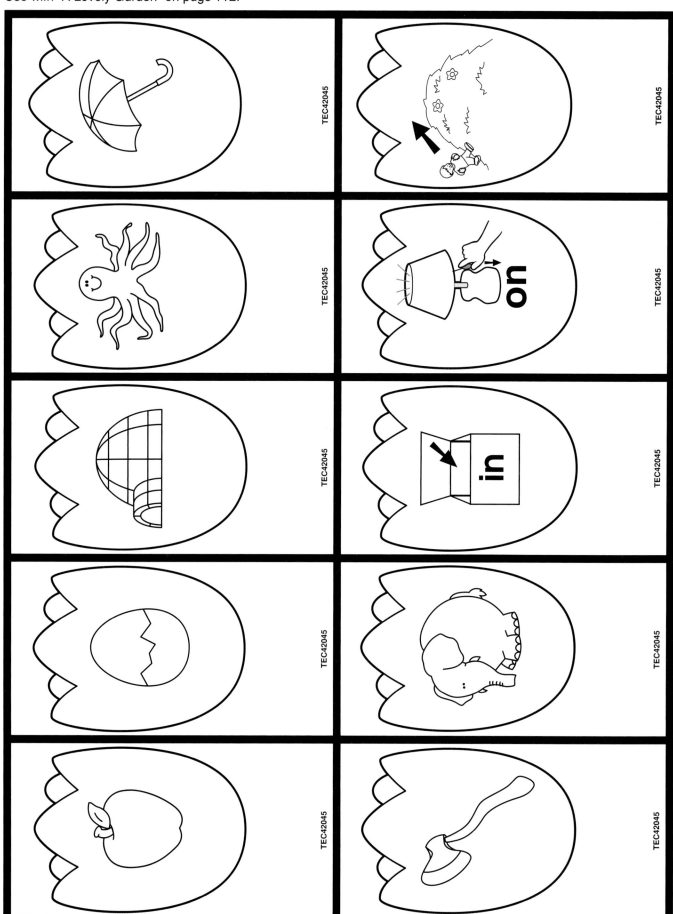

Nighttime Nibbles

Put a number card.
Put the matching corn card.
Check.

Center Cards

Use with "Nighttime Nibbles" on page 112.

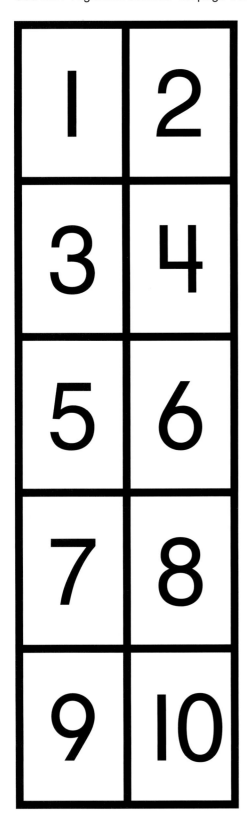

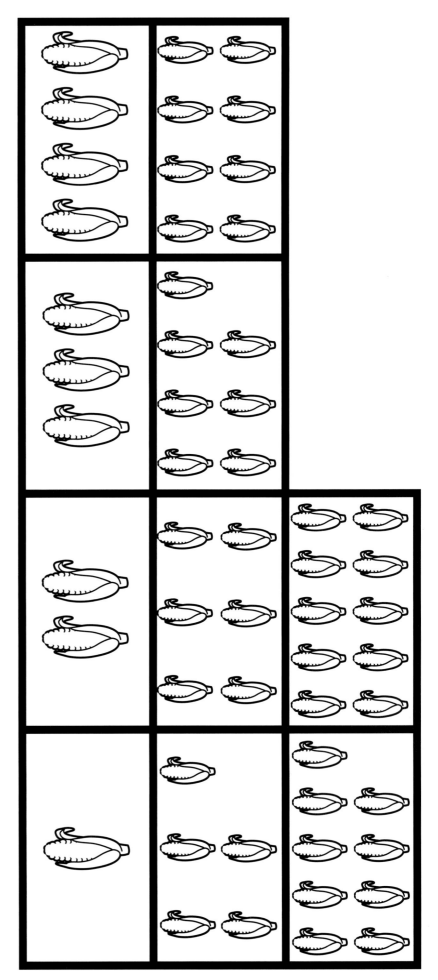

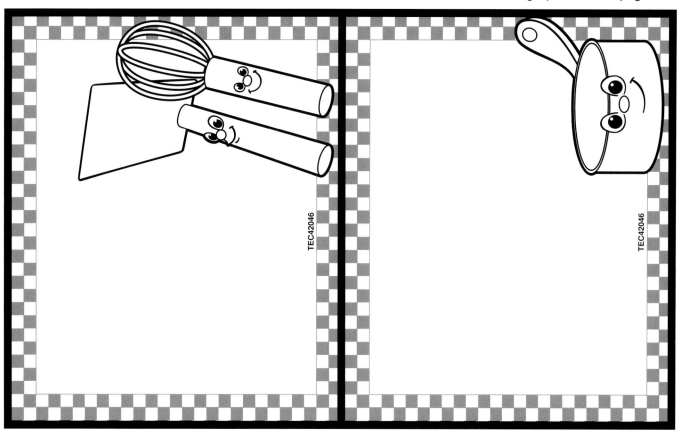

Name _____

From Here to There

Tube	Guess	Check

©The Mailbox® • TEC42046 • Dec./Jan. 2009–10

Note to the teacher: Use with "From Here to There" on page 113.

THE MAILBOX **123**

Picture and Word Cards
Use with "Picture Books" on page 114.

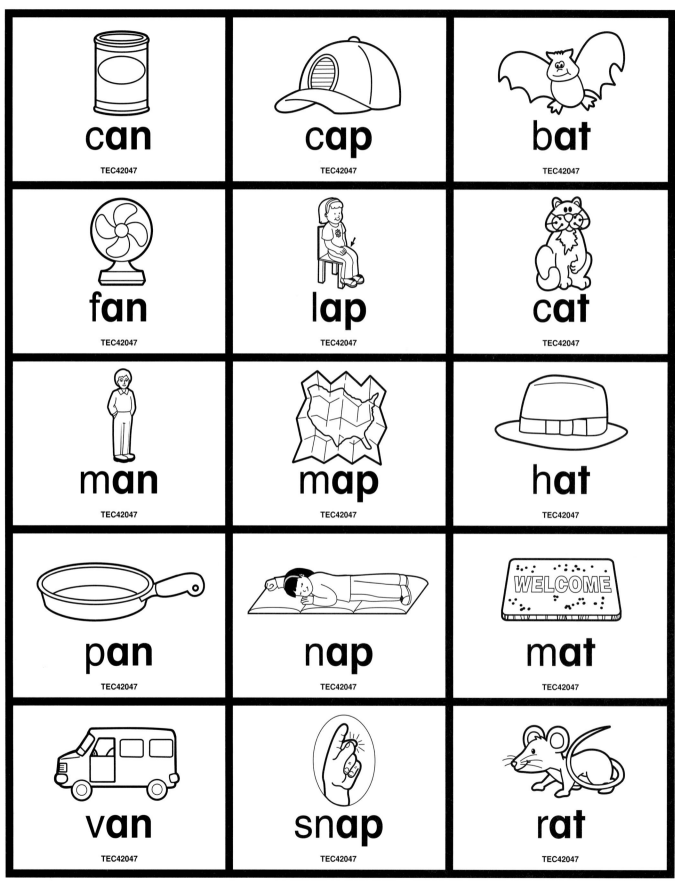

can
TEC42047

cap
TEC42047

bat
TEC42047

fan
TEC42047

lap
TEC42047

cat
TEC42047

man
TEC42047

map
TEC42047

hat
TEC42047

pan
TEC42047

nap
TEC42047

mat
TEC42047

van
TEC42047

snap
TEC42047

rat
TEC42047

©The Mailbox® • TEC42047 • Feb./Mar. 2010

©The Mailbox® • TEC42047 • Feb./Mar. 2010

On the Green!

What You Do

Put a ☐ picture-side up.
Find the matching ◉ .
Flip the ☐ to check.
Repeat.

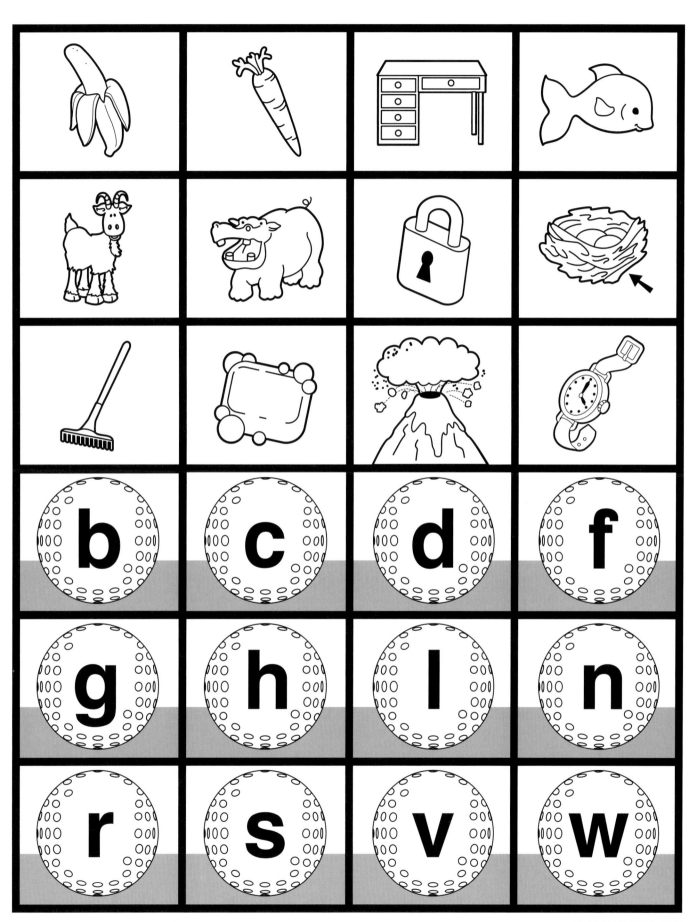

Jelly Bean Measurement

✏️ Write your estimate.
   Measure.
✏️ Write your answer.

Object	Estimate	Measure
🖍️ crayon	about _____ ⬭	about _____ ⬭
〰️ pipe cleaner	about _____ ⬭	about _____ ⬭
🧱 block	about _____ ⬭	about _____ ⬭
📖 book	about _____ ⬭	about _____ ⬭
✏️ pencil	about _____ ⬭	about _____ ⬭

©The Mailbox® • TEC42048 • April/May 2010

128 THE MAILBOX   **Note to the teacher:** Use with "Jelly Bean Measurement" on page 116.

TEC42049

TEC42049

Spill and Sort!

What You Need

15 two-color counters

cup

paper like this: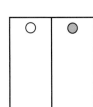

What You Do

① Put the counters in the cup.

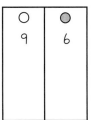

② Shake. Spill.

③ Sort. Line up each set.

④ Count. Write.

⑤ Circle the greater number.

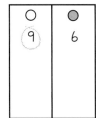

⑥ Do Steps 1–5 again.

©The Mailbox® • TEC42045 • Oct./Nov. 2009

Step-by-step center activity: Make a copy of this activity card and put it in a plastic page protector for durability. Then put the activity card and the needed materials at a center.

Clap and Count

What You Need

grocery store ad

paper

scissors

glue

What You Do

1. Cut out 4 pictures.

2. Draw lines like this.

3. Glue.

4. Clap as you name each picture.

Car-rots.

5. Write how many parts.

Step-by-step center activity: Make a copy of this activity card and put it in a plastic page protector for durability. Then put the activity card and the needed materials at a center.

Stamp It!

What You Need

10 counters in a bag

 1¢ 2¢ 3¢ 4¢ 5¢
6¢ 7¢ 8¢ 9¢ 10¢

2 coin stampers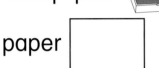

stamp pad

paper

What You Do

① Draw 2 lines.

② Take 1 counter. 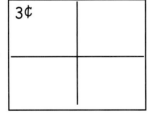 3¢

③ Write.

3¢

④ Stamp coins to match.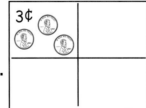

3¢

⑤ Do Steps 2–4 again.

©The Mailbox® • TEC42047 • Feb./Mar. 2010

Step-by-step center activity: Make a copy of this activity card and put it in a plastic page protector for durability. Then put the activity card and the needed materials at a center. (To adapt the activity for different skill levels, adjust the selection of counters and coin stampers.)

LET'S DO SOCIAL STUDIES!

Let's Do Social Studies!

Citizenship Song
Recognizing good citizenship

Promote positive behaviors and good classroom citizens with this song.

(sung to the tune of "London Bridge")

In our class we follow rules,
Follow rules, follow rules.
In our class we follow rules
Like good citizens.

We treat our friends with respect,
With respect, with respect.
We treat our friends with respect
Like good citizens.

In our class we wait our turn,
Wait our turn, wait our turn.
In our class we wait our turn
Like good citizens.

We keep our hands to ourselves,
To ourselves, to ourselves.
We keep our hands to ourselves
Like good citizens.

adapted from a song by Kim Minafo
Apex, NC

Cruising Through the Community
Identifying community helpers

In advance, take pictures of various locations around your school's community, such as a grocery store, doctor's office, police station, and restaurant. Post the pictures along a construction paper road. Then make a pointer by attaching a school bus cutout to a ruler.

To begin, tell students that you are taking them on an imaginary field trip around the community. "Drive" the bus to one picture at a time and ask youngsters to identify each location. Then engage students in a discussion about the community helpers that work at each location. To follow up, have each child draw a picture of a community helper whom he has met.

Erin Bodek, North Cambria, PA

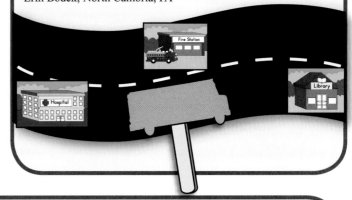

So Proud
Celebrating Constitution Day and Citizenship Day

Commemorate Constitution Day and Citizenship Day on September 17 with this class display. Explain to youngsters that the signing of the constitution in 1787 gave the people in the United States rights and responsibilities as citizens. Then have each child glue a small flag cutout to a craft stick. Along the bottom of a sheet of paper, help him write "Citizen" before his name. Next, direct him to draw a picture of himself that incorporates the flag cutout; then have him glue the cutout to the picture. Display the finished papers with the title "Proud to Be Citizens!"

Citizen Ethan

Let's Do Social Studies!

Who Lives Here?

Knowledge of family

Direct each child to fold a 12" x 18" sheet of construction paper in half and trim it to resemble the structure in which he lives (house, apartment building, mobile home, etc.). Have each child write "Who Lives Here?" on the cover of the resulting booklet and then add details so that it looks like his home. Next, have each youngster open his booklet, write "My Family," and draw a picture of the family members who live in his home. To complete the project, help each student label his family members.

adapted from an idea by Sheli Gossett, Sebring, FL

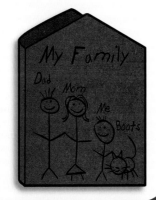

A Decoration to Share

Understanding community

This art project is a picture-perfect way to end a unit on community. Have each student paint or draw on a nine-inch tagboard square a picture of a different community helper or a community building. Glue the completed squares to a large sheet of bulletin board paper and draw stitch marks to make it look like a quilt. Display the quilt with the title shown. If desired, obtain permission to display the quilt in a community building, such as a post office, public library, or town hall.

Amy Rodriguez, Public School 212, Brooklyn, NY

Thankful Pie

Expressing thankfulness

Follow up a discussion on what it means to be thankful with this sweet project. To begin, have each child write, dictate, or draw something she is thankful for on each of several paper strips. Then direct her to fold her strips and put them in an individual-size disposable tart pan. Next, have her paint a tagboard circle (sized to fit inside the rim of the tart pan) with a mixture of equal parts of orange paint and nonmentholated shaving cream plus a dash of pumpkin pie spice. When her circle is dry, have her glue a small piece of cotton batting (whipped cream) to the center and then place it atop the tart pan to make a pumpkin pie. Invite children to take their pies home and share their thankful thoughts with their families on Thanksgiving Day.

Alice McDaniel, Apex, NC

Let's Do Social Studies!

Holiday Candles

Recognizing holidays around the world

Explain to students that many different cultures use candles to represent holiday traditions. Then have each child draw a large candle on the front of a folded sheet of paper and glue on a paper flame. Next, read aloud the poem shown and give each child a copy of the poem to glue inside her paper. Then invite her to take the poem home to share with her family.

Dede Boudinet
Old Bonhomme School
Olivette, MO

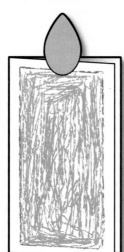

See the candles shine so bright,
Burning, blazing day and night.
On a menorah or on a tree
Or on a kinara for all to see.
See the candles shine so bright,
Welcoming the holidays with their light!

Kwanzaa Kindness

Working toward a class goal

Promote thoughtful behavior this Kwanzaa season. After explaining the seven principles of Kwanzaa (see chart), draw a large kinara on the board or on chart paper. Explain to students that when the class exhibits one of the seven principles, you will color in one candle on the kinara. After all the candles are colored, reward youngsters with a Kwanzaa-related reward, such as a feast of fruits and vegetables or a party to make *mkekas* (woven mats).

Gerri Primak
Charlotte, NC

Seven Kwanzaa Principles
Umoja—unity
Kujichagulia—self-determination
Ujima—collective work and responsibility
Ujamaa—cooperative economics
Nia—purpose
Kuumba—creativity
Imani—faith

Stocking Stuffers

Distinguishing between needs and wants

Display within students' reach two large paper stocking cutouts. Label one stocking "Needs" and the other "Wants." Invite youngsters to cut from magazines pictures of items that are needs or wants. Then gather the class near the stockings and ask each youngster, in turn, to glue his pictures to the correct stockings.

Karen Gore, Dames Ferry Elementary, Gray, GA

Let's Do Social Studies!

Special Badges
Learning about famous Americans

Teach youngsters about famous Americans throughout the school year. To prepare, color and cut out a copy of the badges on page 139. Laminate the badges for durability and attach a pin back to each badge. After reading about and discussing one of the featured famous Americans, have a child wear the badge. Encourage him to tell others about the famous person throughout the day. Have other students wear the badge on subsequent days. Continue this process throughout the year with other badges. **For a home-school connection,** ask youngsters to enlist the help of their families to discover more facts about the featured American.

Ellen Zainea
Knapp Charter Academy
Grand Rapids, MI

If I Were President
Recognizing items used by the president

Use this idea to encourage youngsters to think about the items the president often uses. Help each child make a chart, like the one shown, on a 12" x 18" sheet of paper. Then direct him to cut apart a copy of the cards on page 140. Have him look at each card and determine whether it is an item he would use if he were the president. Have him glue the card on the corresponding side of the chart. Invite each child to share his chart and explain the placement of his cards.

Angie Kutzer
Garrett Elementary
Mebane, NC

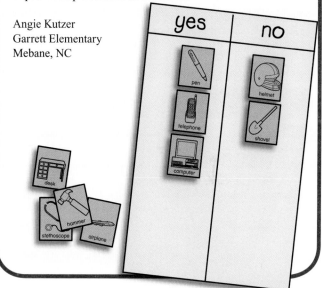

On the Go
Classifying types of transportation

Prior to beginning a unit or an activity on transportation, ask each child to bring a toy vehicle labeled with her name to school. (Have a few extra vehicles on hand in case a child does not have one.) On a large piece of white bulletin board paper, draw a scene with a road, sky, and water; then place the scene on a table. To begin, explain how different types of vehicles travel by land, air, or water. Then invite each youngster, in turn, to place her vehicle on an appropriate area of the scene. **To extend the activity,** make a class chart to list the type of vehicles on each part of the scene.

adapted from an idea by Bonnie P. Munn, First Klass Early Childhood
   Learning Center, Charleston, SC

Let's Do Social Studies!

It's a Community!
Reinforcing the concept of community

In advance, collect a variety of empty food boxes in different sizes. To begin, have youngsters name common buildings and areas found in a community. Then have each child decorate a box to resemble a specific building. Attach the buildings to a length of bulletin board paper placed on your floor. Then prompt students to use craft items and cardboard tubes to add trees, parks, and other areas or items found in a community.

Rosemary Cliburn
Christian Home and Bible School
Mount Dora, FL

Hurrah for Maps!
Reinforcing the parts of a map

Post a map in your classroom. Then lead youngsters in this song, pointing out the different parts of the map when appropriate.

(sung to the tune of "The Ants Go Marching")

We're learning about maps today—hurrah, hurrah!
We're learning about maps today—hurrah, hurrah!
A compass rose and symbols too.
There is a legend to help you.
They are all important parts of a map, of a map,
Map, map, map, map, map, map, map, map.

adapted from an idea by Lisa Dukes
Caldwell Heights Elementary
Round Rock, TX

Good for the Earth!
Learning recycling rules

To prepare for this fun game, gather a class supply of plastic containers that show recycling symbols with various numbers. Have students sit in a circle and then give each child a container. Play a musical recording and direct students to pass the containers around the circle. When the music stops, prompt each child to search for and then identify the number on her container. Have all the youngsters holding containers labeled with the number one stand up. Then tell students that this number is one that most recycling centers will accept. Restart the music and repeat the activity with the number two, explaining this number is also accepted by most recycling centers.

Sarah Hibbett
Henderson, TN

Ask me about
George Washington.

TEC42047

Ask me about
Abraham Lincoln.

TEC42047

Ask me about
Barack Obama.

TEC42047

Ask me about
Martin Luther King Jr.

TEC42047

Ask me about
Rosa Parks.

TEC42047

Ask me about
Betsy Ross.

TEC42047

Ask me about
Alexander Graham Bell.

TEC42047

Ask me about
Helen Keller.

TEC42047

Ask me about
Neil Armstrong.

TEC42047

Ask me about
Benjamin Franklin.

TEC42047

Ask me about
Harriet Tubman.

TEC42047

Ask me about
the Wright brothers.

TEC42047

Cards

Use with "If I Were President" on page 137.

telephone

TEC42047

hammer

TEC42047

computer

TEC42047

stethoscope

TEC42047

helmet

TEC42047

airplane

TEC42047

pen

TEC42047

shovel

TEC42047

desk

TEC42047

Management Tips & Timesavers

Management Tips & Timesavers

Inch by Inch

Here's a positive way to motivate students to follow classroom rules. List different class rewards on a poster-size apple cutout. Divide a green paper strip (grass) into several sections. Display the apple and the grass; then post a worm cutout on the left side of the grass. Each time students exhibit especially good behavior, move the worm to the right one section. After you move the worm to the last section, invite students to choose a reward.

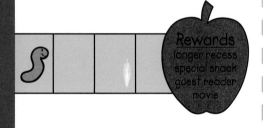

Rewards
longer recess
special snack
guest reader
movie

Check the Cup

Looking for a way to keep small classroom items at your fingertips? Use plastic cups! Pin plastic cups to bulletin boards and place items such as nametags, calendar pieces, or manipulatives inside. Or adhere a strip of magnetic tape to the back of a cup, attach it to the board, and put dry-erase markers inside. *Diane Bonica, Deer Creek Elementary, Tigard, OR*

The First Thing

Help your students remember to write their names on their papers with this catchy tune. Before starting an assignment, lead students in singing the song. If desired, add additional verses for other directions by modifying the ordinal number and task. *Brandy Coker, Boone Trail Elementary, Mamers, NC*

(sung to the tune of "Ten Little Indians")

The first thing you do is write your name on your paper,
Name on your paper, name on your paper.
The first thing you do is write your name on your paper
So we will know it is yours.

In the Bowl

Give each youngster a small paper bowl when it's time for cut-and-paste projects. (The ones with animal prints are fun to use!) The child cuts out the necessary pieces and places them in her bowl for safekeeping until it's time to glue them down. *Mildred Yarborough, Grace Christian School, Cowards, SC*

Picture-Perfect Grouping

Students can practice name recognition while they locate their assigned groups. For each group, list students' names on both sides of an 8" x 10" piece of paper. Slip each paper into an 8" x 10" acrylic picture frame; then place each frame in a different classroom location. When it is time for group work, each child finds his name and then joins his group in the corresponding area. *Suzanne Ward, Caledonia Centennial Public School, Caledonia, Ontario, Canada*

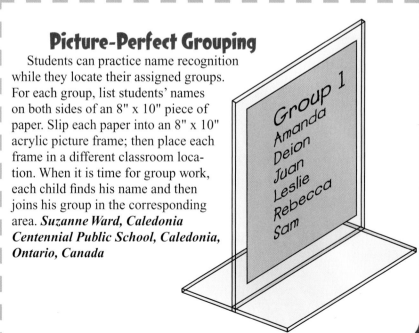

Group 1
Amanda
Deion
Juan
Leslie
Rebecca
Sam

Management Tips & Timesavers

Ready to Work

Looking for a way to keep extra pencils at students' fingertips? Use toothbrush holders! Gather a supply of clean plastic toothbrush holders (such as those found at dollar stores). Store pencils in the toothbrush holders. Then place the holders at centers and other work areas where students may need access to pencils. When a child needs a pencil, she can grab one and get right to work. *Leslie Cedars, Anacoco Elementary, Anacoco, LA*

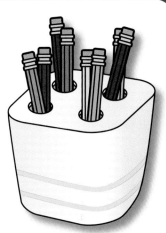

Student Files

Help keep students' paperwork neatly organized with this simple system. Personalize a hanging file folder for each child; then store the folders in alphabetical order in a plastic file crate. Throughout the day, tuck completed papers in the files. You can also file notes to parents and work for absent students. When it's time for students to take their work home, each child's papers will be easy to locate. *Ashlee Williams, Austell Primary, Austell, GA*

Editor's Tip:
As your kindergartners become more familiar with alphabetical order, encourage them to file their own papers.

Treat others with kindness.

Picture-Perfect Behavior

Here's an easy way to provide youngsters with a visual reminder of classroom rules. Take photos of students demonstrating positive behaviors. Mount each photo on a sheet of paper; then label each photo with a short description of the rule. Display the rules to use as a reference throughout the year. *Megan Jones, Old Dominion University, Norfolk, VA*

Prepared Parents

To ensure that parents' questions and concerns are addressed during a conference, send home a copy of page 148 prior to the meeting. Ask each child's family to fill it out and bring it to the scheduled conference. Begin the meeting by having a family member share the information recorded on the sheet. *Cathy Gressley, Jefferson Kindergarten Center, St. Joseph, MI*

Color-Coded Reproducibles

When completing cut-and-glue reproducibles, try this tip to help youngsters avoid mixing their pieces with their neighbors'. Make several different-colored copies of the page and give a different-colored copy to each child at a table. After he cuts the pieces from the page, each child will be able to tell at a glance which ones belong to him. No more mixed-up pieces! *Janice Sutherland, Louisiana Schnell Elementary, Placerville, CA*

Management Tips & Timesavers

A Tidying Tune

Instead of singing a song to designate cleanup time, try using a recorded tune instead. Choose a song that is familiar to your class. When youngsters hear it, they will know it's time to clean up. And since students are familiar with the song, they'll know how much time they have to finish cleaning before the song ends. *Rachel Harrar, Francis Scott Key Elementary, Washington, DC*

Decorate the Tree!

To promote positive behavior, post a large tree cutout. Store colorful paper ornaments near the tree. Each time the class exhibits positive behavior, add an ornament to the tree. When a predetermined number of ornaments adorn the tree, reward youngsters with a special treat or privilege. *Kelly Smith, Marcy Elementary, Marcy, NY*

Fitting Together

Use tray puzzles to divide students into groups. Gather one puzzle for each small group you want to create. (For example, if you have 18 students and want three groups, gather three six-piece puzzles.) Place the pieces from all the puzzles in a container and mix them together. Then place the puzzle trays in separate classroom locations. A child takes a puzzle piece, finds the corresponding tray, and fits his piece inside. Not only will students be divided into groups, but each group will also have a defined workspace. *Jodi Darter, Cabool Elementary, Cabool, MO*

Manipulatives to Go

Easily manage edible manipulatives with the help of a muffin tin and cupcake liners. Place a liner in each section of a muffin tin and scoop a desired number of manipulatives into each liner. Carry the muffin tin to each table to pass out the manipulatives. When the activity is over, students simply dispose of the cupcake liners. *Judy Goldrick, May Academy, Chicago, IL*

Table Toppers

This simple idea for labeling students' work areas reinforces the theme or topic you are teaching. For each table or group of desks in your classroom, attach a card labeled with a different item that corresponds to the theme or topic. Refer to these group names when praising groups of students or calling them to line up. Update the cards as often as needed to match your current theme or topic. *Candace Johnston, Elliston-Lafayette Elementary, Elliston, VA*

pennies   quarter   nickels   dimes

Management Tips & Timesavers

Welcome-Back Buddies

When an absent student returns to school, choose a responsible classmate to be her welcome-back buddy. The buddy reviews important information that was shared during his classmate's absence and explains her makeup work. The returning student gets caught up on what she missed without interrupting the daily classroom routine. *Diane Billman, McKitrick Elementary, Lutz, FL*

A Tall Hat

In honor of Dr. Seuss's birthday (March 2), try this idea to encourage positive behavior. Display a large red and white striped hat cutout. Then post a smiley face cutout at the bottom of the hat. Each time the class exhibits especially good behavior, move the smiley face up one stripe. After moving the smiley face to the last stripe, reward students with a special treat or privilege. *Amy Lawrence, Neason Hill Elementary, Meadville, PA*

Field Trip Folder

Keep field trip necessities at your fingertips with a two-pocket folder. Attach a copy of your class list to the front of the folder and place an envelope inside. When a student turns in his permission slip and field trip money, check off his name on the list. Then tuck the permission slip in a pocket of the folder and place the money in the envelope. When it's time to leave for the trip, simply grab the folder to ensure that you have the items you need. *Jennifer Starcke, Holy Name Catholic School, Kansas City, KS*

Containers for Cuttings

To prevent students from accidentally throwing away important pieces from cut-and-glue projects, try this! Place a plastic container at each table or workstation. As a child works, he places his scrap paper in the container. If he discovers he is missing a necessary piece, he can retrieve it from the container. No more lost pieces! *Terry Schreiber, Holy Family Catholic Academy, Norwood, NJ*

Color-Coded Groups

Manage your reading groups or other small groups with colored sticky dots. Assign each group a different color and attach sticky dots of the corresponding color to students' folders, nametags, or other personalized classroom items. If a student changes to a different group, simply place new sticky dots atop the existing ones. You can also use this idea to limit the number of students out of their seats at a time by using the groups' color names for lining up, gathering for calendar time, or packing up at the end of the day. *Jodi Darter, Cabool Elementary, Cabool, MO*

Management Tips & Timesavers

Get in Shape!

This idea promotes positive behavior and doubles as a seasonal display. Write a different class reward on the backs of several thematic or seasonal cutouts. Then attach the cutouts to the wall or a bulletin board. When your class exhibits especially good behavior, invite a child to choose a cutout. Remove the cutout from the display and announce the reward. *Jennifer Apgar, Grantham, PA*

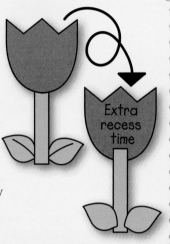

Wiggle Release

Help your kindergartners release excess energy before an extended period of sitting. To begin, invite youngsters to grab some "wiggles" from the air. Name a body part for each child to "place" her wiggles on and then have her wiggle the corresponding body part. Continue in this manner, assigning different body parts, until youngsters have gotten their wiggles out and are ready to sit still. *Janet Galvin, Chamberlin Elementary, Colorado Springs, CO*

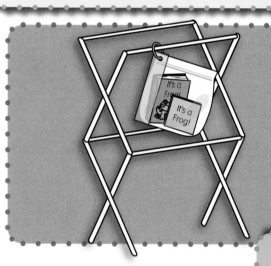

Storage Solution

Here's a simple way to organize books that have accompanying items, such as tapes, CDs, or finger puppets. Place each book and its corresponding items in a gallon-size plastic bag. Reinforce the left side of each bag with packing tape and then punch a hole through the top of each bag as shown. Slip a metal ring through each hole and hang the bags on a laundry-drying rack for easy access. *Kim Minafo, Apex, NC*

Songs on Demand

Keep your song collection organized and at your fingertips. Write each song on a separate index card and organize the cards by song type. Punch a hole in the corner of each card; then slip the cards on a metal ring. Attach a labeled tab to serve as a divider for each new song type. When you're searching for the perfect song to accompany a lesson or fill a few minutes of free time, simply grab the ring! *Kelsea Wright, Seal Elementary, Douglass, KS*

Quiet Butterflies

To help youngsters remember not to talk in the hallway, have them pretend to be butterflies. As students line up, remind them that butterflies are very quiet creatures. When they walk down the hall in a line, have students gently flap their arms like butterfly wings. This simple tip keeps youngsters quiet, as well as occupied, while they walk. *Amy Peterson, The Newfoundland School, Newfoundland, NJ*

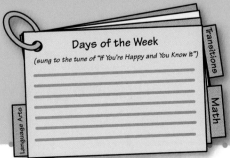

Management Tips & Timesavers

High Five!

Here's a positive way to motivate youngsters to follow classroom rules! Label a supply of handprint cutouts as shown. When you see a student exhibiting especially good behavior, give him a "high five" by attaching a handprint to his work surface. (Write the date on the handprint if desired.) At the end of the week, invite students to take their high five(s) home to share with their families. *Renee M. Plant, Verdigris Elementary, Claremore, OK*

I deserve a high five today!

Collecting Scraps

Add the job of scrap master to your classroom job list. Then place a plastic bucket or container at each table. Throughout the day, have students place any scrap paper in the container at their tables. At the end of the day, the scrap master places the contents of each container in the scrap paper box or the recycling can. *Carrie Knebel, Bethel School District, Eugene, OR*

cat rat

Find Your Match

To partner students for activities or games, write simple rhyming pairs on sun cutouts. Puzzle-cut the suns between the words and give each child a sun half. Have each youngster locate her partner by finding the child with the matching sun half.

What's the Sound?

This attention-getting idea also provides phonemic awareness reinforcement. To begin, repeatedly say a word such as *beep*. As students hear you, they join you in saying the word. After a short amount of time, change the middle sound of the word (such as by saying *bap* or *bop*) and wait for youngsters to begin saying the new word. Continue in this manner until you have each student's full attention. As an alternative, change the beginning or ending sound of the word instead. *Kathie Hilliard, Lake Hazel Elementary, Boise, ID*

Easy Assessment

Try this idea to help keep up with end-of-the-year assessments. Divide a sheet of paper into the same number of sections as you have skills to assess. Then program each section to match a different skill. For each student, personalize a copy of the sheet and attach the copies to a clipboard. As you assess each youngster, highlight the items she still needs to work on. Not only will each child's assessments be on one page, but flipping through the pages will quickly let you know which students still need to be assessed. *Vanessa Rivera, La Luz Elementary, La Luz, NM*

Conference Planning Guide

Child's name: _____

Conference date and time: _____

Child's strengths:	Areas of concern:
Questions:	**Comments:**

OUR READERS WRITE

Our Readers Write

Pick a Pencil!

I assess my students' name–writing skills during the first week of school. To make the assessment enjoyable, I place a variety of novelty pencils in a container. I have a student choose a pencil, and I encourage him to write his name on a sheet of paper. Then he gets to take the special pencil home!

Suzanne Ward, Caledonia Centennial Public School, Caledonia, Ontario, Canada

Keepsake Box

Before our open house, I have each child decorate and attach the poem shown to a box. I give the boxes to parents during open house. Parents tell me that this keepsake box helps reduce clutter and that their youngsters enjoy choosing special school papers to place in the box.

Sue Johnson, Spartanburg Christian Academy Spartanburg, SC

This box can hold special things
I'll make throughout the year.
Papers, letters, crafts, and more—
All things that you'll hold dear.
I know from time to time you'll peek
At all these things I've made.
That's why they are here in this box—
So memories won't fade.

Indestructible Nametags

To make nametags that last all year long, I use a permanent marker to write each youngster's name on a clean margarine lid. Then I punch a hole in each lid. For field trips and other special activities, I simply use a safety pin to attach the appropriate nametag to each child's shirt.

Carole Tobisch, Denmark Early Childhood Center, Denmark, WI

Birthday Backpack

I place a birthday-related book, our stuffed animal birthday mascot, and a notebook in a backpack. On a youngster's birthday, he takes the backpack home and has the mascot join him during his birthday celebration. Then the youngster dictates information about the celebration to be written in the notebook. When the backpack returns to school, I read the youngster's dictation to the class.

Kim Callahan, Cataract Elementary, Cataract, WI

Happy Birthday!

Wishing Tree

At the beginning of the year, the teachers at my school place an artificial tree in front of the school office. We each write items needed for our classrooms on separate apple cutouts and then hang the apples on the tree. When a parent visits the school, he can take an apple, purchase the needed supply, and then drop the supply off at school!

Monica Yankus, St. John the Baptist Catholic School, Plattsmouth, NE

Packs of colorful sticky notes

Ms. Yankus (Kindergarten)

Marvelous Learning Mat

For each child in my class, I make a copy of the table mat shown. As my youngsters learn each shape and color, they color the corresponding picture. Then I laminate the mats and attach each one to the appropriate child's table area. Reviewing the concepts on the mat makes a terrific five-minute filler activity!

Tracy Innes, Emirates National School
Abu Dhabi, United Arab Emirates

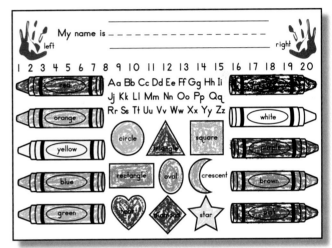

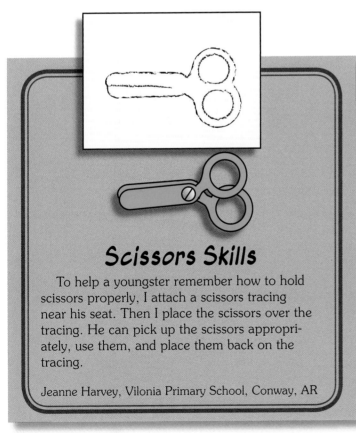

Scissors Skills

To help a youngster remember how to hold scissors properly, I attach a scissors tracing near his seat. Then I place the scissors over the tracing. He can pick up the scissors appropriately, use them, and place them back on the tracing.

Jeanne Harvey, Vilonia Primary School, Conway, AR

Glue Brushes

At the beginning of the year my youngsters have difficulty using glue bottles. When white glue is needed for a project, I pour a little glue on a disposable plate and provide small paintbrushes. My students simply brush the glue on their projects. It's so easy!

Sharon Blackwood, Christ Our King Stella Maris Catholic School, Mount Pleasant, SC

Nice Notes

My students' parents love receiving these simple notes! I take a picture of each youngster participating in a school activity. Then I print out the pictures. When a child does something praiseworthy, I write a quick note on the back of her picture and have her place the picture in her bag to take home.

Millie Morris, Berkmar United Methodist School
Lilburn, GA

Our Readers Write

A New Use

I save unused seasonal napkins from parties and special snacks to use as covers for student-made booklets. I cut student pages slightly smaller than the size of the napkins. Then I staple the completed pages between two napkin covers. Not only are these covers durable, but my students love the colorful designs!

Susan Braverman
Council Rock Primary
Rochester, NY

Fantastic Fire Truck

Sing this toe-tapping tune during Fire Prevention Week to review with youngsters some items found on a fire truck.

(sung to the tune of "The Wheels on the Bus")

The wheels on the truck go round and round,
Round and round, round and round.
The wheels on the truck go round and round
All through the town.

Continue with the following:
The hose on the truck goes spray, spray, spray.
The lights on the truck go flash, flash, flash.
The siren on the truck goes woo, woo, woo.
The ladder on the truck goes up, up, up.

Holly Slama
Hilltop Elementary
Milwaukee, WI

Shapely Diagrams

To make Venn diagrams more meaningful to my students, I draw each side of the diagram in its corresponding shape. Having this visual clue makes it easier for my students to compare and contrast the featured items.

Mary Kibbey
E. J. Arthur Elementary, Athens, NY

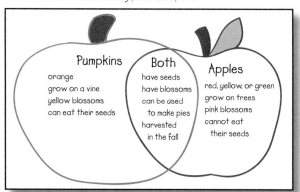

Pumpkins
orange
grow on a vine
yellow blossoms
can eat their seeds

Both
have seeds
have blossoms
can be used
to make pies
harvested
in the fall

Apples
red, yellow, or green
grow on trees
pink blossoms
cannot eat
their seeds

Red and Black Patterns

I keep an eye out at yard sales and discount stores for checkers game pieces. The manipulatives provide unique hands-on practice with patterning skills. My students place the checkers in a row or stack them in a tower to make *AB, AAB,* or *ABB* patterns.

Marie E. Cecchini
West Dundee, IL

What's in the Box?

To help improve my students' reasoning skills, I secretly place a seasonal or theme-related item in a lidded box. Then I show the box to my students and encourage them to ask yes-or-no questions about the characteristics of the object inside. I answer 20 questions about the item, keeping track of the questions and answers as they are asked. After 20 questions have been asked, I review the characteristics that were "yes" answers. Then I encourage each child to guess what is inside the box before I reveal the contents.

Jenny Sims, Dandridge Elementary, Dandridge, TN

Wish Fish

Need extra supplies? Try this! I send a note home to each family to explain that the class occasionally needs extra supplies and to ask whether they are willing to donate items throughout the year. I also program a fish pattern with the rhyme shown, make several copies, and store the cutouts in a nonbreakable fishbowl. Whenever I need a classroom donation, I simply write the item on a fish and send it home with a child whose family offered to contribute.

Jodi Darter, Cabool Elementary
Cabool, MO

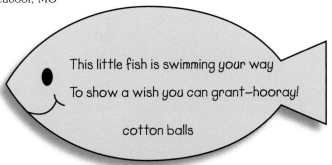

This little fish is swimming your way

To show a wish you can grant—hooray!

cotton balls

Is There a D in Your Name?

| Julia |
Diego	Sam
Cassidy	Robby
Sandra	Beth
Todd	Juanita
Danny	Kyle
Yes	No

Peel and Stick

I encourage literacy development with this idea that's easy to incorporate into my lesson plans. Each week I post a graph similar to the one shown, changing the letter weekly. Nearby I place a sheet of mailing labels programmed with my students' names. A child determines whether her name includes the featured letter, peels her label off the backing, and attaches it to the correct graph column.

Tricia Thissen
Woodbury Elementary, Woodbury, MN

A Special Thank-You

When a parent joins us on a field trip or attends a special school activity, I make sure to snap a picture of him interacting with his child. I glue the photo to the front of a folded construction paper card and write a note of appreciation inside. Parents are thrilled to get a keepsake from the special event they attended.

Amy Rockwood
Grand Traverse Academy
Traverse City, MI

Thank you, Mr. Carter!

Our Readers Write

Who Took My Candy Cane?

To add a seasonal twist to the game Seven Up, I give each child a seasonal cutout. For example, in December I give each child a candy cane cutout. After putting their heads down, my students hold up their cutouts instead of their thumbs. Seven predetermined children secretly take a cutout from a seated student. Each student with a missing cutout guesses which child took her cutout for a chance to switch places with that child.

Barbara Leonhardt, Sewell School, Sewell, NJ

In the Bag

The day before winter break begins, I have each of my students personalize a large paper grocery bag. When he is finished, each child places his bag beside his chair. Throughout the day, students place inside their bags bulky items to be taken home, such as projects and gifts. At the end of the day, each child grabs his bag before exiting the classroom. No more forgotten items!

Cathy Willets
Calvary Christian School
Bellefontaine, OH

Gift Exchange

During the holiday season my class pairs up with another kindergarten classroom. The other teacher and I collect donations from our students' families to purchase a gift for each other's classroom. With our students, we brainstorm items the other class might need and decide which ones we'd like to buy. Then I use the donations to purchase the items. On a designated day we meet with the other class to exchange gifts. Not only do our students learn about the joy of giving, but we also receive much-needed items for our classroom.

Susan Cortright
Pittsford Area Schools
Pittsford, MI

A Peaceful Poem

I share the following poem with my kindergartners to reinforce some of Dr. Martin Luther King Jr.'s beliefs. After my students are familiar with the poem, I have each child take a copy home to share with her family.

Dr. King had a dream
That all people would be fair.
He taught us that if something isn't right,
We should take a stand to show we care.

Lynn Hoseney
Pinckney Elementary
Pinckney, MI

No-Poke Needles

Try using pipe cleaners to make kid-friendly lacing needles. I simply cut a pipe cleaner in half, bend one end to make a loop, and twist the loose end around the pipe cleaner. I thread yarn or other lacing materials through the loop, and the needle is ready to go.

Amy Ryan
Grace Lutheran School
St. Petersburg, FL

Shimmering Paintings

When I want to add some twinkle to my student's paintings, I mix glitter into shallow containers of paint instead of sprinkling it atop projects. When the paint dries, the glitter gives the project a little extra sparkle without the added mess that glitter often brings.

Judy Weber
Evans Falls Elementary
Tunkhannock, PA

Edible Matter

These yummy treats help my students identify three of the states of matter. For each child I place a scoop of ice cream (solid) in a transparent plastic cup. Then I pour some root beer (liquid) on top. The child watches as the carbonation bubbles (gas) rise from the root beer. Before enjoying her root beer float, each child draws a picture of her treat and labels each corresponding state of matter.

Cindy Marshall
Prospect Elementary
Meridian, ID

Write and Play

Rather than having a writing center, I incorporate writing in our dramatic-play center. I label cards with words and pictures that correlate with the current setup of the dramatic-play center. Then I hole-punch the cards and bind them with a metal loose-leaf ring. I place the cards at the center along with paper and pencils. A child visits the dramatic-play center and then uses the cards to write about his experience there.

Blythe Purdin
Rockport Elementary
Rockport, MA

Goodbye Book

If a classmate moves away during the school year, I have my students make a keepsake for him. To begin, we brainstorm different ways to say goodbye, such as "adios," "so long," "farewell," and "see you later." On a copy of a page like the one shown, each child completes the sentence with the word or phrase of her choosing. Then she draws a picture of herself waving goodbye and signs her name. When the pages are complete, I staple them between two construction paper covers and add a title. This book project also makes a nice gift to present to a student teacher who is leaving your classroom.

Beverly Wittes, Deshler Elementary, Deshler, OH

Our Readers Write

A Bright Smile

During National Children's Dental Health Month (February), I teach youngsters this nifty poem to encourage them to brush up on their dental-health habits. It's the perfect reminder for promoting pearly whites and long-lasting smiles!

Brushing, flossing,
And eating right—
These three things
Keep your smile bright!

Marie E. Cecchini, West Dundee, IL

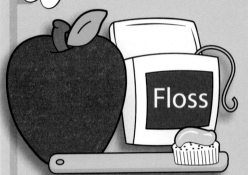

Take a Spin

With this idea, I can quickly make multiple spinners appropriate for students of different ability levels to use with the same game. To make a spinner, I simply draw lines to divide a plate and label the sections as desired. Then, using a brad, I attach a large paper clip to the center of the plate.

Nancy Morgan
Care-a-Lot Daycare and Preschool
Bremerton, WA

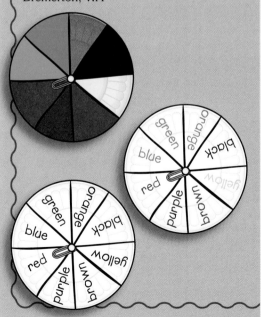

Lovely Decorations

I found a cost-efficient way to provide decorations for students to use when making their valentine card mailboxes. I save old valentine cards along with unused cards parent donate. The following year, I set out the cards and invite students to cut messages and pictures from the cards and use the items to decorate their valentine mailboxes.

Erin Hedstrom
Bright Beginnings Childcare
Princeton, MN

Picture Cards

Looking for ways to use extra border? Try these ideas! I cut the border between pictures so one picture is on each card. Then, when I teach patterns, I encourage my youngsters to use the cards to copy, extend, and create patterns. To make sequencing activities, I cut alphabet or number border apart and place each set of pieces in a separate resealable plastic bag.

Carrie Johnson
Stone Elementary
Crossville, TN

Our Readers Write

Rainy Day Reading

To motivate my blossoming readers, I set up a special indoor flower garden. First, I tape flower cutouts to the outside of a plastic tub or planter. Then I put flashlights and books inside the tub. On rainy spring days, I invite student pairs to choose a book and a flashlight. Students are thrilled to read together by flashlight, and a dreary day becomes much more fun!

Sharron Posey
Double Springs Elementary
Double Springs, AL

Something to Smile About

I make every effort to provide positive feedback to my students. So as I grade a student's work, I draw a small circle next to each answer that needs correcting; then I return the paper to the child. After he corrects his work, I add eyes and a mouth to each circle. That way, when the paper goes home, the student's parents know which problems needed revision and my student knows I'm happy with his efforts.

Sherry Ward
Craigsville Elementary
Craigsville, WV

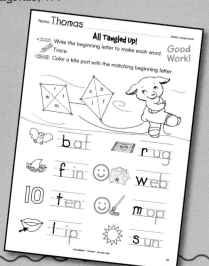

Yardstick Math

To demonstrate how to use a number line for addition and subtraction, I use a yardstick. The numbers are large enough for students to see as I model the process, and it's easy to hold!

Etta Mizell
Bel-Aire Elementary
Gulfport, MS

Pocket Chart Tip

I use my pocket chart to serve as an inexpensive word wall. For each letter of the alphabet, I gather an animal or seasonal cutout that starts with the corresponding letter. I place a few items in each row; then I write the word for each cutout on a separate index card and place the card behind its cutout. What an easy way to utilize a resource I already have!

Charity Snyder, Teravista Elementary, Round Rock, TX

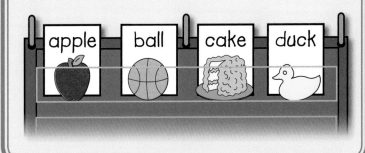

Our Readers Write

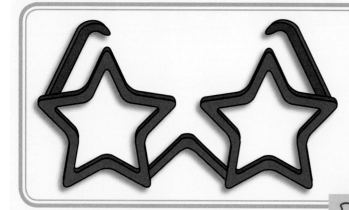

Guided Reading Glasses

I use decorative sunglasses to help my students feel like reading superstars! In advance, I gather enough decorative sunglasses for my largest reading group, and I pop out the lenses. Then I invite each child to wear a pair during guided reading.

Amy Christian
Mesquite, TX

Recess Scramble

When a muddy playground forces my students to play on the blacktop, I organize this fun activity. First, I direct my students to form two lines and face each other. Next, I ask questions such as "Do you have a sister?" and "Is your favorite color pink?" Each time a child answers yes to a question, he runs across to the other line. As we play, I make sure to pose a few all-inclusive questions, such as "Are you wearing shoes?" and "Do you have a belly button?" It's a great way for students to burn some energy and share a few laughs.

Donna Pollhammer, Charles Carroll Elementary
Westminster, MD

Tons of Tracers

With the help of my students' families, my youngsters always have tracers to use. Throughout the year, I request that families save their empty cereal boxes for me. As I receive them, I draw seasonal shapes on each box and cut them out. It doesn't take long to have tracers available for any season or theme.

Suzanne Foote
East Ithaca Preschool
Ithaca, NY

Cutting on the Fold

When my students make a project where they have to cut on a fold to make a whole pattern, I have each child put a clothespin on the fold. This helps the youngster remember where to start cutting and also helps her avoid cutting the shape in two.

Susan Larose
Hubbardston Center School
Hubbardston, MA

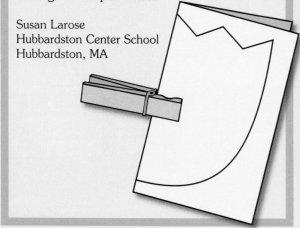

No-Tie Mobiles

To easily hang a student-made project or classroom decorative as a mobile, I use sticker dots! After I cut a length of yarn, I place one end on the front of the project. Then I place a sticker dot atop the yarn. I put the other end on the back of the project and secure it with another sticker dot. With the loop secure, the project is ready to hang—no hole-punching or tying needed. Using sticker dots makes the task so simple that students can do it too!

Christina Garza
Oakwood Terrace Elementary
Euless, TX

Our Readers Write

Picket Fences

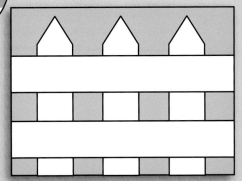

To enhance my garden or farm displays, I reuse old bulletin board border to make a picket fence. To make the fence, I use the white side of the border strips and cut a point at one end to make posts. Then I attach the posts to the display and trim additional border strips to add across the posts as shown.

Shelly Oraze, Challenger Elementary
Everett, WA

A Reading Picnic

This reading center is a favorite among my students. I place inside a picnic basket a checkered blanket, several picnic-themed books, and plastic picnic foods. When a child visits the center, she sets out the blanket and the food. Then she reads one or more of the books while pretending to eat her favorite picnic goodies.

Piper Porter
Mountain Way Elementary
Granite Falls, WA

Little Reporters

To motivate my youngsters to write, I place at the writing center small spiral notebooks with cute characters on the covers. When a child visits the center, he pretends to be a reporter. He walks around the room with a notebook, writing words he recognizes in the notebook. At the end of center time, he reports to me the words he has written.

Rosemary Lehmann, La Rosa Elementary, Ceres, CA

Brush It Away

Over the years I have used several different objects as erasers for individual whiteboards. I have found that foam paintbrushes make the best erasers. After a child has finished writing on a whiteboard, I simply have him brush away the writing.

Jodi Darter
Cabool Elementary
Cabool, MO

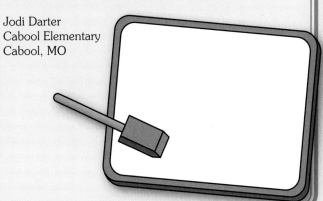

Our Readers Write

A New Use for a Noodle

To make a large number line, I label a swimming noodle as shown. When the group uses the number line, I invite two youngsters to each hold one end of it. I use the number line to reinforce counting, number order, addition, and subtraction.

Jodi Darter
Cabool Elementary
Cabool, MO

Excess Glue

Try this quick tip the next time a child uses too much glue on a project. To keep the glue from dripping on or sticking to anything, I place a piece of waxed paper over the area with excess glue. When the project is dry, I can easily peel the waxed paper away.

Chrystine Haldeman
Hillside Elementary
Berwyn, PA

In the Tent

To encourage my youngsters to read, I set up a small tent in my classroom. Inside the tent I place a few stuffed toy animals and several camping-themed books. A child chooses a book and reads it to the animal campers.

Veronica McElroy
Deposit Central
Deposit, NY

Roll and Review

To prepare for this time filler activity, I program each side of a large cube with a different activity for youngsters to complete. When the group has a few extra minutes, I invite a child to roll the die. Then I lead the group in completing the activity.

Randi Austin
Stoutland R-2 Elementary
Stoutland, MO

A Special Thank-You

I thank my students and their families for a wonderful year with these keepsakes. Prior to the end of the school year, I snap a class photo. Then I take the photo to a photo shop and create a thank-you card. I have one printed for each family. On the last day of school, I send them home.

Kristen Bower
Bradley Beach School
Bradley Beach, NJ

Thank you for a year filled with wonderful memories.

Love,
Ms. Bower

2010

SIMPLE SCIENCE

SIMPLE SCIENCE

Jack and Jill Predictions
Sink and float

Getting ready:
- Set out a pail containing several objects that float in water and several objects that do not.
- Gather paper towels and a pail of water.

Activity: Assign two students the roles of Jack and Jill. Then lead the class in saying the poem shown, encouraging Jack and Jill to pantomime the described actions. Next, instruct Jack to take an object from the pail and show it to the group. Have each class-mate give a thumbs-up if he thinks the object will float in water and a thumbs-down if he thinks it will sink. Then ask Jack to put the object in the water and report the results. After Jack removes the object and sets it on a paper towel, invite Jill to take an object. Have students repeat the predicting and testing process. Then assign different students the roles of Jack and Jill.

Kim Parker
Christian Heritage School
Longview, TX

Jack and Jill went up the hill
To fetch a pail of water.
On the way down, they started to think,
"Will these things float or will they sink?"

Sock Secrets
Sense of touch

Getting ready: Gather a few adult socks. Put a familiar object with a distinctive shape or texture in each sock.

Activity: Have students sit in a circle. Hand the socks to different youngsters. Then ask students to pass the socks around as you lead them in saying the chant below. At the end of the chant, ask each youngster holding a sock to put her hand in it and feel the object it contains. Encourage her to describe how it feels. After she guesses what the object is, ask her to remove it from the sock and show it to the group.

Round or square, smooth or rough.
Clues like these can tell so much.
What's inside? Can you say?
Use your sense of touch today!

adapted from an idea by Tammy Lutz
George E. Greene Elementary
Bad Axe, MI

SIMPLE SCIENCE

Start With a Seed
Understanding the pumpkin life cycle

Getting ready:
- Make one copy of page 168 for each student.
- Set out shallow containers of brown, green, yellow, and orange paint.
- Cut a class supply of 4" x 8" construction paper rectangles.

Activity: Ask each child to follow along on his copy of page 168 as you read the sentences. Then have him use a brown crayon to trace the ground line on each page. Instruct him to use his finger to paint illustrations like the ones shown. After the paint dries, ask him to cut out the pages and put them in numerical order. Next, fold a 4" x 8" rectangle in half and staple the pages inside. Help him title the booklet. Then invite him to sign his name and illustrate the front cover.

Juli Engel
Midland, TX

1. See a pumpkin seed.
2. See two leaves.
3. See more leaves.
4. See a yellow flower.
5. a little green pumpkin.
6. See a big orange pumpkin!

My Pumpkin
Luke

Is it paper? It sounds like you're crumpling it.

Listen and Guess!
Using the sense of hearing

Getting ready:
- Make a recording of familiar school staff members' voices.
- Gather one paper lunch bag for every two students.

Activity: To introduce the activity, play each recorded voice and have students identify the corresponding person. Pair students and give each twosome a bag. Then have each student pair secretly put in the bag a classroom item or a group of like classroom items that can be used to make a distinctive sound. Next, instruct the students in each pair, in turn, to make their chosen sound without revealing its source to their classmates. Once a classmate correctly identifies the corresponding item(s), ask the partners to show the class how they made the sound.

Debbie Patrick
State College, PA

Editor's Tip:
Have partners stand behind an easel to conceal their items as they make sounds with them.

SIMPLE SCIENCE

Time to Hibernate
Animal adaptations

Getting ready: Color and cut out a copy of the picture cards from page 169.

Activity: Explain to students that some animals protect themselves from harsh winter weather by sleeping through much of the season. Discuss examples such as a dormouse sleeping curled up to conserve heat and bats hibernating in groups to share body heat. Then lead students in singing the song below, inviting a youngster to hold up the dormouse picture card during the second verse. Sing the second verse four more times, each time replacing the underlined lines with a different animal fact and having a student hold up the appropriate card.

(sung to the tune of "The Farmer in the Dell")

It's time to hibernate.
It's time to hibernate.
When it's cold and wintry,
It's time to hibernate.

[A dormouse curls up tight.]
[A dormouse curls up tight.]
When it's time to hibernate,
[A dormouse curls up tight.]

Continue with the following:
Some squirrels sleep underground.
Some bat groups sleep in caves.
Some frogs sleep in the mud.
A groundhog goes in its den.

Deborah Gibbone, St. Andrew School, Drexel Hill, PA

A Matter of Colors
Mixing colors, using senses

Getting ready: Bring in ingredients and supplies to make lemon, blueberry, and strawberry gelatin for the class.

Activity: Have youngsters pour each flavor of gelatin powder into a separate clear bowl. Then add water to each bowl as directed on the gelatin packages. Guide students to notice that the powder dissolves and the colors and scents become more intense. Next, have students predict what will happen when a volunteer combines small amounts of lemon and blueberry liquid gelatin. Then instruct the volunteer to mix the liquids in a separate bowl. Discuss the results with students. *(The liquid turns green.)* Repeat the mixing process with strawberry and blueberry and then with strawberry and lemon. After students discuss the color changes, refrigerate the gelatin as directed on the packages. As the gelatin chills, have students recap the changes they observed; then write their observations on chart paper. Later, serve the gelatin to students and have them use sensory words to describe it.

Rochelle White, Early Childhood Center, Poughkeepsie, NY

SIMPLE SCIENCE

Make It Move
Investigating the relationship between force and motion

Getting ready:
- Obtain a handheld fan and an empty squeeze bottle.
- Ball up a tissue or a sheet of tissue paper.

Activity: Display the tissue. Ask students how the tissue can be moved without someone picking it up. Lead them to conclude that air can make the tissue move. Then ask each child to predict which of the following will make the tissue move the most: someone blowing on it, fanning it using a handheld fan, or squeezing the air from an empty squeeze bottle on it. After each child has made her prediction, enlist students' help in testing each type of air-moving force. Then have students make observations, guiding them to conclude that the more force that moves the air, the more an object will move.

Diane Billman
McKitrick Elementary
Lutz, FL

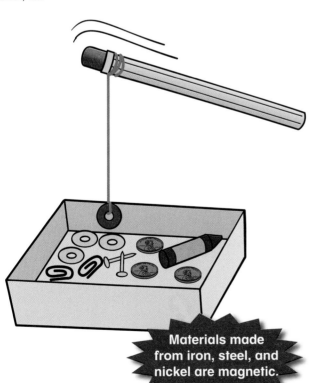

Materials made from iron, steel, and nickel are magnetic.

Magnet Fishing
Making observations about magnets

Getting ready:
- Make a fishing pole by tying a length of yarn to a pencil and attaching a magnet to the free end of the yarn. Repeat to make several poles.
- For each fishing pole, place a variety of magnetic and nonmagnetic items in a shallow box.

Activity: For an introductory activity about magnets, divide students into as many groups as there are fishing poles. Have the youngsters in each group take turns holding their fishing pole over their box and observing which items are attracted to the magnet. Then invite students to discuss their findings and contribute to a class list of magnetic and nonmagnetic items. Encourage students to draw conclusions about the characteristics of magnetic materials.

Barbara Lewis
Hayfield Elementary
Alexandria, VA

SIMPLE SCIENCE

Webbed or Not?
Understanding animal adaptations

Getting ready:
- Partially fill a plastic tub with water.
- Obtain a sandwich-size resealable plastic bag and a rubber band.
- Make a large two-column chart labeled "Has Webbed Feet" and "Does Not Have Webbed Feet."
- Cut out a copy of the cards on page 170.

Activity: In turn, have each child in a small group spread his fingers and move his hand through the tub of water as if he is swimming. Then secure the resealable bag around his wrist with the rubber band and have him move his hand through the water again. After each child has had a turn, lead students in a discussion comparing the amount of water each child moved when he had the bag on his hand to when he did not. Guide students to conclude that animals with webbed feet (similar to their bagged hands) are better swimmers because they move more water when they swim. Finally, present one card at a time and ask students whether the animal has webbed feet; then post each picture in its matching column.

Kelsea Wright, Seal Elementary, Douglass, KS

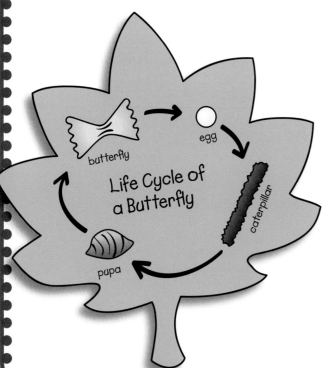

From Egg to Butterfly
Life cycle: butterfly

Getting ready:
- Cut a class supply of large leaf cutouts from green construction paper.
- For each child, gather the following supplies: a small white pom-pom (egg), a piece of brown chenille stem (caterpillar), a shell noodle and a gray tissue paper square (pupa), and a bow tie noodle (butterfly).

Activity: Have each youngster glue a gray tissue paper square around a shell noodle to complete the pupa. Then have each student glue her supplies to a leaf cutout as shown. Review the life cycle of a butterfly with youngsters as you guide them in drawing arrows on their leaves to illustrate the sequence of the cycle. **For an added challenge,** have students refer to a word bank to label each step of the cycle.

Bernadette Hoyer, H. B. Brunner Elementary, Scotch Plains, NJ

SIMPLE SCIENCE

Lots of Rocks
Investigating physical properties

Getting ready:
- Gather a supply of different rocks.
- Obtain several paper plates and a marker.

Activity: Gather a small group of students and set the rocks in front of them. Discuss with youngsters the physical properties the rocks could be sorted by—such as size, shape, color, or texture. Have students decide on a sorting criterion; then label the plates accordingly. Guide youngsters in sorting the rocks onto the appropriate plates. After all the rocks have been sorted, invite students to examine the rocks on each plate as you discuss the results.

Tammy Willey
Pine Street Elementary
Presque Isle, ME

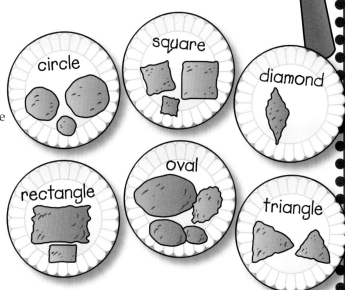

An Edible Root
Investigating plants

Getting ready:
- Tint a glass of water with blue food coloring.
- Place a whole carrot (leaves attached) in the tinted water.
- Make a chart similar to the one shown.

Activity: Show students the glass with the carrot. Ask them to predict what will happen to the carrot and the water. Then list their responses on the chart. Encourage students to watch the carrot for a few days, and each day have youngsters make observations and compare them to their predictions. After several days, cut the carrot in half lengthwise. Lead students to realize that a carrot is a root that stores food and water for the plant. Then explain that a carrot is not only a root, it is also an edible vegetable. **To extend the activity,** invite youngsters to name other edible roots, such as radishes or turnips.

Sharon Hackley
Kingman, AZ

What will happen to the carrot?
- The leaves will turn blue.
- It will drink all the water.
- It will get squishy.

Pumpkin Booklet Pages

Use with "Start With a Seed" on page 163.

See a pumpkin seed.

1

See two leaves.

2

See more leaves.

3

See a yellow flower.

4

See a little green pumpkin.

5

See a big orange pumpkin!

6

dormouse

TEC42046

squirrel

TEC42046

frog

TEC42046

groundhog

TEC42046

bats

TEC42046

Animal Picture Cards
Use with "Webbed or Not?" on page 166.

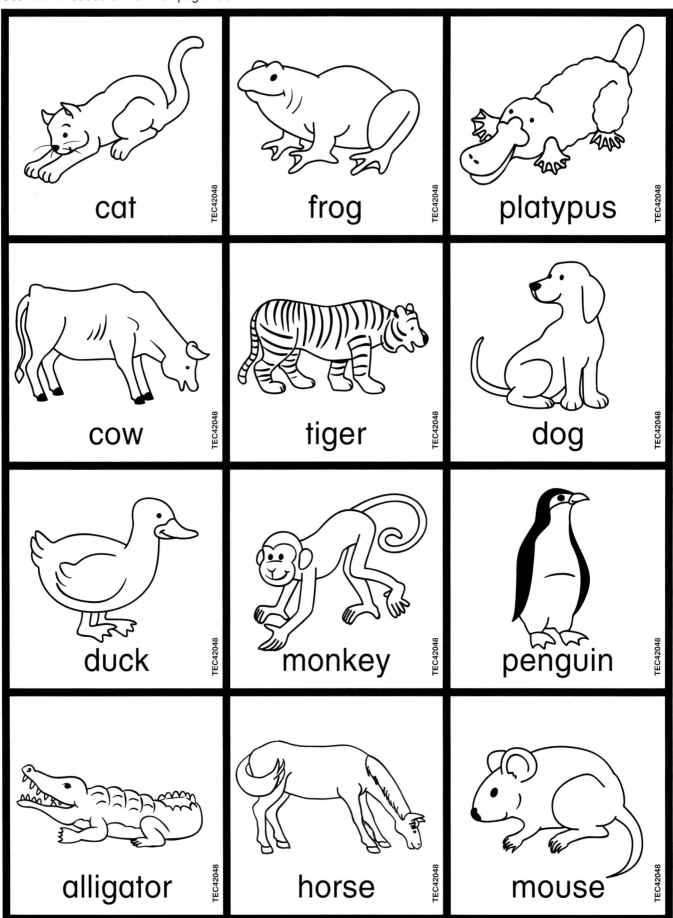

cat

frog

platypus

cow

tiger

dog

duck

monkey

penguin

alligator

horse

mouse

'TIS THE SEASON

'Tis the Season

How Many Seeds?

Engage students in comparing sets with this partner game. For each twosome, mask one side of a large die with a picture of a watermelon. Then give each child in the duo a green paper oval (watermelon) and a supply of small black paper squares (seeds). To take a turn, a child rolls the die and places the corresponding number of seeds on her watermelon. If a student rolls the watermelon picture, she removes all the seeds from her watermelon cutout. After a predetermined amount of time, direct students to stop and count the seeds on their watermelons. Then have partners compare their numbers using the terms *more* and *fewer.*

adapted from an idea by Jennie Jensen, North Cedar Elementary, Lowden, IA

All About Me

Invite youngsters to introduce themselves to their classmates by making these one-of-a-kind posters. Give each child labeled die-cut shapes, similar to those shown, and a 12" x 18" sheet of construction paper. Have him draw, help him write, or have him glue photos on each shape to tell about himself. Then encourage each student to glue the shapes to his construction paper to make a poster. After each youngster's poster is complete, invite him to share it with the class.

Maureen Glennon, Faller Elementary, St. Ridgecrest, CA

Bushels of Sounds

Youngsters pretend to go apple picking at this seasonal center! To prepare, cut out a copy of the cards on page 178. At a center, place the cards on a large tree cutout along with two basket cutouts labeled as shown. A child picks an apple card from the tree and says its name, stressing the beginning sound. If the picture begins with one of the featured letter sounds, she places the card above the appropriate basket. If it does not, she puts it back on the tree. She continues with the remaining cards until only the two distracter cards remain on the tree. **For an easier version,** do not use the two distracter cards.

Julie Vickery, International Children's Language School
Yangju-Si, Gyeonggi, South Korea

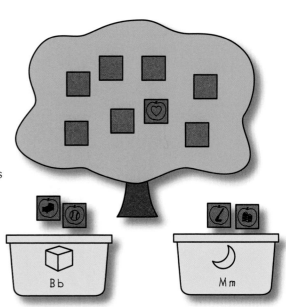

'Tis the Season

Eight Legs

Youngsters practice letter recognition with this small-group game. To prepare, have each child draw a spider face on a black paper circle. Then have her attach eight sticky dots, each labeled with a different letter, to her spider as shown. Give each student eight black paper strips (spider legs) to use as game markers. To play, announce a letter (keep track of the letters you call). Each child who has that letter on her spider covers it with a spider leg. When a child has all eight legs on her spider, she announces, "Spider!" After checking for accuracy, have students trade spiders to play another round. **For a more challenging version,** announce sounds rather than letters.

Susan Servin, Oracle Ridge School, Oracle, AZ

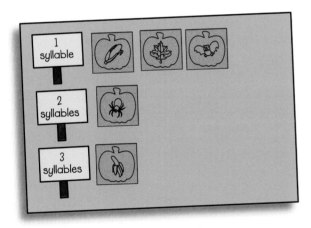

In the Pumpkin Patch

Counting syllables helps this pumpkin patch grow! To prepare for this center, program a large sheet of green paper (pumpkin patch) as shown. Place the pumpkin patch at a center along with a cut-out copy of the cards from page 180. For each card, a child names the picture, quietly claps once for each syllable, and then places the card in the matching row.

Kathryn Davenport, Partin Elementary School, Oviedo, FL

Hide and Hunt

To prepare for this small-group game, cut out the pilgrim hat and turkey from a copy of page 181 for each student. Then program the patterns as described in one of the options below. Hide the turkeys around the classroom while students are out of the room. To complete the activity, give each child in the group a hat and encourage him to hunt for the corresponding turkey. After checking each child's match, direct youngsters to swap hats to prepare for another hunt.

Matching numbers: Program each hat with a different numeral and each turkey with an identical numeral.
Matching numbers to sets: Program each hat with a different numeral. For each number, draw a matching dot set on a turkey.
Number words: Program each hat with a different numeral. Then write each matching number word on a different turkey.

adapted from an idea by Laurie Gibbons, Huntsville, AL

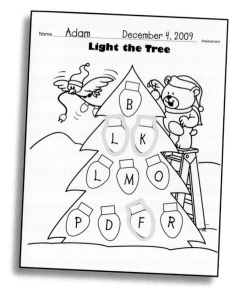

Name Adam   December 4, 2009   Assessment
Light the Tree

Light the Tree

Add a twinkle to assessments with this easy-to-adapt activity. Program the bulbs on a copy page 184 as described in one of the options below. Working with one student at a time, assess the skill as described. Then highlight the bulb for each correct answer to "light" the tree.

Initial consonants: Program each bulb with a different letter. Name a word and have a child point to the beginning letter.
High-frequency words: Write a different word on each bulb. Ask a child to read each word.
Number identification: Program each bulb with a different number and have a child name each number.
Coin identification and value: Use an ink pad and coin stampers to stamp a different coin (front or back) on each bulb. Have a youngster name each coin and its value.

adapted from an idea by Ilene Bickel, Naples Park Elementary, Naples, FL

A Brand-New Year

Kick off the new calendar year with this class writing activity. To begin, ask students to help compile a class list of things they have learned since the beginning of the school year. Then make another list of things they would like to learn during the remainder of the school year. Display the lists with the poem shown.

Jodi Darter, Cabool Elementary, Cabool, MO

As the clock strikes twelve on the last day of December,
We say goodbye to the old year and pause to remember.
In January, we welcome a brand-new year
Full of learning fun and plenty of cheer.

A Tall Snowman

Review ordinal numbers with this frosty friend! For each child, fold a 12" x 18" sheet of construction paper in half and then cut the top flap to make a five-section booklet like the one shown. Also write the ordinal number words *first* through *fifth* on the board. Have each child draw a large snowball on the front of each flap and add details to the snowballs to make a snowman. Beginning at the top of the booklet, have her say each ordinal number as she writes it under the corresponding flap. To follow up, pair students and have partners take turns pointing to chosen snowballs and asking their partners to name the corresponding ordinal numbers.

Jill Thomas, Torrence Creek Elementary, Huntersville, NC

Groundhog Graph

Was the groundhog's weather prediction correct? Try this graphing activity to find out! On Groundhog Day, tell students about the groundhog's prediction and then post a graph like the one shown. Each school day for the next six weeks, invite students to observe the weather conditions and share their findings. If the weather is springlike, have a student draw a sun in the corresponding row. If the weather is wintry, have a child draw a snowflake in the corresponding row. After six weeks, use the graph to guide students in determining whether the groundhog's prediction was correct.

Gracye McCoy, Kendall-Whittier Elementary, Tulsa, OK

What's the Weather?								
Spring ☀	☀	☀	☀	☀	☀	☀		
Winter ❄	❄	❄	❄					

Heartfelt Math

Serve up a "heart-y" portion of addition practice with this center. Set out a large heart cutout (folded in half and opened so that it is creased down the center) and ten smaller heart cutouts. A student places a desired number of smaller hearts on each side of the large heart. On a sheet of paper, he writes and solves the resulting addition problem. He removes the hearts and then repeats the activity, placing a different number of small heart cutouts on each side.

Alyson Severino, Ocean Day School, Lakewood, NJ

Lucky Shamrocks

To prepare for this partner activity that reinforces initial consonants, cut out a construction paper copy of the shamrock cards on page 187. Program the back of each card with the picture's beginning letter for self-checking. Spread the cards picture-side up on the floor. Also provide a large gold coin or a yellow sponge cut in a coin shape. A child tosses the coin onto a shamrock and names the beginning letter of the pictured item. He checks his answer and then passes the coin to his partner, who takes a turn in the same manner. Students continue as time allows.

Barbara Descavish-Bloom, Resica Elementary, East Stroudsburg, PA

G!

'Tis the Season

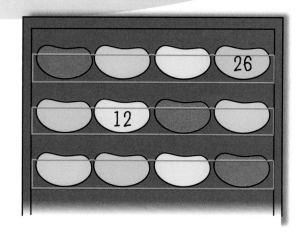

Jumping for Jelly Beans

To prepare, write each number from 1 to 30 on a separate jelly bean cutout. Arrange the jelly beans at random in a pocket chart with the blank sides facing out. Invite a child to turn over a jelly bean and read the number aloud. Then have him lead the group in jumping that number of times. Continue with the remaining jelly beans as time allows.

adapted from an idea by Rosa Ungurait
Senatobia Elementary
Senatobia, MS

Lots of Eggs

Crack open a variety of skills practice at this center! Choose a skill below and follow the directions for programming a supply of paper egg shapes. Then cut each egg in half and place the egg halves at a center. If desired, make the center self-checking by color-coding the back of each egg half. A child finds a match and places the halves together to make a whole egg. He continues as described until all the egg halves are correctly paired. **For an easier version,** use a different puzzle-cut for each egg.

Word families: Write two words from the same word family on an egg. Repeat with different word families for the remaining eggs.
Ending consonants: On each egg, glue a simple picture and write the matching ending consonant.
Uppercase and lowercase letters: On each egg, write an uppercase letter and its corresponding lowercase letter.
Addition: Write a different addition problem and its sum on each egg.
Money: Use a coin stamper to stamp a different money amount and its value on each egg.

adapted from an idea by Vatesha Bouler
Sara Lindemuth Elementary, Harrisburg, PA

I'm a little seedling,
Small and young.
Plant me in your garden.
The bees will surely hum!
When I get some water
And lots of sun,
We will grow together
For years to come!

Small Seedlings

This planting activity teaches youngsters the importance of giving back to the earth. In advance, gather potting soil and a class supply of seedlings (perennials), plastic flowerpots (or plastic cups with holes cut in the bottoms), and craft sticks. Give each child a copy of the poem shown, a craft stick, and a pot. After reading the poem aloud, help each child transplant a seedling to a pot. Then have her tape her copy of the poem to a craft stick and insert the stick into the pot. Encourage youngsters to transplant their seedlings near their homes so they can watch them grow for years to come.

Laurie Carrera, Barton Elementary, Patchogue, NY

'Tis the Season

Icy Lemonade

To prepare for this addition center, cut four drinking-glass shapes from yellow paper to make glasses of lemonade and label the glasses as shown. Also cut apart a copy of the ice cube patterns on page 189. (If desired, label the backs of the ice cubes for self-checking.) A child takes an ice cube, reads the problem, and determines the answer. Then he places the ice cube on the glass labeled with the matching sum. He continues until all the ice cubes are correctly placed on the glasses.

Marie E. Cecchini, West Dundee, IL

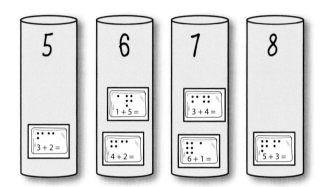

Picnic Fun

Youngsters practice several skills with this easy-to-adapt idea. Program cards as described in one of the options below and store the cards in a picnic basket. Place a blanket on the floor and set the basket nearby. Invite a group of youngsters to join you on the blanket and complete the chosen activity.

Color words: Program each of several cards with a different color word. A child takes a card and names an item of that color that she might see at a picnic.
Initial consonants: Program each of several cards with a different consonant. A child takes a card and names a picnic food or activity whose name begins with the chosen letter.
Descriptive words: Attach to each of several cards a picture of a picnic food. A child takes a card and uses descriptive words to describe the food.

Marie E. Cecchini

Take a Dip

Prepare your little swimmers for an imaginary dip in the pool with this action rhyme.

Suzanne Moore, Tucson, AZ

The water's fine; dive right in.	*Pretend to dive.*
Stand in the water up to my chin.	*Point to chin.*
I'll swim forward: one, two, three.	*Pretend to swim forward.*
Swimming forward is fun for me.	
I'll swim backward: one, two, three.	*Pretend to swim backward.*
Swimming backward is fun for me.	
I'll do the side stroke: one, two, three.	*Pretend to do the side stroke.*
Swimming to the side is fun for me.	
I'll go underwater: one, two, three.	*Pretend to go underwater.*
Holding my breath is fun for me.	
I love swimming, yes sirree!	*Pretend to swim.*
Going swimming is fun for me.	

Apple Picture Cards
Use with "Bushels of Sounds" on page 172.

TEC42044

TEC42044

TEC42044

TEC42044

TEC42044

TEC42044

TEC42044

TEC42044

TEC42044

TEC42044

TEC42044

TEC42044

Plenty of Nuts

What comes next?

 Cut. Glue.

Pumpkin Picture Cards

Use with "In the Pumpkin Patch" on page 173.

TEC42045 TEC42045 TEC42045

TEC42045 TEC42045 TEC42045

TEC42045 TEC42045 TEC42045

TEC42045 TEC42045 TEC42045

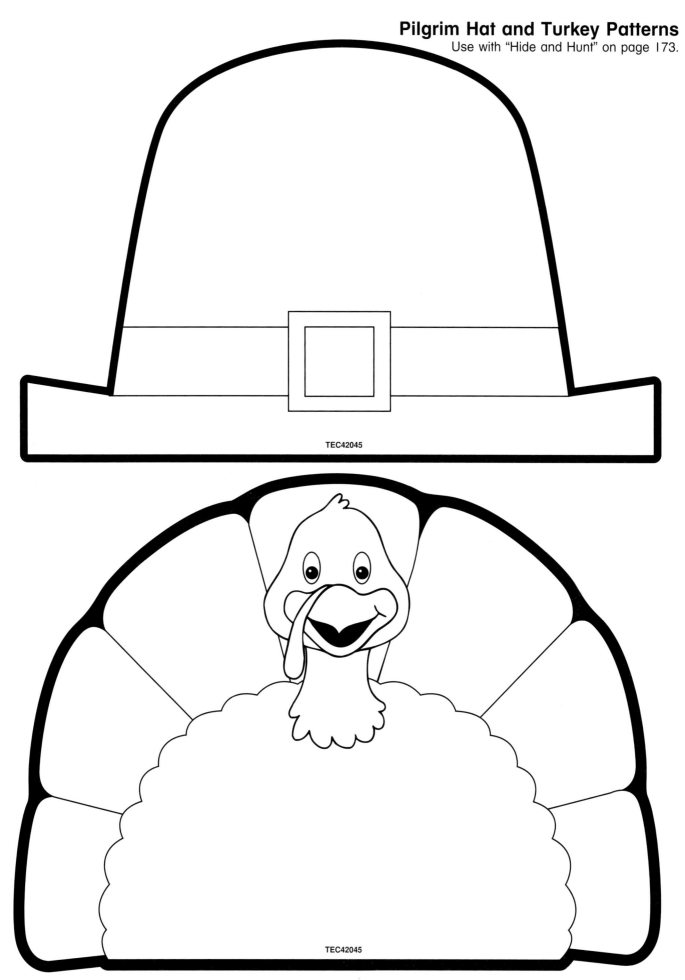

TEC42045

TEC42045

Can you see pumpkins?

1

Can you see apples?

2

Can you see leaves on the ground?

3

Note to the teacher: Have each child cut out a copy of pages 182 and 183. Then help her sequence the booklet pages and staple them between two construction paper covers.

Can you see squirrels?

4

Can you see acorns?

5

Yes! I can see fall all around.

6

©The Mailbox® • TEC42045 • Oct./Nov. 2009

Note to the teacher: Use with the directions on page 182.

THE MAILBOX 183

Light the Tree

Note to the teacher: Use with "Light the Tree" on page 174.

Decorating a Gingerbread Man

Item	Guess	Actual

Note to the teacher: List four different items (such as small crackers, cereal pieces, Unifix cubes, or paper clips) on a copy of this page. Then place at a center a container of each item and a class supply of the programmed page. For each item, a child guesses how many will fit on the gingerbread man without overlapping and records his guess. Then he fills the shape and records the actual number of items that fit.

M Is for Menorah

✏ Write each beginning letter.

✂ Cut. 🧴 Glue the words that start with **m**.

___ oon

___ ug

___ un

___ op

___ an

___ at

___ ap

©The Mailbox® · TEC42046 · Dec./Jan. 2009–10

Note to the teacher: Have each child follow the directions on the page. Then have him glue the remaining two cards to the back of his paper.

Shamrock Cards
Use with "Lucky Shamrocks" on page 175.

TEC42047

TEC42047

TEC42047

TEC42047

TEC42047

TEC42047

TEC42047

TEC42047

TEC42047

TEC42047

TEC42047

TEC42047

Up, Up, and Away

✂ Cut. Sort.

Glue.

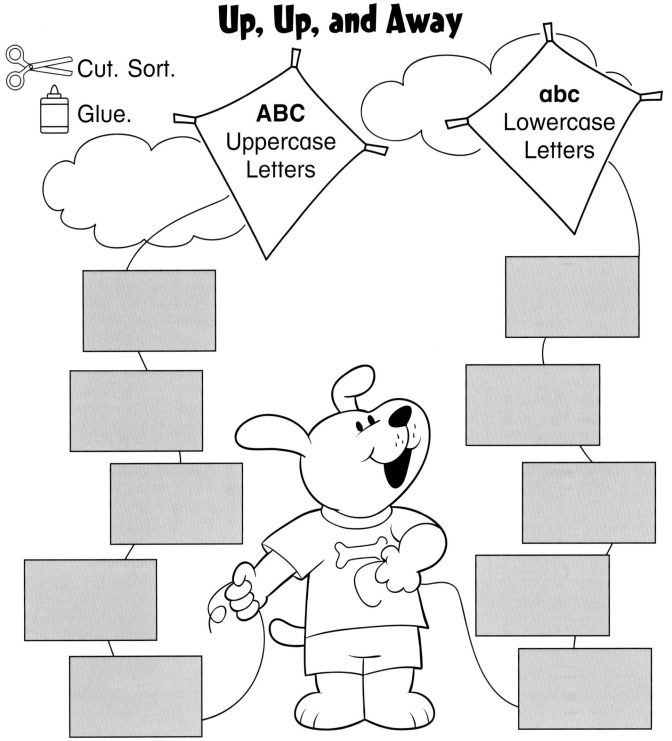

ABC
Uppercase
Letters

abc
Lowercase
Letters

©The Mailbox® • TEC42047 • Feb./Mar. 2010

G	T	m	L	t
M	I	g	R	r

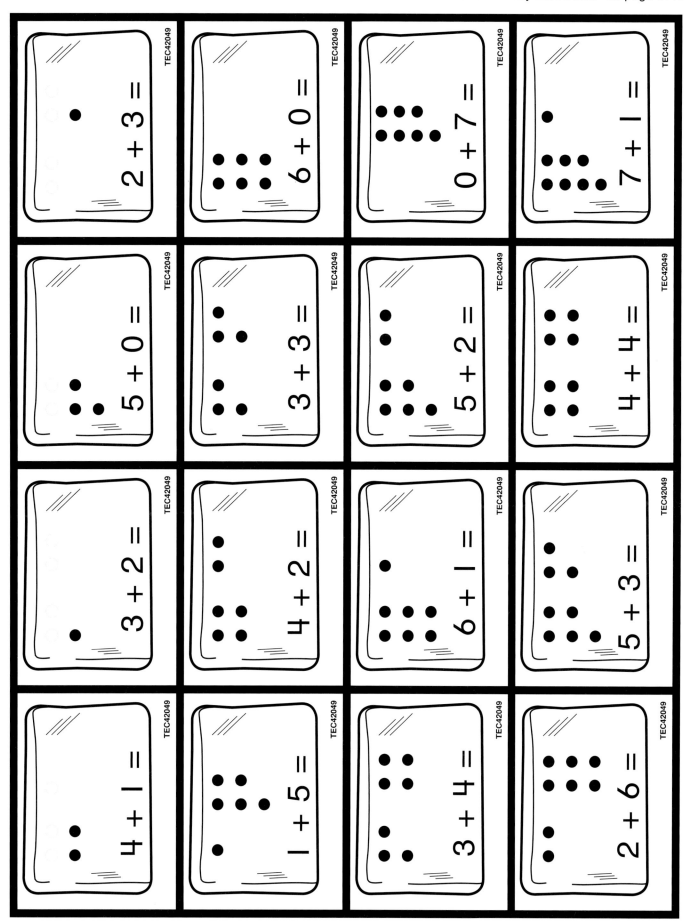

Have each child cut apart a copy of pages 190 and 191. Then help her sequence the booklet pages and staple them between two construction paper covers. For additional skill reinforcement, ask students to complete text-related tasks, such as, for page one, "Circle the word *dog*" and, for page two, "Find the word that rhymes with *dog*. Circle it."

The dog is hot.

1

The frog is hot.

2

The sun is hot. Is the pool cool?

3

©The Mailbox® • TEC42049 • June/July 2010

The dog and frog get in the pool!

4

Look! The dog is cool.

5

Look! The frog is cool.

6

©The Mailbox® • TEC42049 • June/July 2010

Note to the teacher: Use with the directions on page 190.

THE MAILBOX **191**

Initial and final consonants

Super Sand Castle

 Write each beginning and ending letter.

 a ____    ____ i ____

____ U ____   ____ e ____

 ____ o ____    ____ U ____

 ____ i ____   ____ a ____

 ____ e ____   ____ o ____

Name _____

Join the Pack!

Lotto game: counting and shapes or rhyming Cut out a copy of one set of cards from page 194 to make caller's cards. (For math, call the corresponding shape and number. For rhyming, call a word that rhymes with the picture name and have students identify the correct picture.) Give each child a copy of this page and a copy of the appropriate game cards. Instruct her to cut out the cards and glue each card to a randomly chosen board space. Then have students play the game like traditional lotto.

Game Cards

Use with "Join the Pack!" on page 193.

Math Cards

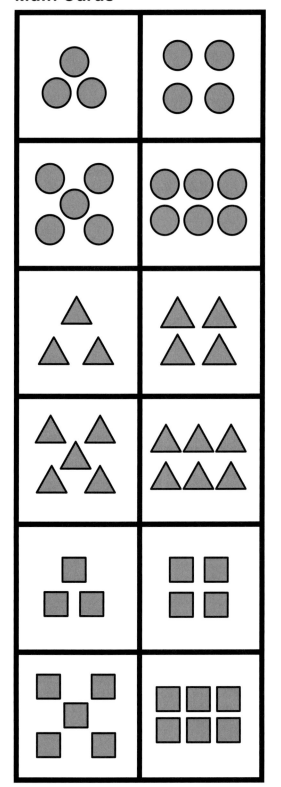

Rhyming Picture Cards

 Tips

- **For an easier rhyming game,** call a space by naming a picture. After each child marks the picture on her board, have students name rhyming words.
- **For added fun,** use stickers to mark a free space on each child's gameboard. After she glues a card in each blank space, have her discard the extra card.

©The Mailbox® • TEC42044 • Aug./Sept. 2009

The Biggest and Best

Lotto game: positional words or initial consonants Cut out a copy of one set of cards from page 196 to make caller's cards.
(For a seed card, describe where the X is in relation to the awake or sleeping seed. For a picture card, name the item's initial consonant and
write it on the board.) Give each child a copy of this page and a copy of the appropriate game cards. Instruct her to cut out the cards and
glue each card to a randomly chosen board space. Then have students play the game like traditional lotto.

Game Cards
Use with "The Biggest and Best" on page 195.

Seed Cards

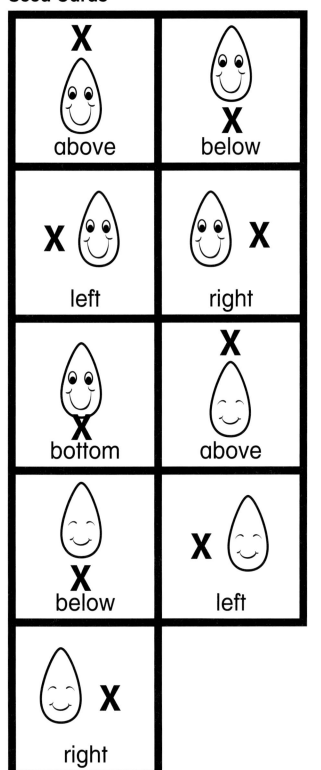

Picture Cards

 Tips
- Give students orange squares to use as game markers. As they play, their pumpkins will appear to ripen!
- For a phonemic awareness version, call a space by naming a word that is not pictured. Ask students to find the picture with the same beginning sound.

 ©The Mailbox® • TEC42045 • Oct./Nov. 2009

Ready to Ride

Lotto game: ending consonant sounds Cut out a copy of the caller's cards from page 198. Give each child a copy of this page and of the player's cards from page 198. Ask him to cut out the cards and glue each one to a randomly chosen board space. Then give him 12 game markers. To begin, name the picture on a caller's card and have each player mark the picture on his board that has the same ending sound. Continue as in the traditional game of lotto.

Game Cards

Use with "Ready to Ride" on page 197.

Caller's Cards

Player's Cards

Editor's Tip:
Use the cards for a Concentration game too! Simply cut out a copy of each set of cards, back the cards with tagboard for durability, and have students play as in the traditional game.

Name _____

Love You!

Lotto game: equal/unequal parts or blending onsets and rimes Cut out a copy of one set of cards from page 200 to make caller's cards. (For math, call the item and tell whether it has equal or unequal parts. For literacy, segment the onset and the rime. Have students blend the word parts and find the matching picture.) Give each child a copy of this page and a copy of the appropriate game cards. Instruct her to cut out the cards and glue each card to a randomly chosen board space. Then have students play the game like traditional lotto.

Game Cards

Use with "Love You!" on page 199.

Math Cards

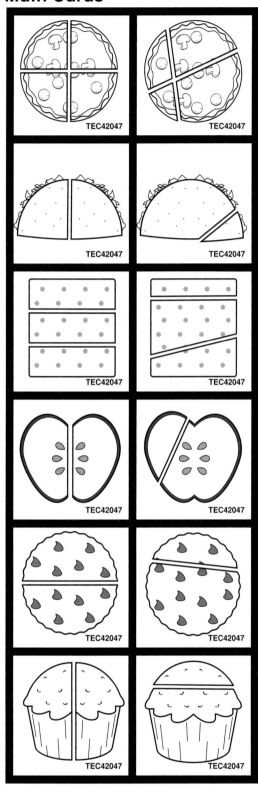

Short-Vowel Rime Picture Cards

Tip: For added fun, give each child a heart-shaped sticker to mark a free space on her gameboard. After she glues a card in each blank space, have her throw away the extra card.

Name _____

Munch! Crunch!

©The Mailbox® • TEC42048 • April/May 2010

Lotto game: solid shapes or word recognition To make caller's cards, cut out a copy of one set of cards from page 202. (For the solid shape cards, call the solid shape and a descriptor, such as a cone that holds ice cream or a cylinder that makes music.) Give each child a copy of this page and a copy of the appropriate game cards. Ask her to cut out the cards and glue them to randomly chosen board spaces. Then give students game markers and play the game like traditional lotto.

Game Cards

Use with "Munch! Crunch!" on page 201.

Solid Shape Cards

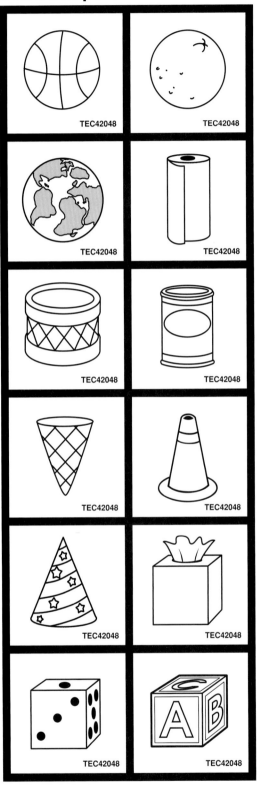

TEC42048 (basketball)
TEC42048 (ball)
TEC42048 (globe)
TEC42048 (paper towel roll)
TEC42048 (drum)
TEC42048 (can)
TEC42048 (ice cream cone)
TEC42048 (traffic cone)
TEC42048 (party hat)
TEC42048 (tissue box)
TEC42048 (dice)
TEC42048 (block)

Word Cards

one	red
TEC42048	TEC42048
two	blue
TEC42048	TEC42048
three	yellow
TEC42048	TEC42048
four	green
TEC42048	TEC42048
five	brown
TEC42048	TEC42048
six	black
TEC42048	TEC42048

Busy Bees

Lotto game: addition to ten or -ip and -it words To make caller's cards, cut out a copy of one set of cards from page 204.
Give each child a copy of this page and a copy of the appropriate game cards. Instruct her to cut out the cards and glue each card to a
randomly chosen board space. Then give students game markers and play the game like traditional lotto. (To call a space for the math
game, name a problem. Students find the matching problem on their gameboards and say the sum.)

Game Cards

Use with "Busy Bees" on page 203.

Addition Cards

• • 1 + 1	•• •• •• •• 4 + 4
• • • • • • 2 + 3	• •• • •• • •• 3 + 6
•• •• •• •• • • 3 + 5	• • • • 1 + 3
•• •• •• •• • • 5 + 5	•• ••• •• • 6 + 1
• • • • 2 + 2	• • • • • 3 + 3
• • •• • •• 3 + 4	• • • • 1 + 2

-ip and *-it* Word Cards

it	dip
bit	hip
fit	lip
hit	rip
kit	sip
sit	zip

WRITING

"Bear-y" Fun for Young Writers!

Give fine-motor skills an entertaining twist with this version of the traditional "Going on a Bear Hunt" story.

ideas contributed by Kathy Ewert, Heller Elementary, Neodesha, KS

Getting the Booklet Ready

For each student, accordion-fold a 6" x 18" strip of white paper into three sections (pages). Number the pages, using the front and back of the paper. Stick to the first page an adhesive label with the title shown. Then have each child complete her booklet pages as described.

Page 1: Write your name. Draw two green horizontal lines and add short and tall grass as shown.

Page 2: Draw brown hills.

Page 3: Draw purple mountains.

Page 4: Use an orange crayon to write *S*s (curvy roads).

Page 5: Draw wavy, vertical blue lines (water in a stream). Draw black pawprints beside the stream.

Page 6: Use a brown crayon to write *C*s (caves) and draw a bear.

Telling the Story

Have students refer to their booklets as you lead them in an imaginary bear hunt as described below.

Page 1: Rub your fingers together as you pretend to walk through short grass. Rub your hands together as you pretend to walk through tall grass.

Page 2: Pat your legs slowly as you pretend to go up hills; pat them quickly as you pretend to go down hills.

Page 3: Pat your legs loudly as you pretend to climb mountains.

Page 4: Put your hands together and then make back and forth motions as you pretend to walk the curvy roads.

Page 5: Pantomime swimming. Then pantomime looking through binoculars at pawprints.

Page 6: Use your fingers to pantomime tiptoeing around the caves. When you find the bear, make a hasty retreat to page 1!

Name _____

Draw and Write!

My Family

©The Mailbox® • TEC42044 • Aug./Sept. 2009

Note to the teacher: Give each child a copy of this page. Ask her to draw her family members and then write about them. If desired, save students' papers and also have youngsters complete the activity in the spring to show their writing progress.

Name _____

Pumpkin Plans

Think: How would you decorate a pumpkin?

Draw.

Write.

_____

- -

- -

- -

- -

- -

Name _____

Warming Up

Think: What are two things you do to get warm?

Draw.

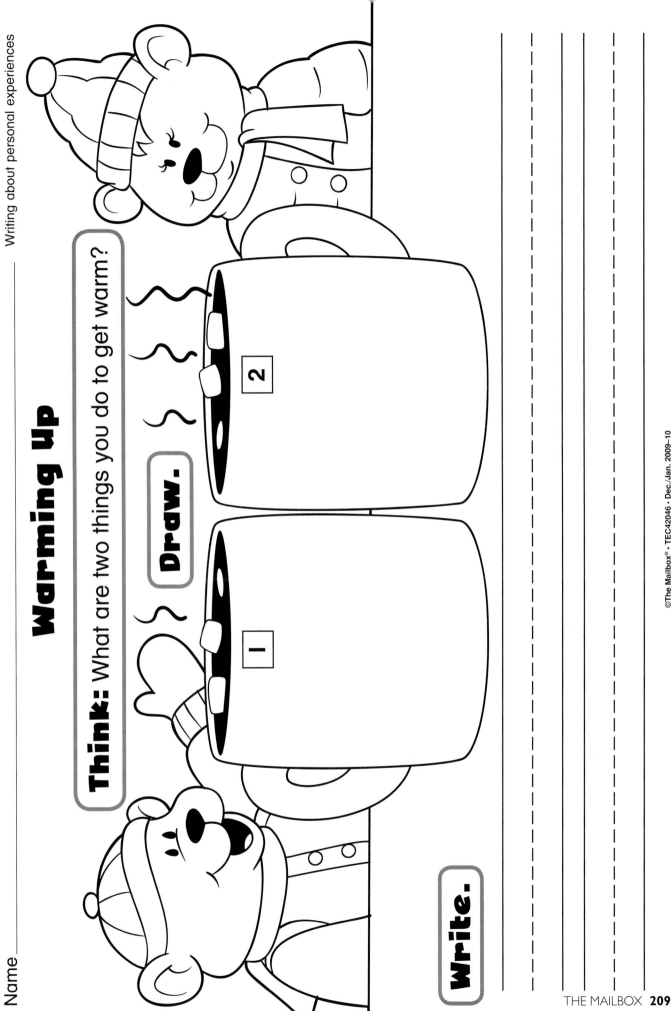

1

2

Write.

- - - - - - - - - - - - - - - -

- - - - - - - - - - - - - - - -

- - - - - - - - - - - - - - - -

Name _____

Pick a Prompt

©The Mailbox® • TEC42047 • Feb./Mar. 2010

The Yummiest Candy

My Best Friend

A Valentine's Day Party

A Lucky Day!

Think: Think about a time you felt lucky.

Draw.

Where were you?

What happened?

Write.

_____

- -

_____

_____

- -

_____

_____

- -

_____

Name____

A Springtime Delivery

Think: How would you fill this basket for your family?

Draw.

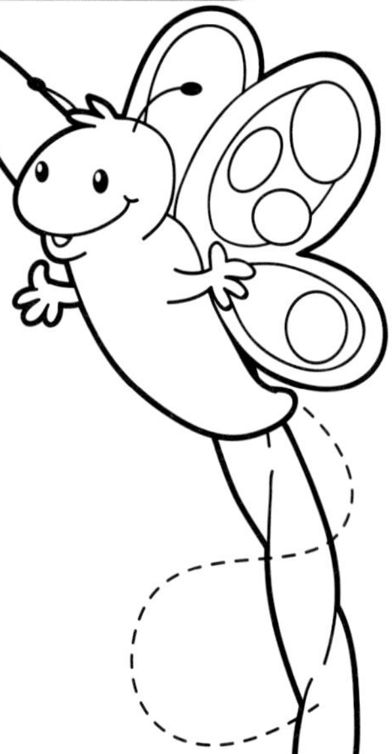

Write.

Name _____

Pick a Prompt

A Sneaky Garden Visitor

A Magic Seed

The Very Best Garden

Splish! Splash!

cloud

house

rainbow

flowers

puddle

sun

frog

rain

towel

☐ A rainy day means…   ☐ Mud makes…

☐ When it rains,…   ☐ The sound of rain…   ☐ I wish…

©The Mailbox® • TEC42048 • April/May 2010

Note to the teacher: Have each child keep a copy of this page in his journal-writing folder. After he uses a prompt, ask him to draw a check mark in its box.

A Yummy Cookout

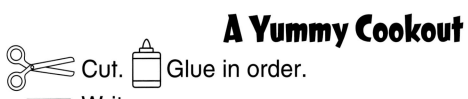 Cut. Glue in order.

Write.

1	2	3

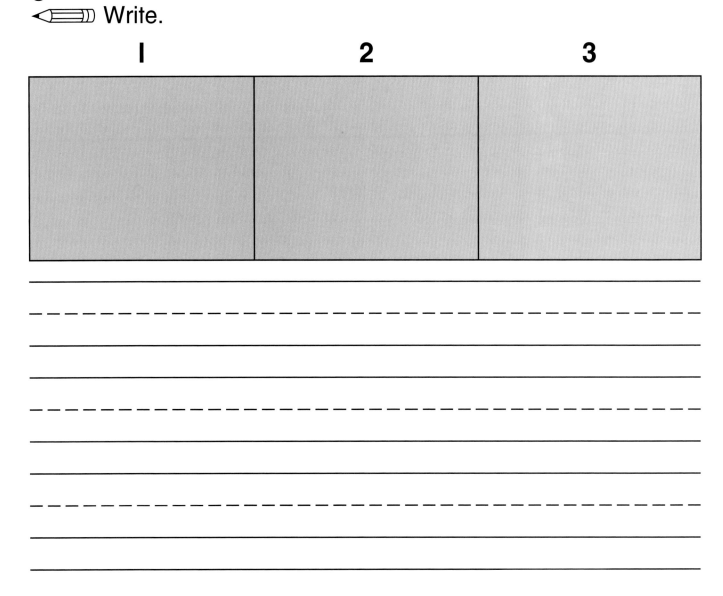

_____

- -

_____

- -

_____

- -

_____

- -

_____

Summer Fun!

Think: What two things do you hope to do this summer?

Draw. Show yourself doing each thing.

Write.

- -

- -

- -

LITERACY UNITS

From **A** to **Z**

Part One

Kick off your school year with these alphabet activities! On the following pages, you will find the letters *A* through *M*; then look for the letters *N* through *Z* in the next unit.

A Is for *Alligator*

To make an alligator puppet, have each child round the bottom corners of a 5" x 6" rectangle, set vertically. Next, give him paper shapes to make a head similar to the one shown. After he glues the head to the flap of a lunch sack, help him name an object that begins with /a/ to complete the sentence "My alligator ate an _____." Write the sentence on the bag. Then have him lift the head and draw the named object. ***Letter-sound association, sentence completion***

DeAnna Martin, Hargett Elementary, Irvine, KY

B Is for *Beehive*

Cut out copies of the picture cards on page 222 to have one card per child. Gather students in a circle and place in the middle a large hive cutout labeled as shown. Give each child a card. In turn, have her name the object on the card. If the object begins with /b/ as in *beehive,* she buzzes to the hive and places her card faceup on it. If the object does not begin with /b/ , she buzzes to the hive and places her card facedown. ***Distinguishing beginning sounds***

Sarah Huntley, Kelleytown Baptist Kindergarten Hartsville, SC

The **Bb** Hive

218 ©The Mailbox® • Aug./Sept. 2009

🅲 Is for *Cupcakes*

For each student, draw a large *c* on a sheet of construction paper. Provide paper cutouts for each child to make five cupcakes. Encourage her to use craft materials to decorate her cupcakes. Then have her glue the cupcakes on her paper to form the letter *c*. ***Letter-sound association, letter formation***

Sue Fleischmann, Catholic East Elementary, Milwaukee, WI

🅳 Is for *Dinosaur*

Give each child a cutout copy of the dinosaur pattern on page 223 and a paper oval slightly larger than the pattern. Instruct him to label the dinosaur "Dd" and then cut the oval to make cracked egg halves. Next, have him glue the bottom of the dinosaur to the back of one egg half. Then help him use a brad to attach the cracked eggs as shown. Each time a student opens his egg, he says, "/d/." ***Letter formation, letter-sound correspondence***

Debbie Newsome, Dolvin Elementary, Cumming, GA

🅴 Is for *Eggs*

Have each child label each of three egg shapes with *E*s as shown. Have her glue the eggs to the center of a sheet of paper, keeping the letters right-side up. Next, instruct her to glue brown paper strips below the eggs to make a nest. Then have her underline each *e* on a copy of the sentence shown and glue it to her paper. ***Letter formation, recognizing the letter* e**

Patty Henderson, Early Childhood Learning Center, Titusville, PA

I see three Ee eggs in the nest.

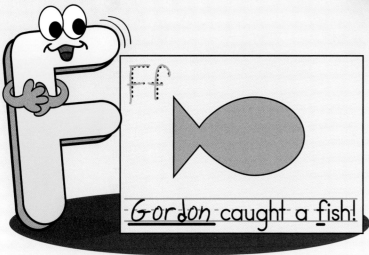

Ff

Gordon caught a fish!

🅵 Is for *Fishing*

To make a fishing pole, use string to tie a magnet to a stick. Attach individual paper clips to a class supply of fish cutouts and place the magnetic fish on a blue paper pond. To begin, invite each youngster, in turn, to go fishing. When he catches a fish, have him chant, "/f/, /f/, fish!" Next, instruct him to remove the paper clip and then glue his fish to a sheet of paper programmed as shown. To complete the paper, have him write his name on the line, trace the dotted letters, and underline the *f* in *fish*. ***Letter-sound association, letter identification***

Nicole Bennington, St. John Neumann Academy, Blacksburg, VA

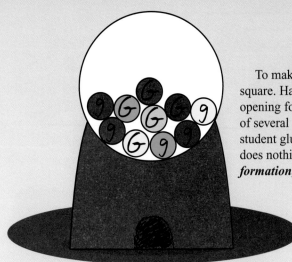

🄶 Is for *Gumballs*

To make a gumball machine, help each child round two corners of a six-inch square. Have her glue the trimmed shape to a seven-inch paper circle and draw an opening for the gumballs. Next, direct her to write a capital or lowercase *g* on each of several small circles (gumballs). Announce a word. If it begins with /g/, each student glues a gumball to her gumball machine. If it begins with another sound, she does nothing. **For an easier version,** only announce words that begin with *g*. ***Letter formation, letter-sound correspondence***

🄷 Is for *Hat*

Have each child write on a hat cutout an uppercase and lowercase *h* several times. After each child writes his name on the back of his hat, collect the hats. While students are out of the room, randomly place the hats around the room. When the class returns, say the chant shown, emphasizing each *h*. Then have each student repeat the sound of *h* until he finds his hat. ***Letter formation, letter-sound association***

Hurry! Hurry! Find your hat.
Someone hid it, just like that!

Melissa Huff, Fair View R-XI, West Plains, MO

🄸 Is for *Ice Cream*

Have each child write "Ii" on each of three ice cream scoop cutouts. Then have her trim two corners of a rectangle to make a dish. Instruct her to glue the scoops to the dish to make an ice cream sundae. Encourage her to embellish her craft with art supplies. ***Letter formation***

Sue Fleischmann, Catholic East Elementary, Milwaukee, WI

🄹 Is for *Jell-O Gelatin*

Write "Jj" in bubble letters on a sheet of construction paper for each student. Next, direct each child to use a paintbrush to apply a thin layer of diluted glue on the inside of each letter. Then have her shake Jell-O powder onto the glue. When the glue is dry, shake off the excess powder. **For an added challenge,** ask each youngster to draw on her paper pictures of items that begin with *j*. ***Letter formation***

Jodi Darter, Cabool Elementary, Cabool, MO

🄚 Is for *Kite*

Have each youngster draw lines to divide a kite cutout into four sections. Then announce two words, one that begins with /k/ and one that does not. Ask students which word begins with /k/, as in *kite*. After they identify the correct word, have each child write a *k* in one section of her kite. Continue in the same manner for each remaining kite section. Then invite each child to glue a ribbon tail to her kite. ***Distinguishing beginning sounds***

🄛 Is for *Lollipop*

Give each child a tagboard circle. Have her draw a picture that begins with /l/ on one side of the circle. Encourage her to decorate the other side to resemble a colorful lollipop. Then help her glue the circle to a craft stick to make a lollipop. ***Letter-sound association***

Karen Bryant, Miller Elementary, Warner Robins, GA

🄜 Is for *Mouse*

Have each youngster color and cut out the mouse pattern and picture cards on page 223. Help him stack the cards and staple them on the mouse as shown. After he glues on a yarn tail, have him name each picture, emphasizing the /m/ at the beginning of each word. ***Letter-sound association***

Picture Cards

Use with *"B* Is for *Beehive"* on page 218.

TEC42044

TEC42044

TEC42044

TEC42044

TEC42044

TEC42044

TEC42044

TEC42044

TEC42044

TEC42044

TEC42044

TEC42044

TEC42044

TEC42044

TEC42044

TEC42044

TEC42044

TEC42044

TEC42044

TEC42044

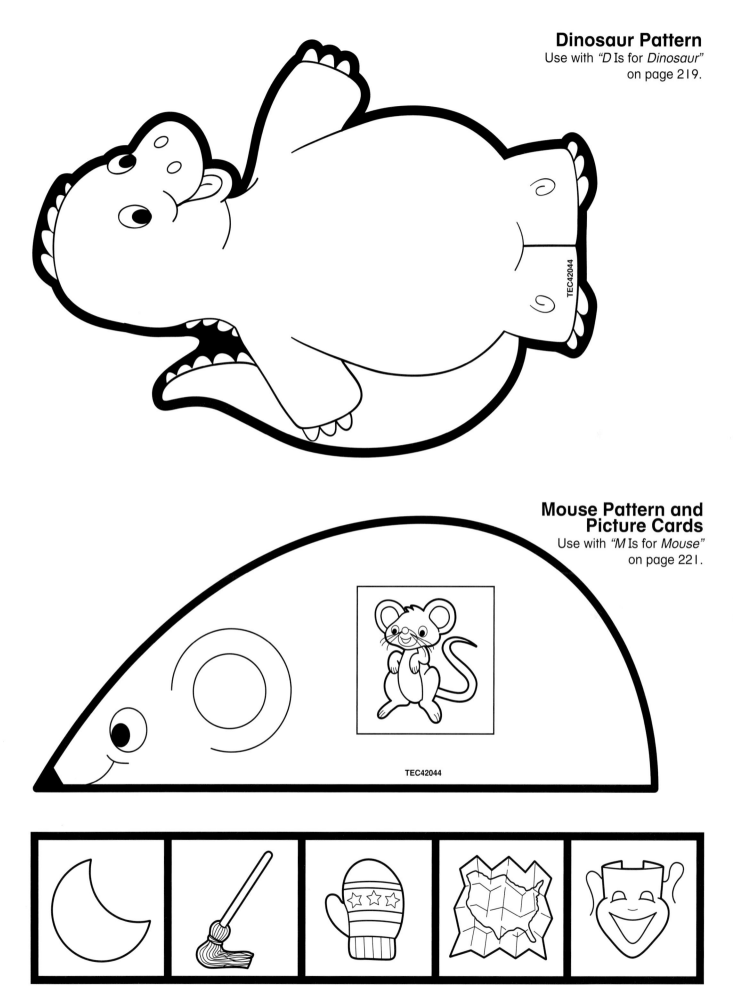

Dinosaur Pattern
Use with *"D* Is for *Dinosaur"*
on page 219.

TEC42044

**Mouse Pattern and
Picture Cards**
Use with *"M* Is for *Mouse"*
on page 221.

TEC42044

From A to Z

Part Two

In the previous unit, we served up activities to use with the letters *A* through *M*. Now it's time to continue the fun with ideas that focus on the second half of the alphabet!

N Is for *Net*

To prepare, write *Nn* on a simple net cutout for each student. To make a net, have each child draw net lines on her cutout, taking care not to draw over the letters. Help her glue a craft stick to the top to make a handle. Then have her cut out the letter *N* in various fonts from a newspaper and glue the cutouts to the back of her net.
***Recognizing the letter* n**

October.

O Is for *Octopus*

Give each youngster a paper circle (body), eight strips of crepe paper (arms), and a supply of O-shaped cereal (suckers). Instruct each child to draw facial features on the body and then glue the arms on the lower half. Have him glue suckers on the back of each leg. To use the octopus, announce words that do and don't begin with the letter *O*. Each time a youngster hears a word beginning with /ŏ/, he moves his octopus so it looks like it's swimming.
Distinguishing beginning sounds

Abby Clark, Sandoval Elementary
Sandoval, IL

P Is for *Pie*

Set out an empty disposable pie tin. Have students name different words that begin with /p/. Then have each child draw on an index card a picture whose name begins with /p/. When everyone is finished, have each student share her drawing. Direct classmates to say /p/ and repeat the featured word as each child drops her picture in the pie tin. If desired, write *Pp* on a circle cutout and lay it atop the stuffed tin to serve as the piecrust. ***Beginning sound /p/***

adapted from an idea by Andrea Lovejoy
Goodrich Elementary, Milwaukee, WI

/p/, /p/, puppy.

Q Is for *Quack*

Invite your students to act like ducks as they quack and waddle to the group-time area. To begin, announce a word that either does or doesn't begin with the sound of *Q*. If the word begins with /*kw*/, students quack and waddle like a duck. If the word does not begin with /*kw*/, they remain silent. Continue for several words. ***Distinguishing beginning sounds***

adapted from an idea by Mary Ruth Downs, Community Christian School Metcalfe, Ontario, Canada

Quack!

R Is for *Rainbow*

The result of this activity is a colorful classroom display. Have each child color and cut out a copy of the rainbow pattern on page 228. Then ask him to draw on each of two cloud cutouts a picture that begins with /r/. Help him label each picture and then have him glue a cloud to each end of his rainbow. Display the rainbows to showcase the student-generated collection of *R* words. ***Letter-sound association, writing***

adapted from an idea by Susan Brown
Central Elementary, Palmyra, VA

rose   rock

S Is for *Sock*

Give each child a simple sock cutout. Have her practice writing *Ss* on one side of the sock. Then have her flip the sock and use a variety of craft materials to make a silly sock design. ***Letter formation***

Jodi Darter, Cabool Elementary
Cabool, MO

T Is for *Terrific T*

Have each child glue tissue paper to a *T* cutout. After it dries, help her attach the *T* to a craft stick to make a pointer. Then encourage her to tiptoe around the room and point to objects and words that begin with /t/. *Letter-sound association*

Andrea Lovejoy, Goodrich Elementary
Milwaukee, WI

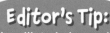

Up.

U Is for *Umbrella*

Have each child cut out a copy of the *U* and umbrella patterns on page 228. Ask him to write *U*s on the umbrella. Then direct him to glue the umbrella to one end of a craft stick and the *U* cutout to the other end to make a handle. After each child has completed his craft, ask him to hold up his umbrella as he names one or more words that begin with *U*. *Letter formation, letter-sound association*

V Is for *Vegetables*

Give each child a can of vegetables. Then have students work together to use the cans to form the letter *V* on the floor. *Letter formation*

Jodi Darter, Cabool Elementary, Cabool, MO

W Is for *Wagon*

Help each child write *wagon* on a rectangle and *W* on each of two circle cutouts. Have her glue the shapes to a sheet of paper to make a wagon. If desired, encourage her to use paper scraps to make a handle. Then have her draw a picture of a word that begins with /w/ above her wagon. *Letter formation, letter-sound association*

X Is for X-ray

Give each child a copy of page 229. Have her cut out the bone patterns and glue the cutouts to a 6" x 18" sheet of black construction paper so they resemble an arm X-ray. Then name words that do or don't have the sound of X. If a child hears /ks/ in a word, have him hold up the X-ray and say "/ks/." ***Distinguishing sounds***

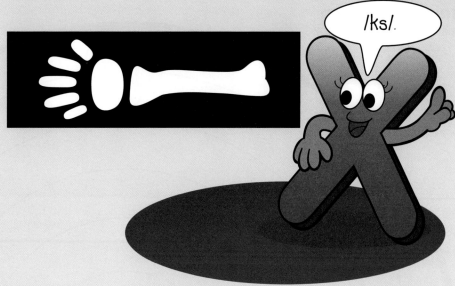

/ks/.

Y is for yellow boots.

Y Is for Yellow

Have each child complete the sentence "*Y* is for yellow…" Then help her write her sentence on a sheet of story paper. After she illustrates the sentence, collect each student's paper and bind the stack into a class book. Then read the book aloud, emphasizing the /y/ in *yellow* on each page. ***Letter-sound association, writing***

Z Is for Zebra

To make a zebra head, have each child trace the outline of her shoe on white paper and cut it out. Then have her cut black paper to make zebra stripes, ears, eyes, a nose, and hair. With a white crayon, have her write *Z* on each ear and draw pupils on the eyes. Then have her glue the details in place. ***Letter formation***

Betty Lynn Scholtz
St. Ann Catholic School
Charlotte, NC

Rainbow Pattern
Use with *"R* Is for *Rainbow"* on page 225.

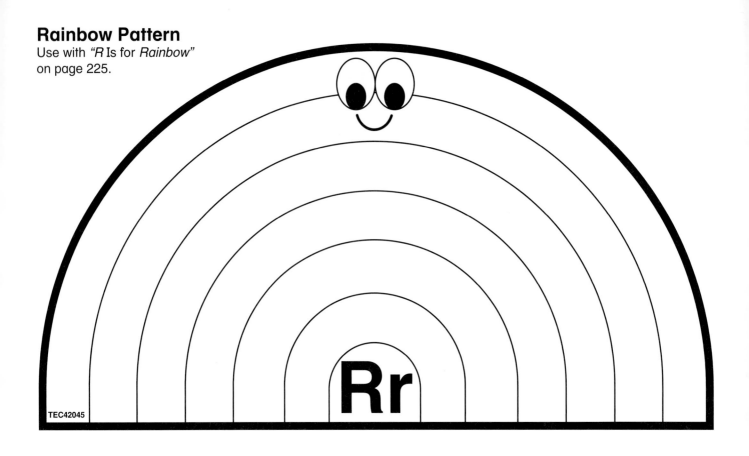

TEC42045

U and Umbrella Patterns
Use with *"U* Is for *Umbrella"* on page 226.

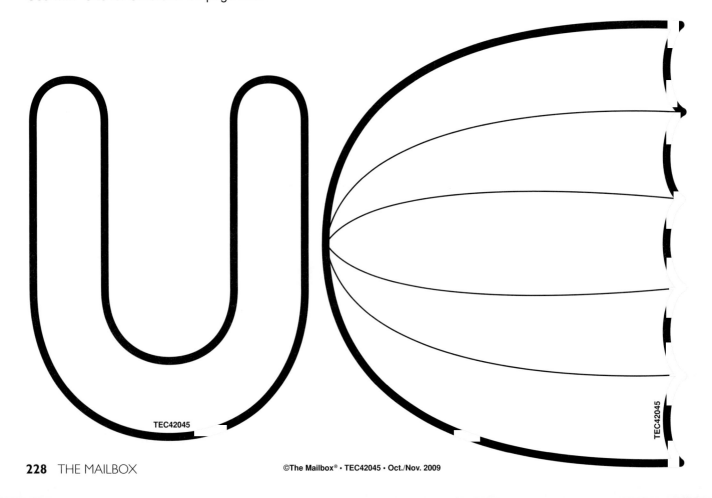

TEC42045

TEC42045

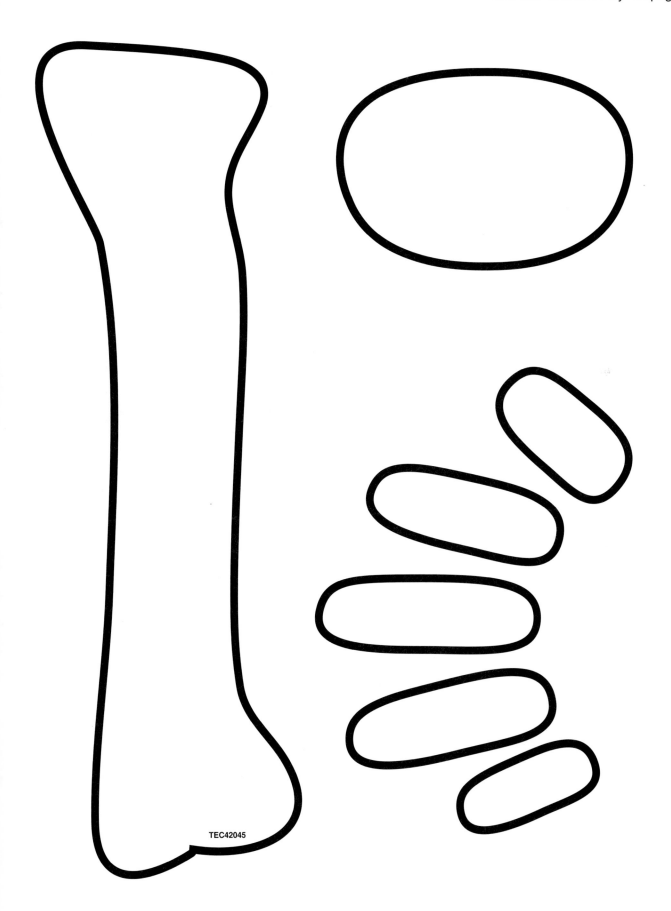

TEC42045

Blast Off With
High-Frequency Words

ideas contributed by Angie Kutzer,
Garrett Elementary, Mebane, NC

Like!

Countdown!
Spelling

Youngsters are sure to reach for the stars after naming each letter in a featured word. Point to a word on your word wall or another high-frequency word list. Then lead youngsters to spell the word aloud, crouching a little closer to the floor for each letter named. After spelling the word, encourage students to "blast off" toward the sky as they repeat the word aloud.

The

Spotlight on Words
Reading words

High-frequency word cards and a flashlight are all you need to put this review in galactic motion. Invite a child to hold a flashlight (sunlight), pretending to be the sun. Then give each remaining youngster a word card and have the group stand around the sun to form a circle. Lead youngsters to circle around the sun, pretending to be planets, while chanting the rhyme shown. At the end of the rhyme, the planets stop and the sun reads the word (with assistance from the group as needed) on which his sunlight shines. When the word is correctly named, the two students switch places. Continue with additional rotations.

Round and round the sun we go,
With lots of words that we now know!
When we stop, the light will shine
On a word. Will it be mine?

To the Moon
Motivation

Inspire youngsters to achieve a class goal with this motivational display. Write a desired goal, such as "We know our sight words!" on a moon cutout. Color and cut out a copy of the shuttle pattern on page 232; post the shuttle a predetermined distance away from the moon. As students demonstrate progress toward the goal, move the shuttle closer to the moon. Reward students' success when the shuttle lands on the moon. **To motivate independent progress,** give each child a shuttle pattern and have her color sections as she moves closer to her goal. When her shuttle is completely colored, have her post it on a space-related display.

We know our sight words!

Alien on the Loose!
Reading

For this small-group activity, write a different high-frequency word on each of several paper plates (UFOs). Arrange the plates in rows on the floor. Then secretly hide an alien cutout (pattern on page 232) behind one of the plates. To find the alien, invite each student, in turn, to read a word on the UFO behind which he thinks the alien is hiding. After he reads the word, he lifts the UFO to search for the alien. Continue to review words in this manner until the alien is found. Then secretly hide the alien behind a different UFO for a new round.

Word Constellations

These star-studded flash cards are the perfect tool to review high-frequency words. To make one card, write a word on black construction paper. Then place star stickers on the letters to resemble a constellation. Use the prepared cards and the ideas below for dazzling word practice.

Reading: Give each youngster a constellation card. Then pair youngsters and set a timer. Encourage partners to read and spell each word, in unison, before the time runs out.

Writing: Put the cards at a center with paper and crayons. A child selects a card, makes a crayon rubbing, and connects the stars to write the word. For an added challenge, the child writes each word in a sentence.

Assessment: Arrange the constellation cards in random order in a child-friendly location. Instruct a youngster to point to each matching word after you name it. Or have her read each word to you independently.

Shuttle Pattern
Use with "To the Moon" on page 231.

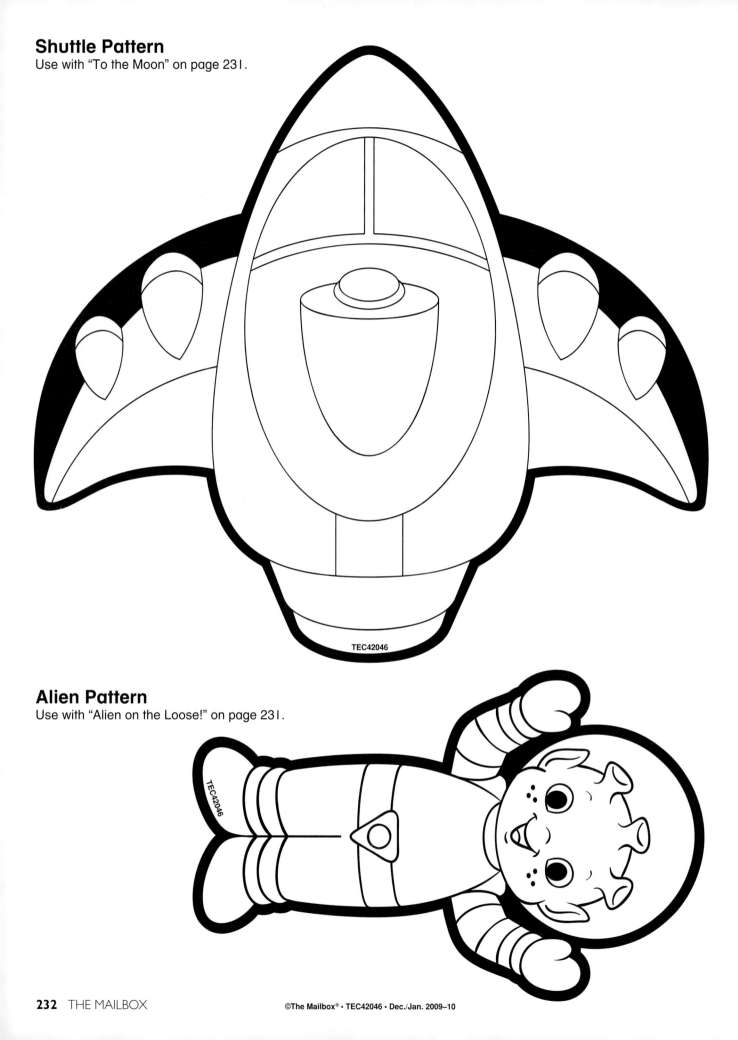

TEC42046

Alien Pattern
Use with "Alien on the Loose!" on page 231.

TEC42046

A Special Delivery of Short-Vowel Word Families

Check out these first-class ideas that can be used with any word family!

Come on In!
Sorting words

Invite your little postal workers to deliver mail each morning! Write on a small card each rime you would like to feature and attach each card to a small box to make sorting bins. Also write on a class supply of cards different words that contain the rimes. When each child enters the room, have him take a card and drop it into the matching bin. Later, gather youngsters to read the mail in each word family bin as part of your daily routine.

adapted from an idea by Robyn Pryor
Prestonwood Christian Academy, Plano, TX

Stuff the Envelopes
Reading words

For this class activity, write a different rime on each of two envelopes and corresponding words on individual cards. Then display the words near the envelopes. To begin, sing the first verse of the song shown. Then have the class sing the second verse in response. After singing the response, help a child find a word in the named word family, read it, and place the card in the corresponding envelope. After each card has been stuffed, encourage youngsters to review each word family by reading the mail.

(sung to the tune of "The More We Get Together")

Oh, can you find a word, a word, a word?
Oh, can you find a word in the [*-ip*] family?

Oh, yes! We'll find a word, a word, a word.
Oh, yes! We'll find a word in the [*-ip*] family.

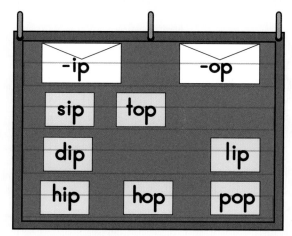

Peek Inside!
Making words

At this center, students manipulate letters to make words. Program an envelope with a rime. Inside the envelope, insert onset cards that form real words when coupled with the rime. Place the envelope and a supply of paper at a center. A child removes the cards from the envelope. He places each card on the envelope to form a word and records each word on a sheet of paper. **For a more advanced version,** provide onset cards that do not form real words for youngsters to differentiate.

Robyn Pryor

Mixed-Up Mail
Real and nonsense words

Program a class supply of cards with real and nonsense words from a chosen word family. Draw on the board two simple mailboxes labeled as shown. To begin, give each child a card. In turn, have each student read her word aloud and tell if it is a real or nonsense word. Then have her "deliver" the card by taping it to the matching mailbox. After each youngster has had a turn, lead the class in rereading the mail in each box. **For added fun,** have youngsters deliver their mail to pretend mailboxes (shoeboxes that you've covered with paper and cut slits in the lids).

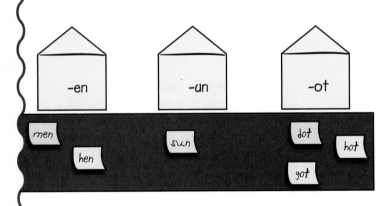

Door to Door
Recognizing and writing words

Students are sure to enjoy delivering words to the houses on this road! Program simple house cutouts with different rimes. Display the houses along a length of black paper (road). Then encourage each child to use books, posters, and charts to find words in each posted word family. When a word is found, have her copy it onto a sticky note and "deliver" it to the matching house. After a predetermined amount of time, lead youngsters in reading the words posted by each home.

Robyn Pryor, Prestonwood Christian Academy, Plano, TX

Helpful Bear Paws
Writing words

To prepare this reproducible booklet from page 235, program a copy of the mailbag on the booklet cover with a rime. Then program each of the bear paws on the booklet pages with different onsets that form real words when combined with the rime. (Be sure the resulting words on pages one and two can be illustrated.) Next, make a copy of the programmed page for each child. A child combines the onset on each paw with the rime to write each word. Then he illustrates each word on pages one and two. To complete the booklet, he cuts apart the cover and pages and staples them in order. **For more advanced students,** simply provide the rime on the mailbag.

Name _____

©The Mailbox® • TEC42047 • Feb./Mar. 2010

1

2

3

Storytime Solutions

Help your students improve their comprehension of just about any story with these follow-up activities.

This story reminds me of when we got our first pet. It is a cat too! His name is Tabby.

Human Hot Potato
Making connections

Motivate students to make story connections with this game variation. After reading a story aloud, gather youngsters in a circle. Quickly walk around the circle while the group says, "Hot potato stop!" Then stop and face the child closest to you and ask her to make a text-to-self connection. After sharing, switch places with the child and have her begin a new round. Continue as time permits, switching to text-to-text or text-to-world connections.

Alicia K. Shaffer
Mechanicsburg, PA

Build a Sandwich
Story elements

The elements of a story are the perfect ingredients for this literary sandwich. Give each child two tan paper squares (bread slices) and four different-colored papers trimmed to make sandwich ingredients. Help him write the title and author of a story on one bread slice and his name on the other. Then help him label each sandwich ingredient with one of the following words: *Setting, Characters, Problem,* and *Solution.* To make a sandwich, the student draws the corresponding element on each ingredient and then staples the ingredients between the bread slices. **For a class book variation,** supersize each page for small groups to complete.

Alicia K. Shaffer

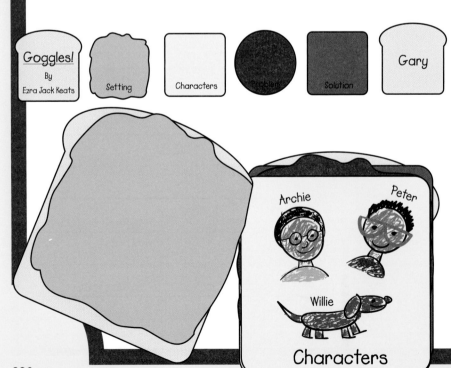

Read, Roll, and Respond!
Comprehension

> I liked the story because it made me laugh!

In advance, choose a skill below. Then prepare the cards as described and glue each card to a different side of a cube. After reading a story aloud, have youngsters roll the cube, in turn, and respond to the prompt that lands faceup.

Literary response: Cut out a copy of the literary response cards on page 238.
Making connections: Cut out two copies of the making connections cards on page 238.
The Five *W*s and *How*: Label each of six blank cards with one of the following questions: Who? What? When? Where? Why? How?

Alicia K. Shaffer, Mechanicsburg, PA

> How else might the story have ended?

> The best part of the story is

Meaningful Monkeys
Literary response

One of these little monkeys is sure to prompt a lively discussion! Cut apart a copy of the monkey cards on page 239. Then decorate a large can to resemble a barrel and put the cards in the barrel. After storytime, invite a child to remove a card from the barrel to prompt a follow-up discussion. **For a writing extension,** help each child write and illustrate a completed sentence about the prompt.

Alicia K. Shaffer

Picture Booklet
Retelling

For each child, fold a paper to make six boxes. In the first box, guide him to write the title of a selected story. After reading the tale aloud and listing a review of story events as a group, have him draw in each remaining box a different picture that will help him retell the story. Then have him cut along the fold lines, sequence his story behind the title page, and staple it together. Encourage youngsters to use their booklets to retell the story to a friend or family member.

Amy Rodriguez
P.S. 212
Brooklyn, NY

> How Froggy Grew Up

Literary Response Cards

Use with "Read, Roll, and Respond!" on page 237.

Would you like to be the main character? Tell why.

TEC42048

Who else might like to read the story?

TEC42048

What is your favorite part? Tell why.

TEC42048

How else might the story have ended?

TEC42048

Do you like the story? Tell why.

TEC42048

Would you read the story again? Tell why.

TEC42048

Making Connections Cards

Use with "Read, Roll, and Respond!" on page 237.

Text-to-World

TEC42048

Text-to-Text

TEC42048

Text-to-Self

TEC42048

The best part of the story is when…

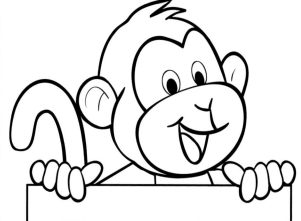

The end of the story made me feel…

If I could be in the story, I would like to…

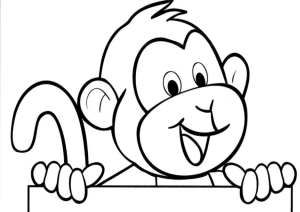

A different ending to this story could be…

TEC42048

TEC42048

TEC42048

TEC42048

Abuzz About Writing

Your students are sure to buzz about these literacy activities!

ideas contributed by Alicia K. Shaffer, Mechanicsburg, PA

"Bee" on the Lookout!

These handy bee puppets are sure to help your kindergartners check their writing. In advance, cut a half-inch hole in the center of a four-inch yellow oval for each child. To make a bee, a child draws two eyes and black stripes on his oval. He cuts wings and antennae from scrap paper or craft supplies and glues them on his bee. Then he glues the lower half of his bee to a craft stick. To use his bee, he "flies" the bee over his sentence(s) to find each capital letter and the ending punctuation, viewing them through the open circle. **For a circle-time alternative,** make a larger bee to use with chart paper and big books.
Capitalization, punctuation

I see five bees by the

Name Alicia

I am a busy bee!

Busy as a Bee

Abuzz About Writing
Responding to a prompt

I am busy when I help feed my dog.

Busy Bees

To begin, ask youngsters to tell what they think it means to be a busy bee. Then invite them to share things they do each day that keep them busy. Next, give each child a copy of page 242 and read the prompt aloud. Have each student write and draw to respond to the prompt. If desired, create a summery scene by displaying the completed pages above colorful paper flowers and adding the title "Busy Bees in 'Kinder-garden.'"
Responding to a prompt

Buzzy Bee's Week

Students write a book about Buzzy Bee with this repetitive writing prompt! To make a book for each child, staple five or seven sheets of paper between construction paper covers. Before writing, have youngsters tell about different places they have seen bees as you record their responses on chart paper for future reference. For daily writing, have each child complete the prompt "On [day of the week], Buzzy Bee…" Then have her illustrate her sentence(s). If desired, encourage students to include in their writings additional characters such as talking flowers, animals, and bugs. *Creative writing*

Flying to Flowers

To prepare, program a class supply of flower cutouts with writing prompts that encourage students to write about familiar experiences. Place the flowers, writing side down, in a pocket chart. During writing time, invite each child, in turn, to "buzz" to the chart and take a flower. Have her glue her flower to a sheet of paper and then write and/or draw to respond to the prompt. **To extend the activity,** display the papers around the room and invite your little bees to buzz around the class and read each other's papers. *Writing about a familiar experience*

Writing prompts:
I was happy when…
I was sad when…
Describe your favorite toy.
Describe your bedroom.
Tell about a pet you would like to have.
Tell about your favorite season.
What do you like to do on the weekends? Why?
What is your favorite meal? Why?

Word Hives

Follow up this group activity with a writing center. First, label the top of a hive cutout with a rime of your choice. Invite youngsters to name words in the word family, and record each correct response on the hive. Then place the hive and writing paper at a center. A child selects words from the hive to form rhyming sentences and phrases or a rhyming song. If desired, set out crayons for him to draw pictures or a scene to match his writing. *Writing simple rhymes*

Editor's Tip:
This can be easily adapted to review high-frequency words too!

Busy as a Bee

I am a busy bee!

I am busy when I

©The Mailbox® · TEC42049 · June/July 2010

Note to the teacher: Use with "Busy Bees" on page 240.

LITERATURE UNITS

Miss Bindergarten Gets Ready for Kindergarten

Written by Joseph Slate
Illustrated by Ashley Wolff

Miss Bindergarten's students have a lot to do to get ready for kindergarten. As they wake up, brush their teeth, and find their sneakers, Miss Bindergarten completes several chores of her own! This simple, engaging book soothes kindergarten jitters and helps youngsters develop rhyming skills.

ideas by Ada Goren, Winston-Salem, NC

Getting Ready

Writing

To prepare for this adorable class book, have someone take several photos of you getting ready for kindergarten. Then take a photo of each student. Arrange each two-page spread of your class book as shown, with student photos to the left and a photo of yourself to the right. As each child describes something he does to get ready for kindergarten, write his words next to his photo. Then caption each photo of yourself as shown and bind the pages together. After you read the book aloud, place it in your reading center.

Emily eats her oatmeal.

Jack goes to bed early.

Ms. Taylor gets ready for kindergarten.

Student Name Game

Matching letters

From Adam the alligator to Zach the zebra, Miss Bindergarten's students cover the entire alphabet! That makes the class photos on the final page of the book perfect for this letter-matching game. Place a set of small uppercase letter cards at a center along with the book opened to the final page. Two students take turns choosing cards, identifying the letters, and placing them over the matching pictures.

Find the Rhyme

Identifying rhyming words

Cut out a copy of the cards on page 245 and place them in your pocket chart. During a second reading of the story, pause before each rhyme that has a corresponding card. Encourage a student to find the card to complete the rhyme. Have youngsters help you recite the sentence with the rhyme included. Then have the student turn over the card. "Jessie Sike pedals her…bike!"

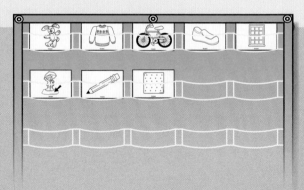

TEC42044

TEC42044

TEC42044

TEC42044

TEC42044

TEC42044

TEC42044

TEC42044

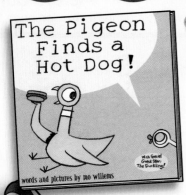

The Pigeon Finds a Hot Dog!

By Mo Willems

A tricky duckling tries to persuade a pigeon to give up his hot dog, but the pigeon is just too smart. No doubt a bit of sharing will solve the problem!

ideas contributed by Lynn Wagoner, Greensboro, NC

Quiet and Loud

Varied speaking tones in reading

In advance, prepare paper strips with different type sizes like the ones shown. After a read-aloud of the book, help youngsters notice the differences in type size throughout the story. Guide students to conclude that the type size indicates whether the words should be spoken quietly or loudly. Have students repeat several of the characters' words with the appropriate volume. Then show youngsters the paper strips and prompt them to read each sentence using the appropriate speaking volume. **For an easier version,** show youngsters letter cards with different type sizes and prompt them to name each letter using the appropriate speaking volume.

> This is a hot dog.
>
> This is a hot dog.
>
> This is my hot dog.
>
> This is my hot dog.
>
> This is the hot dog.
>
> This is the hot dog.

Pigeon and Duckling

Beginning sounds

Youngsters focus on the two fine-feathered characters with this activity. Cut out copies of the picture cards on page 247 to make a class supply and give each child a card. Help youngsters sort themselves into two groups: those with picture names that begin with /p/ as in *pigeon* and those that begin with /d/ as in *duckling*. Have students sit down. Then reread the book, prompting each group to stand when the appropriate character is talking.

Mustard or Ketchup?

Graphing

At the end of the story, the duckling shows a preference for mustard on his hot dog. Give youngsters the opportunity to share which condiments they prefer too! Make a class supply of hot dog cards (patterns on page 247) plus three extras. Color three cards appropriately and use them to make a simple graph programmed as shown. Then have each child personalize a card to show his preferred condiment. After students add their cards to the graph, help them compare the results.

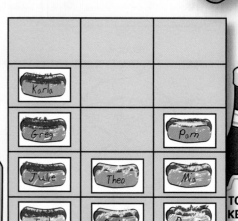

TEC42045

TEC42045

TEC42045

TEC42045

TEC42045

TEC42045

TEC42045

TEC42045

Hot Dog Cards
Use with "Mustard or Ketchup?" on page 246.

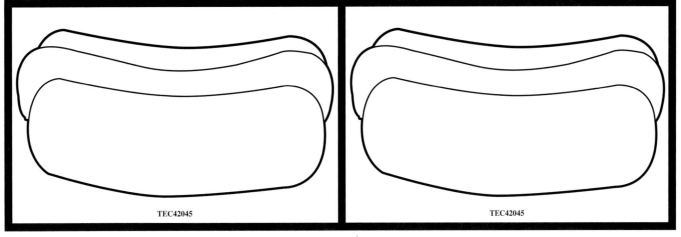

TEC42045

TEC42045

Bear Snores On

Written by Karma Wilson
Illustrated by Jane Chapman

While Bear takes his winter nap, forest animals take shelter in his nice warm cave. Their impromptu party eventually wakes Bear, but instead of being angry with his uninvited guests, he just wants to be included in the fun!

ideas contributed by Lynn Wagoner, Greensboro, NC

Rhyme Time
Developing rhyming skills

Kindergartners are sure to enjoy this interactive rereading of the story! As you read the story aloud, pause before each rhyming word and then prompt youngsters to supply the word. Also encourage students to add sound effects to the rereading by having them snore loudly each time you read the words "But the bear snores on." What fun!

Pretend Bears, Real Bears
Distinguishing real from pretend

Bear cries, talks, and drinks tea! Help youngsters sort these pretend bear behaviors from real bear behaviors. In advance, draw two simple caves on a sheet of chart paper and label the caves as shown. Then program paper strips naming real bear behaviors and the pretend behaviors of the bear in the book. After a read-aloud of the story, have students help you sort the strips onto the caves.

Bears have babies called cubs.
Bears can be dangerous.
Bears eat berries and fish.

Real Bear

Bear snores.
Bear cries.
Bear drinks tea.
Bear talks.

Pretend Bear

Aaaa-choooo!

The bear snez and wacs up. The bear is hape.

Pepper Project
Writing, retelling a story

At the end of the story, a small fleck of pepper causes Bear to sneeze and wake up. Help youngsters retell the story up to the appearance of the pepper. Then have each child write about the ending with this adorable project! To make the project, a child colors and cuts out a copy of the stew pot on page 249. Then he glues the pot to a sheet of construction paper programmed as shown. He brushes glue above the pot and sprinkles black hole-punched dots (pepper) over the glue. Then he writes or dictates a sentence or two to describe the end of the story.

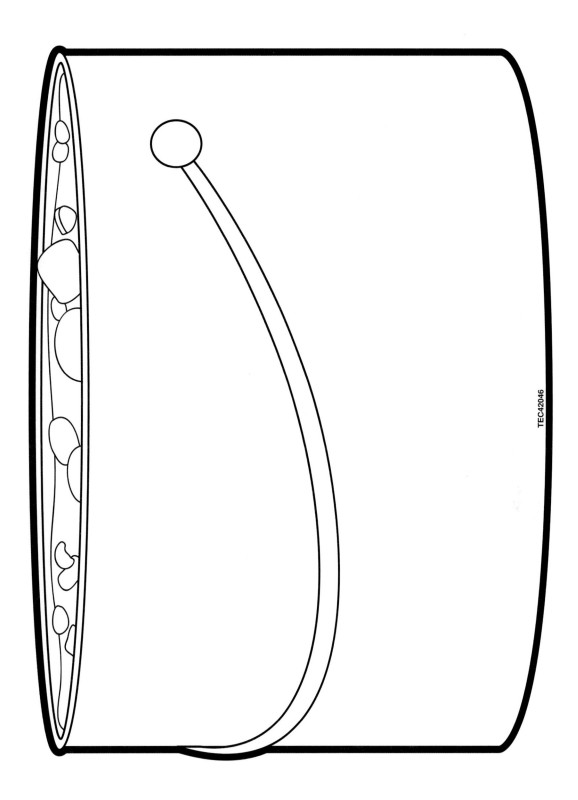

TEC42046

I Can Read With My Eyes Shut!

by Dr. Seuss

The zany Cat in the Hat proves to youngsters that the best type of reading is done with open eyes. This classic story is sure to tickle your students and urge them to open books.

ideas contributed by Katie Zuehlke, Bendix Elementary, Annandale, MN

Sing and Rhyme
Reinforcing rhyming words

After a read-aloud of the story, place pairs of rhyming word cards in your pocket chart. Help students read the first pair of rhyming words aloud. Then lead them in singing the song shown, inserting the appropriate words. Repeat the process with each remaining pair of cards.

(sung to the tune of "If You're Happy and You Know It")

Oh, it's very hard to read with my eyes shut.
Oh, it's very hard to read with my eyes shut.
But when my eyes open wide,
I can read [rhyming word] and [rhyming word].
Oh, it's very hard to read with my eyes shut.

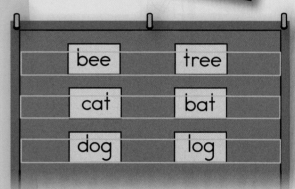

bee	tree
cat	bat
dog	log

So Many Possibilities!
Writing

The story names a variety of topics one might find in books. Have youngsters name additional topics for this class book! Encourage students to explore books in both your classroom and the library. Then give each child a copy of page 251. Help each student finish the prompt with the name of a potential topic. Then encourage her to add an illustration to her work. Bind the finished pages together with a cover labeled "What Can We Read About?"

Name Sammie

We can read about frogs and turtles

Open Eyes
Identifying sight words

Gather a supply of jumbo wiggle eyes. Write sight words on a sheet of paper and make several copies. Then gather a small group of youngsters at a table and give each child a paper. Name one of the words and encourage each child to place a wiggle eye on the word. Congratulate youngsters for reading with their eyes open. Then continue until all the words are covered with eyes.

and   are
at   or
is   it
        the

We can read about _____

_____.

Duck & Goose

Written and illustrated by Tad Hills

When Duck and Goose happen upon what they believe is an egg, they fight over the opportunity to tend to it until it hatches. They learn, however, that things are not always what they seem!

Duck, Goose, or Other?

Making predictions

Youngsters guess what will hatch from the egg with this simple graphing activity! Cut out a copy of the graph labels from page 253. Then label a large graph as shown and display it in your classroom. Read the story aloud, stopping at the page that says, "It's time, Goose, it's time!" Have each child write his name on an egg cutout. (See the egg patterns on page 254.) Prompt him to guess what will happen next and place his egg on the graph accordingly. Then read the end of the story and have students compare the actual ending with their predictions.

Angie Kutzer, Garrett Elementary, Mebane, NC

What Will Happen?

A duck will hatch.	A goose will hatch.	Something else will happen.
Joelle	Jose	Michelle
Aaron	Derrick	
Julian	Jon	
Alyssa		

Egg or Ball?

Making comparisons

Duck and Goose mistake a ball for an egg. Your youngsters can help them distinguish between the two objects with this simple Venn diagram. Label a Venn diagram with the headings shown. Then show youngsters a ball and an egg. Prompt students to describe characteristics of the ball and the egg and encourage them to help you write the characteristics in the appropriate section of the Venn diagram.

Ball — Egg

- bounces
- used to play

look similar
can buy in a store

- breaks easily
- has a baby inside

Play Ball!

Comprehension, speaking to answer questions

Use the main object in the story, a ball, to ask students questions about the book. Roll a ball to a child and then ask him a question such as one of the ones shown. If he doesn't know the answer, encourage him to roll the ball to a classmate to help him answer the question. When the question is answered correctly, have the child roll the ball to another student. Continue until each child has had a turn.

Angie Kutzer

Questions

What do Duck and Goose do to pass the time?
Why do Duck and Goose start to get along?
How does the story end?
What is your favorite part of the story?
Which story character do you like the best—
 Duck, Goose, or the blue bird?
When have you had to share something?
 Describe how you felt.

What is the setting of the story?
What is the problem?
Who are the main characters?
Who sees the egg first?
Who touches the egg first?
What is something Duck and Goose say they
 want to teach the baby bird?

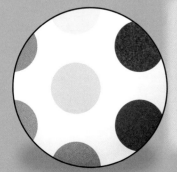

A duck
will hatch.

©The Mailbox®

A goose
will hatch.

©The Mailbox®

Something
else will
happen.

©The Mailbox®

Egg Patterns
Use with "Duck, Goose, or Other?" on page 252.

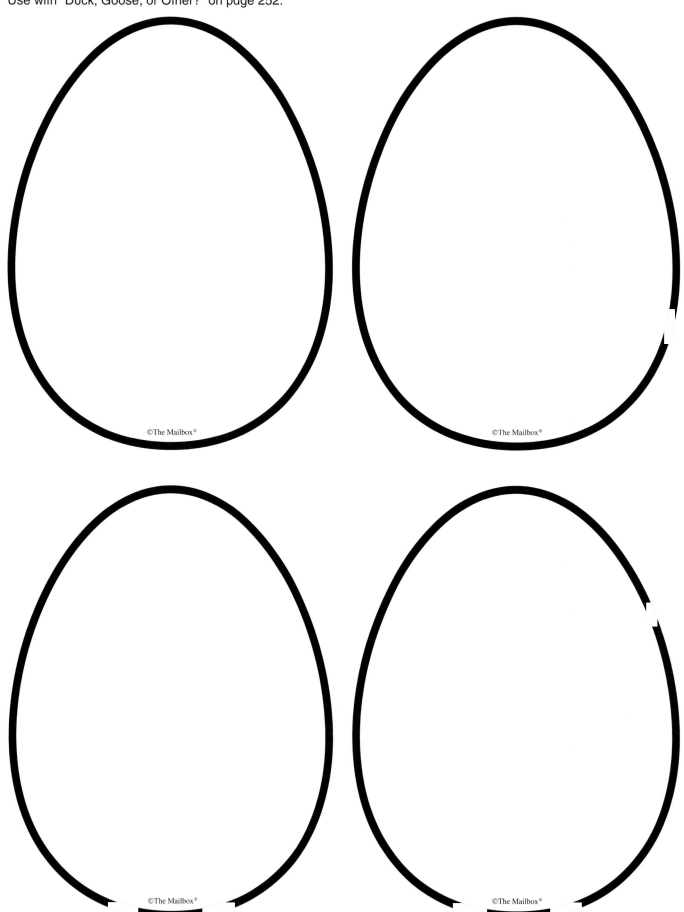

©The Mailbox®

©The Mailbox®

©The Mailbox®

©The Mailbox®

The Rainbow Fish

by Marcus Pfister

Rainbow Fish has many beautiful, flashy scales, but he refuses to share with the other fish. When they ignore him for his lack of kindness, he discovers from the wise old octopus that sharing can make one happy indeed.

ideas contributed by Kathy Ginn
Miami Trace Elementary
Washington Court House, OH

A Sparkling School

Identifying the main idea and details

In advance, display a large fish cutout. After reading the story aloud, have each child color and cut out a copy of the fish pattern from page 256. Encourage him to glue an aluminum foil scale to his fish. Next, have students help determine the main idea of the story. Write the main idea on the large fish. Then prompt each child, in turn, to stand with his fish and name a detail from the story. Help him attach his fish to the display.

You should always brush your teeth because it keeps them clean.

Octopus Is Wise

Writing

The octopus in the story gives very good advice. No doubt your kindergartners will be eager to share other thoughts from this wise animal! Have each youngster draw an octopus on a sheet of paper. Encourage her to draw a speech bubble above her octopus. Then prompt her to write advice from the octopus in the speech bubble. If desired, bind the finished papers together to form a class book.

Sharing Time

Making real-life applications

With this activity, youngsters identify sharing behaviors that Rainbow Fish would approve of. In advance, write the suggested sharing scenarios on separate fish cutouts (pattern on page 256) and place the fish in a decorative gift bag. Put the headings shown in your pocket chart. To begin, have a child draw a fish from the bag and help him read the scenario. Then prompt him to place the fish beneath the correct heading. When the fish are sorted appropriately, revisit the fish beneath the "Not Sharing" heading and encourage students to discuss a better way to handle each situation.

Sharing scenarios:
Jenna has two cookies. She gives one cookie to a friend.
Sam has many different blocks. He won't give any blocks to his brother.
Jason has played on the swing throughout recess, so he gives his swing to Hannah.
Shana has the bottle of glue. She keeps it on her side of the table so others can't use it.
D'Juan has a new toy. He asks Conner whether he wants to play with him.
Courtney is pouring juice for herself and her friend. She makes sure they each get
  equal amounts.

Fish Pattern
Use with "A Sparkling School" and "Sharing Time" on page 255.

TEC42049

MATH UNITS

Ideas You Can Count On!

ideas contributed by Angie Kutzer, Garrett Elementary, Mebane , NC

Classroom Collections

Making sets to ten

Give each child a lunch-size paper bag labeled with a numeral from one to ten. Then direct her to place in her bag a set of small objects from the classroom that matches the number on her bag. After all students have finished, invite each youngster, in turn, to share her collection with the group. As the child pulls each item out of the bag, lead the class in counting aloud. **To vary the difficulty and skill of the activity,** label some bags with dot sets, some bags with numerals, and some bags with number words.

1, 2, 3, 4, 5, 6, 7.

Three.

Find a Number!

Identifying numbers to ten

To prepare this small-group game, program for each group member a sheet of construction paper with a different number from one to ten. Then mix up the numbers and place them on the floor in a circle. Play a recording of soft music and invite the group to slowly walk around the outside of the circle. When you stop the music, instruct each youngster to pick up the nearest paper. Have each student, in turn, display his number for the group as he says it aloud. **To practice ordering numbers,** have students arrange themselves in sequential order based on the numerals on their papers.

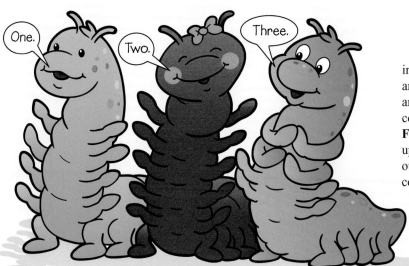

Sound Off
Counting

Turn a frequent classroom occurrence—getting in line—into a teachable moment! Once students are in a line, the first child begins counting by announcing "one." Each subsequent student continues counting by saying the next number. **For an alternate version,** have boys and girls line up in separate lines and direct each line to count out loud in turn. Then have a student volunteer compare the number of students in each line.

Card by Card

One-to-one correspondence, sorting, ordering numbers

The only thing you'll need for the following small-group activities is a deck of playing cards.

One-to-one correspondence: Ask one child to be the dealer and give him the deck of cards. He gives each child in the group a facedown card as he counts along. Then collect the cards and invite another child to be the dealer.

Sorting: Prepare the deck of cards so that students can sort by one attribute, such as suit or color. Then have the group work together to sort the cards as designated.

Ordering numbers: Remove the picture cards and aces from the deck. Give each child in the group a card. The youngsters arrange the cards in order from least to greatest.

Classroom Sets
Modeling numbers

To prepare, write on a sheet of paper a sentence starter similar to the one shown; then copy the page to make a class supply. To begin, point out sets of items in the classroom, such as three shelves on a bookcase or four desks in a group. Then have each child find a set of items in the room and draw it on a copy of the prepared page. When his drawing is finished, help him complete the sentence to match his drawing. Bind the completed pages into a class book titled "Sets in Our Classroom."

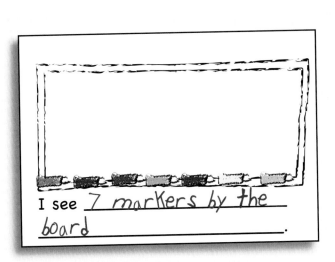

I see 7 markers by the board.

Lots of Spots

Draw ○ to match the number on each .

5

7

9

8

10

Math Roundup

Roll, Count, Corral!
Counting

To prepare for this small-group game, have each group member cut out a set of the cow cards from page 263. Then give each child a construction paper corral similar to the one shown. To take a turn, a player rolls a die and places the corresponding number of cows in her corral. Play continues until a player has corralled all her cows. If a player rolls a number higher than the number of cows she has left to corral, she loses that turn.

Randi Austin, Stoutland R-2 Elementary, Stoutland, MO

Western Wear
Patterning

The result of this center is a hat fit for a little cowpoke! Make a class supply of large cowboy hat patterns like the one shown. Have each child cut out a hat pattern and use two crayon colors to draw on his hat an *AB* pattern of a symbol such as an X, a dot, or a star. Encourage each child to read his color pattern to a classmate before he glues his hat to a tagboard strip. Staple the ends of the strip to make a hat headband.

Rope 'em In!
Sorting geometric shapes

For this small-group activity, gather a variety of square, circular, triangular, and rectangular blocks such as attribute blocks. Have the group work together to sort the blocks by shape. Then give one student a length of yarn and ask her to round up a set of shapes by forming a matching-shaped lasso around the set. Continue until each set of shapes has been lassoed.

Jennie Jensen, Clarence, IA

A Spotted Cow

Modeling numbers, comparing sets

To prepare, program the cowbell on each of several cow patterns (see page 263) with a different numeral. Place the cows at a center along with a supply of black felt shapes (spots). Then choose one of the ideas below.

Modeling numbers: A youngster chooses a cow and reads the number on the cowbell. Then she places the matching number of spots on the cow.

Comparing sets: Each student in a pair takes a cow, reads the number on the cowbell, and places the matching number of spots on her cow. Then the two youngsters compare the number of spots on their cows. The child whose cow has more spots says, "Moo!"

Jennie Jensen
Clarence, IA

Moo!

Editor's Tip:
To reinforce larger numbers and keep the spots from getting too small, simply enlarge the cow pattern.

Shorter Than My Lasso	Longer Than My Lasso

Shorter or Longer?

Nonstandard measurement

Have each student cut a desired length of twine or yarn to make a lasso. Then give him a recording sheet similar to the one shown. With his lasso untied, have him compare the length of several classroom items to his lasso. Direct him to write or draw each item in the appropriate column of his recording sheet. If he finds an item that is exactly the same length as his lasso, have him write or draw the item on the back of his paper.

adapted from an idea by Cindy Barber
Fredonia, WI

Cow Cards

Use with "Roll, Count, Corral!" on page 261.

Cow Pattern

Use with "A Spotted Cow" on page 262.

How Tall? How Heavy?

By the Card
Comparing lengths

No advance preparation is needed for this idea. Simply give each child an index card and ask her to find an object in the classroom that is about the same length as the card. When she finds an item, have her draw it on a piece of paper. Then have students search for items that are longer than and shorter than their cards in the same manner. After a predetermined amount of time, invite students to share their findings.

Marie E. Cecchini, West Dundee, IL

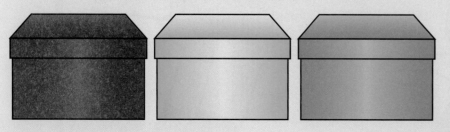

Deshawn

Boxes to Lift
Ordering by weight

Choose three items of various weights, such as cotton balls, small wooden blocks, and hardback books. Place a few of each item inside separate lidded boxes, ensuring that each box feels obviously different in weight. Wrap each box (wrapping the lid separately) in a different color of paper and place the boxes at a center. A child compares the weight of each box and places the boxes in order from lightest to heaviest. Then he draws three boxes on a strip of paper and colors them to show the order of the boxes. After recording his answers, he removes the lids to see what items made the boxes have different weights.

Marie E. Cecchini

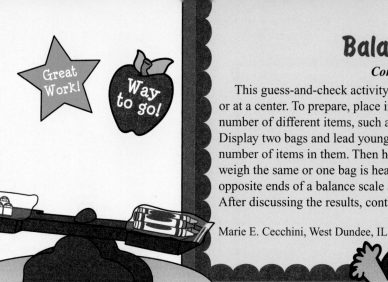

Balancing Bags
Comparing weights

This guess-and-check activity can be done in a whole group, a small group, or at a center. To prepare, place in separate resealable plastic bags the same number of different items, such as paper clips, beans, pennies, or crayons. Display two bags and lead youngsters to realize that the bags have an equal number of items in them. Then have youngsters predict whether the bags weigh the same or one bag is heavier, and if so, which one. Place each bag on opposite ends of a balance scale and have students check their predictions. After discussing the results, continue with different combinations of bags.

Marie E. Cecchini, West Dundee, IL

An Arm's Length
Comparing lengths

For each child, cut a piece of yarn equal to the length of his arm and a different-colored piece of yarn equal to the length of his leg. Encourage students to explore length using one or more of the options below. After students have made several comparisons, invite them to share their observations.

- Compare the length of your arm to your leg.
- Compare the length of your arm to your classmates' arms.
- Compare the length of your leg to your classmates' legs.
- Find objects that are shorter or longer than your arm.
- Find objects that are shorter or longer than your leg.

Kristin Bauer Ganoung, Sandhills Public Schools
Halsey, NE

Shorter and Taller
Comparing heights

Making a page for this class book encourages students to examine their heights. Give each child a copy of page 266 and have her draw herself in the box labeled "Me." Next, direct her to find in the classroom something that is shorter than her and something that is taller than her and draw each item in the corresponding box. Have her write her name to complete the first sentence and then help her write the name of each item drawn to complete the other sentences. Bind the completed pages between two construction paper covers to make a class book.

Katie Zuehlke, Bendix Elementary, Annandale, MN

Taller	Me	Shorter

My name is _____.

_____ is shorter than me.

_____ is taller than me.

©The Mailbox® • TEC42046 • Dec./Jan. 2009–10

Note to the teacher: Use with "Shorter and Taller" on page 265.

Let's Celebrate the 100th Day

A Number Lineup

Matching numbers, number order

Number 100 sticky dots from 1 to 100. Attach each dot to a small object and store the objects in a container. Place a number line from 1 to 100 on the floor and set the container nearby. Have a child take an object, find the matching number on the number line, and place the object below the number. Have students take turns until all the objects are correctly placed.

Jody Carlson
Smith Elementary
Berea, OH

Editor's Tip:
If you don't have a number line to 100, attach a long strip of masking tape to the floor and write the numbers on it.

Dear Family,
Our class will be celebrating the 100th day of school on
January 11 . Please have your child put 100 of
the same object in the paper bag. Then help him/her write three
clues about the object. Please return the bag and clues on 100th
Day. Thanks for your help.

Sam 's Clues
name
1. They are soft.
2. They are white.
3. They look like a bunny's tail.

Three Clues

Counting, critical thinking

Prior to the 100th day of school, send home with each child a paper lunch bag and a copy of the note at the top of page 269. Invite a family member to help the child place 100 like objects in the bag, write three clues about the objects, and return the note and bag to school. On 100th Day, encourage the child to share his clues. Then choose volunteers to name what they think is in the bag. **For an added challenge,** later in the day, direct each child to arrange and count his items in sets of ten.

Blythe Purdin, Rockport Elementary, Rockport, MA

Chicks Aplenty

Counting, tally marks

Prior to the 100th day of school, have youngsters decorate yellow paper ovals to make 100 chicks like the one shown. On 100th Day, hide the chicks around the room before students arrive. To begin the activity, read aloud *The Wolf's Chicken Stew* by Keiko Kasza and then invite youngsters to find the chicks. Next, make a tally chart to count the chicks found. Lead students in counting the tallies. If all 100 chicks have not been found, help students determine how many chicks are missing. Then invite youngsters to find the remaining chicks. If desired, display the chicks for an eye-catching reminder of 100th Day and the value of teamwork!

Suzi Boyett, Harney Elementary, Lebanon, IN

31. Julius
32. Donovan
33. Kara
34. Elise
35. Jake
36. Keida
37. Anna
38. Steve
39.
40.

An Autograph Collection

Counting, writing

Number ten half sheets of paper from 1 to 100, putting ten numbers on each sheet. For each child, staple a copy of the sheets between two half sheets of construction paper. Have each child personalize a copy of the cover at the bottom of page 269 and glue it to the front of his book. Next, read aloud the poem on the cover and have each child sign his name in his book. During the day, encourage students to ask their classmates, teachers, and students in other classes to write their names in his book. At the end of the day, direct him to count the number of autographs he has collected. If his book has fewer than 100 signatures, encourage him to take it home and collect the remaining signatures from family and friends.

Jodi Darter, Cabool Elementary, Cabool, MO

Hop to 100

Counting by tens

For this center activity, program each of ten large construction paper squares as shown. Laminate the squares for durability and tape them to the floor to form a hopscotch board. To count by tens to 100, a child hops on the board and names the numbers.

Susan Miller Geisler
Oakmont Elementary
Fort Worth, TX

Dear Family,
   Our class will be celebrating the 100th day of school on
_____. Please have your child put 100 of
the same object in the paper bag. Then help him/her write three
clues about the object. Please return the bag and clues on 100th
Day. Thanks for your help.

_____'s Clues

name

1. _____

2. _____

3. _____

_____'s Autograph Book

Today is the 100th Day.

Hip hip hooray!

I'm collecting autographs all day.

There are 100 places for people to sign.

Make that 99—one place is mine!

Note to the teacher: Use the top half of the page with "Three Clues" on page 267. Use the bottom half of the page with "An Autograph Collection" on page 268.

Sailing Into Addition!

Ahoy! Set sail into beginning addition with these hands-on ideas!

There are two turtle sailors and one duck sailor in the boat. How many sailors are there in all?

All Hands on Deck!
Beginning addition

You can count on these crewmates to provide practice with the concept of addition! Use the patterns on page 272 to make a supply of sailor cards. Then draw a simple boat on the board and place the cards nearby. As you announce a story problem about the sailors, have student volunteers tape sailor cards to the boat to match the problem. Then lead the class in counting the sailors to find the sum. Repeat the activity as time allows.

One, two, three, four, five.

Gone Fishin'!
Beginning addition

Youngsters act as fishermen with this catchy tune. Cut out several copies of the fish cards on page 272 in two different colors. Place each colored set on a separate sheet of blue paper (sea). To begin, invite a child to "catch" a desired number of fish from each sea and then place them in front of the group. Lead youngsters in singing the song shown. During the third line in the second verse, guide students in counting the fish to find the sum.

(sung to the tune of "Mary Had a Little Lamb")

[Child's name] caught [three] little fish,
Little fish, little fish.
[Child's name] caught [three] little fish
And then [she] caught [two] more!

[Child's name] has [three] and [two],
[Three] and [two], [three] and [two].
[Child's name] now has [five] in all—
[Five] fishies by the shore!

Lynn Wagoner, Greensboro, NC

Ten Little Fishies
Ways to make ten

Fish-shaped crackers make perfect manipulatives! Give each child a blue piece of paper (ocean), ten fish-shaped crackers, and a recording sheet similar to the one shown. Have her arrange the crackers in two groups. Then have her write the number of crackers in each group on her recording sheet. She continues in the same way, making as many different combinations that equal ten as she can.

_5_ and _5_ is 10.
_2_ and _8_ is 10.
___ and ___ is 10.
___ and ___ is 10.

Ava

Four turtle sailors and three duck sailors make seven sailors.

How Many Sailors?
Addition combinations

To prepare this center, copy the sailor cards on page 272 so there are ten of each sailor. Then cut out the cards and number ten boat cutouts with a different number from 1 to 10. Place the boats and cards at a center. A child takes a boat and places sailors above it to make the featured number. Then she counts each type of sailor she used and says the addition problem. She repeats the activity with different boats as time allows. **For an added challenge,** have her write each addition sentence on a sheet of paper.

adapted from an idea by Lynn Wagoner
Greensboro, NC

Boxes Overboard!
Writing addition sentences

Oh no! A cargo ship dropped a load of boxes into the ocean and your youngsters have to clean it up! To prepare, cut squares from two different colors of craft foam. Float the squares (boxes) in a water table or large shallow container and place a plastic scooper nearby. Invite a student to help "clean up" the spill by scooping up some boxes. Have her announce how many of each color she removed. Then enlist students' help in writing the corresponding addition sentence on the board. Return the boxes to the water and repeat the activity as time allows.

3 + 3 = 6

Sailor Cards

Use with "All Hands on Deck!" on page 270 and "How Many Sailors?" on page 271.

Fish Cards

Use with "Gone Fishin'!" on page 270.

TEC42047
TEC42047
TEC42047
TEC42047
TEC42047
TEC42047
TEC42047
TEC42047
TEC42047
TEC42047

Land Ho!

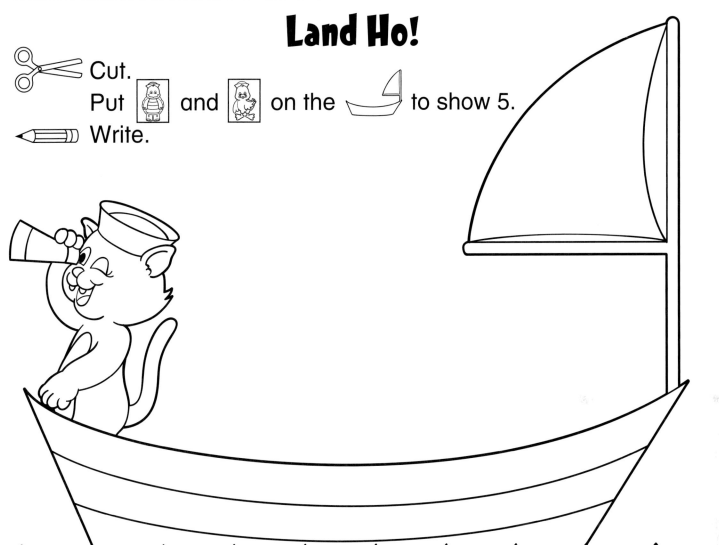

✂ Cut.

Put 🐱 and 🐦 on the ⛵ to show 5.

✏ Write.

___ + ___ = 5   ___ + ___ = 5

___ + ___ = 5   ___ + ___ = 5

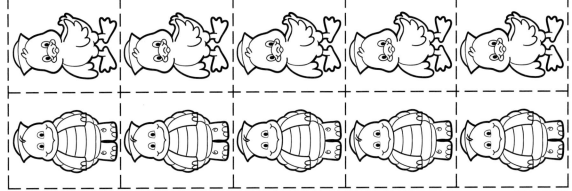

Take It Away!

What's packed into this fun-filled unit? A load of skill-boosting subtraction ideas!

Toss and Count
Beginning subtraction

It's easy to make subtraction problems during parachute play! Have youngsters stand in a circle, holding the edge of a parachute or a bedsheet. Toss a desired number of small balls on the parachute as you tell students the number. Next, direct the group to shake the parachute until you say to stop, allowing some of the balls to fall off. After the parachute has stopped, have youngsters help you count the balls that are on the floor. Then guide students to use the information to make a subtraction problem as you write it on the board. Repeat the activity with a different number of balls.

Kathy Shaw, Highland Park Learning Center, Roanoke, VA

There are seven ants on the picnic blanket. Four ants leave. How many ants are left on the blanket?

7 – 4 = 3

The Ants Go Marching
Beginning subtraction

For this small-group activity, prepare several ant cutouts. Then spread a picnic blanket on the floor and place the ants nearby. Gather a small group of youngsters around the blanket. As you announce a picnic-related story problem, have student volunteers move ants on and off the blanket to match the problem. Write the corresponding subtraction sentence on a sheet of chart paper. Then lead the group in counting the ants to find the difference.

Ada Goren
Winston-Salem, NC

Cover and Solve
Solving subtraction sentences
This reproducible helps students understand the concept of subtraction. Give each child a copy of page 276 and have her cut along the dotted lines, making five flaps. To complete each problem, a youngster folds each flap along the solid line to cover the corresponding illustration(s). Then she counts the remaining illustrations to determine the difference and writes the number on the answer blank.

Wilma Droegemueller
Zion Lutheran School
Mt. Pulaski, IL

Eight minus five is three.

Polly Wants a Cracker
Modeling subtraction
Have youngsters pretend to be Polly the hungry parrot as they practice subtraction skills. Give each child in a small group a paper plate and a cup of small crackers. Say a subtraction story about Polly, such as "Polly has eight crackers. She eats five. How many crackers are left?" Have each student place the corresponding original number of crackers on his plate and pretend to eat the appropriate number of crackers to match the problem. Then have youngsters count the remaining crackers to find the difference. Repeat with different problems. Then invite your little parrots to eat their crackers. **For more advanced students,** have them write each subtraction problem on a sheet of paper.

Diane Dorais, Patrick Henry Elementary, Heidelberg, Germany

A Pet Story
Writing number sentences
To begin, show the group a stuffed animal pet. Tell students a story involving the pet and a number of items it has (such as dog bones or toys). Have each child draw an illustration to match your description. Then tell youngsters that the pet lost a number of its items and direct each child to cross off on her drawing the corresponding number of items. Finally, guide each child in writing a number sentence to match her illustration.

Angie Kutzer, Garrett Elementary, Mebane, NC

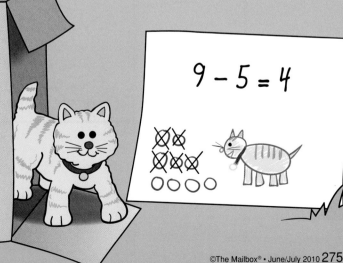

Name _____

Move It!

Listen and do.

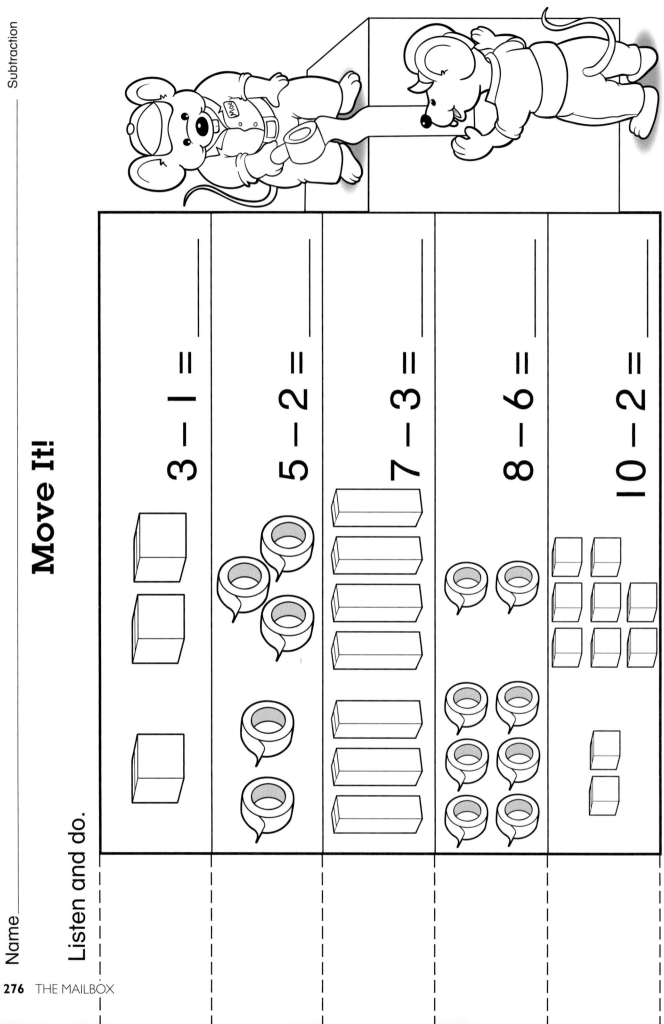

3 – 1 = ___

5 – 2 = ___

7 – 3 = ___

8 – 6 = ___

10 – 2 = ___

©The Mailbox® • TEC42049 • June/July 2010

Right On Time!

Give your students high-flying math practice with these timely ideas.

ideas by Kathy Ginn
Washington Court House, OH

Which Nest?
Estimating time

For this small-group activity, cover the clock on a copy of the bird pattern from page 279 and make a copy for each child. Cut out the birds and give one to each child, along with two lengths of brown yarn and two small sticky notes. Direct each child to use the yarn to make two circles (nests). Then have him label the sticky notes as shown and place one in each nest. For each nest, announce an activity that is taking place. (See the suggestions below.) Then direct each child to "fly" his bird to the nest of the fastest (or slowest) activity. After confirming the answer, continue in the same manner, naming different activities each time.

> In nest one, the birds are taking a bath. In nest two, the birds are drinking water. Put your bird in the nest where the activity will take a shorter amount of time.

Suggested Activities

drinking water
taking a bath
building a nest
waiting for an egg to hatch

chirping hello
feeding baby birds
eating a worm

Match 'em Up!
Reading analog clocks

Youngsters help birds fly to their nests with this partner activity. For every two students, label a brown paper semicircle (nest) with a time to the hour. For each nest, draw the matching time on a bird cutout (pattern on page 279). If you have an odd number of students, program two birds for one of the nests. Randomly distribute the birds and the nests. Then have each youngster search for the classmate with the matching nest or bird. When a child finds her match, have the twosome sit down and put the bird "in" the nest. After confirming each match, redistribute the cutouts for additional practice.

2 o'clock

Home, "Tweet" Home
Matching analog clocks and digital times

Lead your flock in playing this whole-class game! Cut out an equal number of birdhouses and birds (patterns on page 279). Draw clock hands to show a different time on each bird; then write each corresponding digital time on a separate birdhouse. Randomly arrange the cutouts face-down in a pocket chart. To begin, have a child turn over a birdhouse and read the time. Then ask another student to turn over a bird and read the time. If the bird and the birdhouse show the same time, each partner keeps a cutout. If not, they flip the cutouts back over. Students alternate turns until the pocket chart is empty.

A Bird's Day
Ordering events based on time

Invite your students to help a busy bird organize the events of its day. Have each child color and cut out a copy of the daily activity cards from page 279. The youngster orders the cards from the earliest time to the latest time. Then she glues the cards in this order to a 3" x 18" construction paper strip. **For an added challenge,** have each child write the corresponding digital time below each card.

| wake up | take a bath | rest on a branch | fly around | tidy nest | eat worms |

Check the Clock
Modeling time

To prepare, draw the minute hand pointing to the 12 on an enlarged copy of the bird pattern from page 279. Laminate the pattern and display it in an accessible location. Have a youngster use a wipe-off marker to draw the hour hand to show the time of his choosing. Invite his classmates to chirp like a bird if they know the time. Then ask a volunteer to announce the time shown. After confirming her answer, invite her to wipe off the clock and draw the hour hand to show a different time.

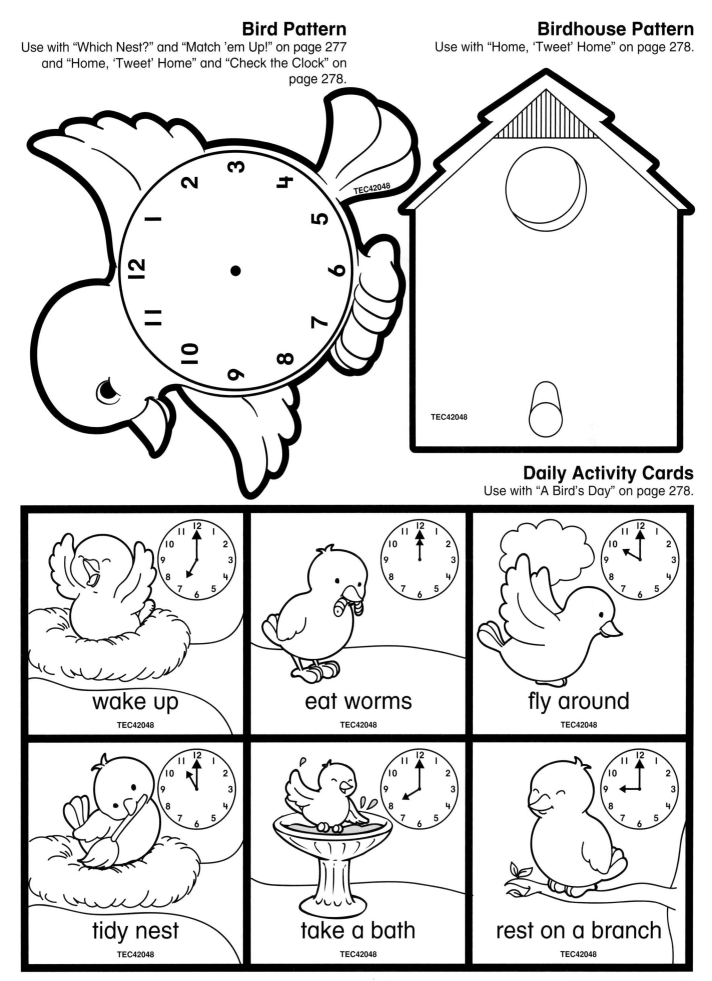

Bird Pattern

Use with "Which Nest?" and "Match 'em Up!" on page 277 and "Home, 'Tweet' Home" and "Check the Clock" on page 278.

TEC42048

Birdhouse Pattern

Use with "Home, 'Tweet' Home" on page 278.

TEC42048

Daily Activity Cards

Use with "A Bird's Day" on page 278.

wake up

TEC42048

eat worms

TEC42048

fly around

TEC42048

tidy nest

TEC42048

take a bath

TEC42048

rest on a branch

TEC42048

Find the Nest

✏️ Draw a line to match each bird to a nest.

Some nests will have more than one bird matched to them!

6 o'clock

11 o'clock

2 o'clock

9 o'clock

4 o'clock

7 o'clock

SEASONAL UNITS

Treasured Back-to-School Ideas

All Aboard!

Name display

Welcome your students aboard with this get-acquainted activity. Post an enlarged copy of the pirate ship pattern from 284. Also cut out a class supply of the parrot pattern on page 284. On each parrot, write a different student's name. Encourage each child to lightly color his parrot. Then attach the parrots to the ship. Invite each child, in turn, to point to his parrot and introduce himself to the class.

Kim Hintze, Show Low, AZ

Peter

Welcome Aboard!

X Marks the Spot

School tour, snack

Take youngsters on a treasure hunt to help them become familiar with the school. Plan to lead students to several locations before concluding the hunt in the lunchroom. For each location, write a simple clue on a sheet of paper and hide it in the location described by the previous clue. In the lunchroom, leave a treasure-themed snack for each student, such as a cup of chocolate pudding with a candy buried in it, topped with graham cracker crumbs.

To begin the treasure hunt, read the first clue aloud. Have youngsters give suggestions about where the clue may lead and then take them to the correct location, stopping to allow them to hunt for the next clue. Continue until the snacks are found. Then give each child a spoon (shovel) to dig into her snack to find her own buried treasure.

Kim Hintze

Clue 1: Go where there are lots of books. It's a place where you should always use your quiet voice.

Clue 2: Go to the playground to find the next clue. It's at the bottom of something that you can slide down.

A Big Catch
Name recognition

For this class activity, write each child's name on a separate fish cutout. Place the fish facedown on a large blue paper pond. To begin, turn over a fish and show the name on it to the class; have the corresponding student read her name aloud. Then lead students in the rhyme shown, inserting the child's name where indicated in the first three lines. While the class recites the last line, have the named student turn over a fish. Then insert the new name in the last line. To play again, use the name of the student whose fish was just drawn in the first three lines and have him pick a fish during the last line.

Marla Cobb, Barhitte Elementary, Burton, MI

[Mary] over the ocean,
[Mary] over the sea.
[Mary] caught a big fish,
But [she] didn't catch [Robert]!

Terrific Treasures
Writing

Who or what do your youngsters treasure? Find out with this writing project! Engage students in a conversation about the people and things that are important to them. Then have each student draw a corresponding picture on a copy of page 285. (If desired, have each child bring in photos for the project.) Direct her to write her name and dictate a description of her treasure. After students share their work, bind the pages together in a class book titled "Our Treasures."

Kim Hintze, Show Low, AZ

Rectangle Roundup
Matching shapes

Use this idea to pair students for introductions or partner work. For each twosome, cut from construction paper an identical pair of rectangles. (Vary the colors of the pairs to make matching easier.) Place the rectangles in a bag and then invite each child to take one. On your signal, have each student find his match. For an introduction activity, have partners tell each other about three of their favorite things. For partner work, have the partners sit together and wait quietly for further instructions.

Paula Uthoff, Amvet Boulevard School, North Attleboro, MA

Kindergarten Treasure
Making a keepsake

Have students make these keepsakes to take home on the first day of school. To begin, have each child fold a 12" x 18" sheet of construction paper in half. Help him round the corners of the folded edge and add details to look like a treasure chest. For each student, write a brief note on a copy of page 286. Give each youngster his paper; have him write his name and then draw to complete the rest of the page. Next, have him cut on the bold lines. Then have him glue the piece with his name to the front of his treasure chest and the other piece on the inside.

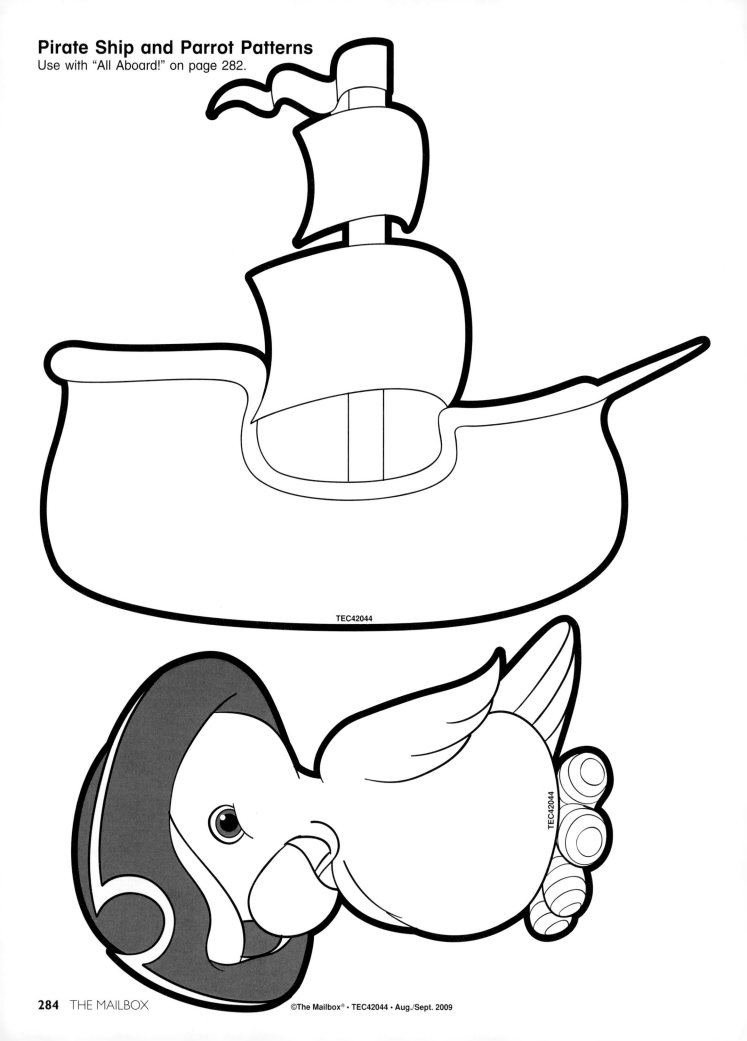

TEC42044

TEC42044

©The Mailbox® • TEC42044 • Aug./Sept. 2009

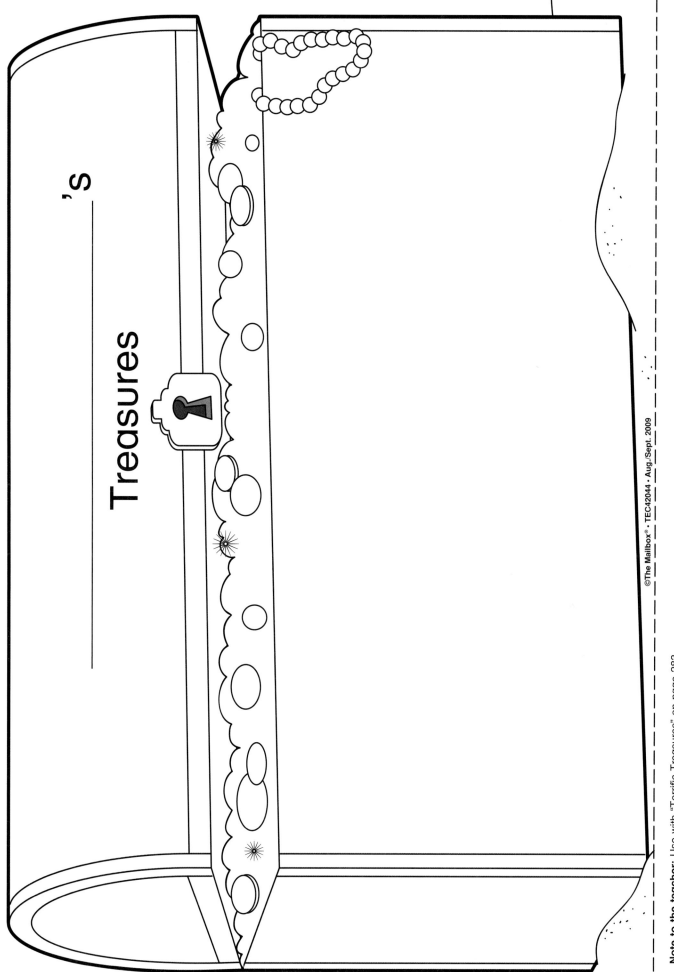

Treasures

's

©The Mailbox® • TEC42044 • Aug./Sept. 2009

Note to the teacher: Use with "Terrific Treasures" on page 283.

Treasures From
My First Day of Kindergarten

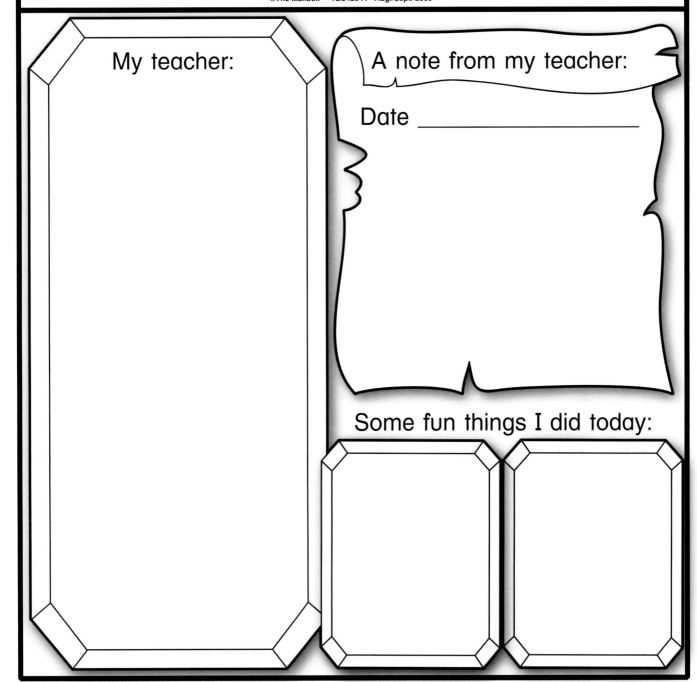

My teacher:

A note from my teacher:

Date _____

Some fun things I did today:

Seasonal Skill Practice
Bats

MATH AND SCIENCE
Yes or No?

Activate students' prior knowledge and reveal bat facts with this simple graphing activity. Write on the board a bat-related question and draw a two-column cave-shaped chart labeled as shown. Give each child a bat cutout (pattern on page 289). Read the question aloud. Have each child indicate her response by placing a bat in the corresponding column. Then use the provided information to guide a class discussion about students' answers. Encourage students to discuss the results of the graph and then reveal the correct answer. Remove the bats and continue with more bat-related questions. *Activating prior knowledge, graphing*

adapted from an idea by Christine Kellerman
Grandma's House, Brookfield, WI

Bat Facts
Bats sleep during the day and fly around at night.
Bats eat fruit or insects.
Bats have fur.
Bats sleep in caves.
Bats hang upside down.

> Do bats sleep at night?

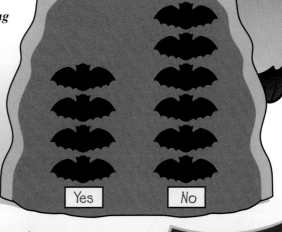

Yes   No

LITERACY
Wing by Wing

For this center, trace a copy of the bat pattern on page 289 onto black tagboard. Then cut out the tracing and draw a face. Place the bat at a center along with a cutout copy of the rhyming cards on page 289. A student chooses a picture and places the card on a wing. Then she finds the rhyming picture and places it on the other wing. After quietly saying the rhyming words, she removes the cards and continues with other rhyming pairs. **For an added challenge,** have the student write each rhyming pair on a sheet of paper. *Rhyming*

rock   lock

adapted from an idea by Jennie Jensen
Clarence, IA

Bats in Their Places

Give each child a copy of page 290. Have him cut out the bat cards at the bottom of the page. Then read aloud the directions below to direct students where to glue their bats. After they complete the page, encourage pairs of students to use positional words to tell each other about the location of the bats. *Positional words, following directions*

Ada Goren, Winston-Salem, NC

Directions:
1. Put a bat *above* the small tree.
2. Put a bat *below* the stars.
3. Put a bat *next to* the owl.
4. Put a bat *between* the trees.
5. Put a bat *on* the fence.
6. Put a bat *to the right* of the large tree's hole.

SCIENCE

Batty Facts

With this action poem, your youngsters will learn several facts about bats. For a literacy connection, give each child a copy of the poem. Have students circle "bat" or "bats" each time it appears in the poem. *Characteristics of bats*

Ada Goren

Bats fly around at night	*Flap arms.*
And sleep throughout the day.	*Rest head on folded hands.*
If a bat flies too close to you,	
You may want to run away!	*Run in place.*
Bats are helpful creatures.	*Put up index finger.*
They eat bugs, you know.	*Make eating motion with hand.*
But do not call a bat a bird.	*Wag finger back and forth.*
It has no feathers—no!	
Bats have furry bodies	*Flap arms.*
And hang down by their feet.	*Point to feet.*
Now, tell me, don't you think	*Shrug shoulders.*
That bats are kind of neat?	

LITERACY

Batty About Words

Use the bat pattern on page 289 to make several templates. Also display a large bat cave shape cut from bulletin board paper. Have each child trace a bat template, cut out the shape, and add facial features. Then choose an idea below.

Initial consonant *b*: Have students name words that begin with *b* like *bat*. Record students' responses on the board. After rereading the list aloud, direct each child to draw on a two-inch white paper square a word that begins with *b*. Help her add a label and glue the square to her bat. Display the bats on the cave with the title "Batty About *B*s."

Word family *-at*: Assign each student an onset that makes a word when combined with *-at*. Have her blend her onset with *-at* and use a white crayon to write the resulting word on her bat. Display the bats on the cave with the title "The *-at* Cave."

Kathryn Davenport, Partin Elementary, Oviedo, FL

Bat Pattern

Use with "Yes or No?" and "Wing by Wing" on page 287 and "Batty About Words" on page 288.

TEC42045

Rhyming Cards

Use with "Wing by Wing" on page 287.

bat TEC42045	hat TEC42045
car TEC42045	star TEC42045
bell TEC42045	shell TEC42045
pig TEC42045	wig TEC42045
lock TEC42045	rock TEC42045
bun TEC42045	sun TEC42045

Name _____

©The Mailbox® • TEC42045 • Oct./Nov. 2009

Note to the teacher: Use with "Bats in Their Places" on page 288.

Wrapped Up for the Holidays

ideas contributed by Ada Goren, Winston-Salem, NC

Add a Bow

For this center, use a black marker to write a different color word on each of several paper lunch bags. Place inside each bag a piece of construction paper in the corresponding color. Fold each bag to close it and slide a paper clip onto the fold. Also color a copy of a bow pattern from page 293 to match each bag. Place the bows and bags at a center. A child reads each color word and slides the matching bow under the paper clip. To check her work, she opens the bag to see whether the paper inside matches the bow. ***Color words***

red
yellow
green

Editor's Tip:
To keep the bags from easily tipping over, place a small wooden block in each one.

MATH

Gifts Galore

Wrap up lots of learning with activities that are easy to adapt to different skills! To prepare, gather holiday gift wrap in four different designs. Help each child wrap a large wooden block to make a pretend gift. Then use the gifts in the ideas below.

Graphing: Arrange graph labels, like the ones shown, on the floor. In turn, ask each youngster to place his gift in its corresponding graph column. After the object graph is complete, ask students graph-related questions.

Ordinal numbers: Have each child color a unique design on a copy of the bow pattern on page 293. Then have her tape it to her gift. Collect the gifts and line up ten of them. Next, ask ordinal number–related questions, such as, "Which gift has holly paper and a green and yellow bow?"

Patterning: Use some of the gifts to start a pattern. Then ask student volunteers to continue the pattern. For an added challenge, invite students to create patterns for their classmates to continue.

Giving gifts is fun to do.
Here's a gift from me to you.

Giving the Alphabet

These student-made gifts are full of letter practice! To make a gift, have each child fold a sheet of construction paper in half vertically. Then give used magazines and a different letter manipulative to each student. Direct her to cut out pictures of items whose names begin with her letter. Then have her glue the pictures to the inside of her paper. (Collect the letter manipulatives.) Encourage her to decorate the front of her folded paper to resemble a gift.

After students finish making their gifts, invite a child to stand as you lead the class in the rhyme shown to the right. At the end of the rhyme, instruct the child to open her gift and show her classmates. Have students name the pictures and identify their beginning letter. *Letter-sound correspondence*

I made a flower for Grammy.

MATH AND LITERACY

In the Bag

For this center, put a supply of pattern blocks in a gift bag. Place the bag, blank paper, and writing materials at a center. A child arranges the blocks on a sheet of paper to make a gift. He traces the outline of his creation and colors it. Then he writes or dictates a sentence about his gift. *Shapes, writing*

This gift is for
Mom

I will help set the table.

LITERACY

Priceless Presents

Incorporate gift giving and writing! Help youngsters understand that they can give gifts that don't cost money. Enlist students' help in coming up with a list of some of these special gifts, such as giving hugs and helping around the house. Then have each child write or dictate on a sheet of paper a sentence about a gift she would like to give to someone. Have her draw the gift. Then direct her to glue her drawing to a slightly larger sheet of gift wrap. Have her cut out and complete a copy of a gift tag pattern from page 293 and glue it on the gift. Invite students to share their finished projects with the class before giving them to their intended recipients. *Writing*

Gift Bow Patterns
Use with "Add a Bow" and "Gifts Galore" on page 291.

TEC42046

TEC42046

Gift Tag Patterns
Use with "Priceless Presents" on page 292.

This gift is for

_____.

TEC42046

This gift is for

_____.

TEC42046

Name _____

Wrap It Up!

✂ Cut.

🖊 Glue in order.

✏ Write. Use the word bank.

1	2	3

Word Bank

wrap

cut

tape

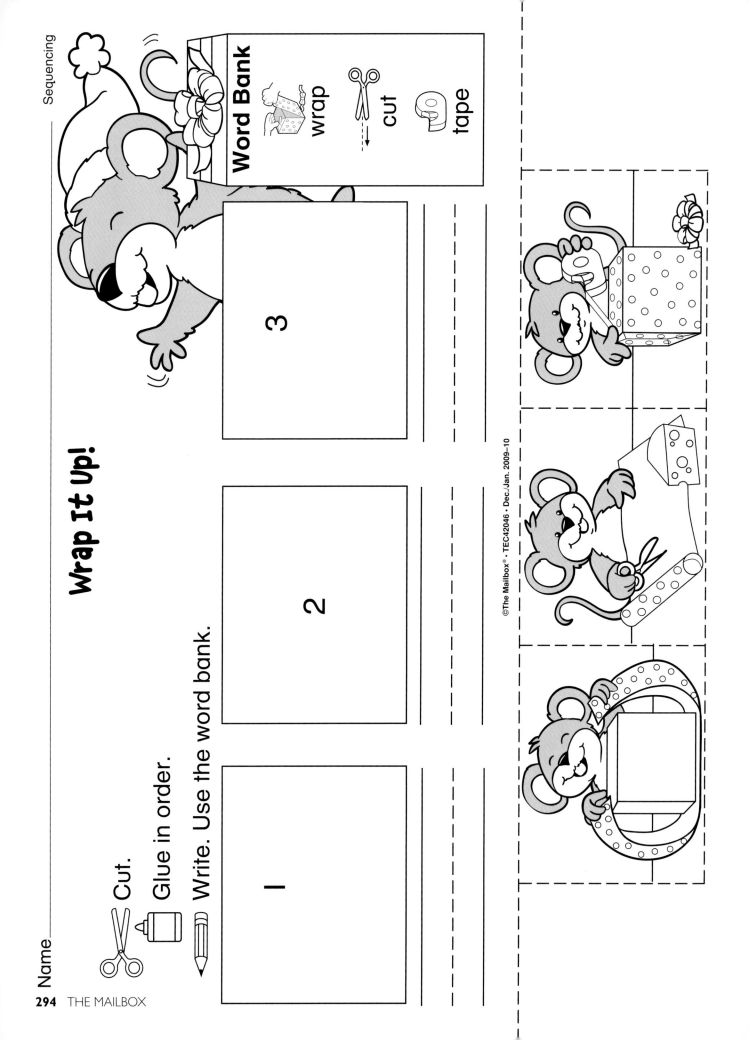

Pattern Wrap-Ups

 Color. ✂ Cut. Glue to finish the pattern.

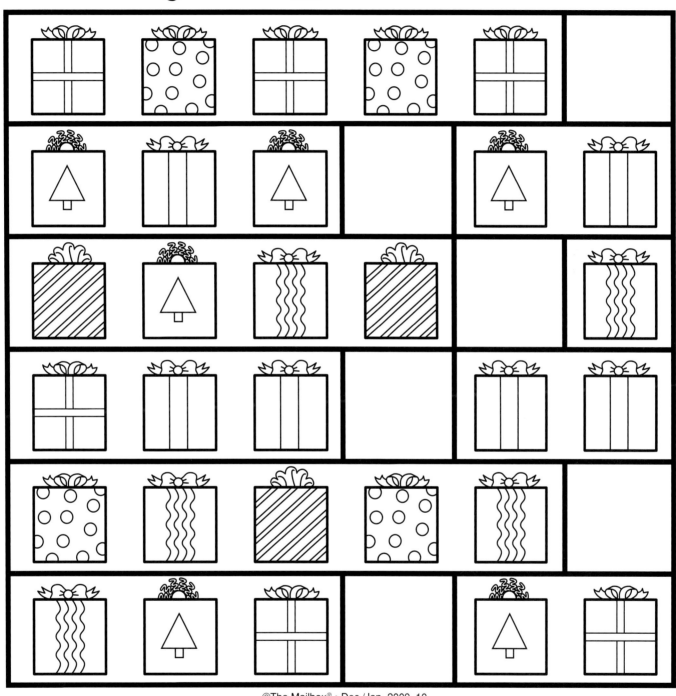

Seasonal Skill Practice
Candy

This delicious assortment of math and literacy ideas is sure to bring sweet success to your kindergarten classroom!

ideas contributed by Ada Goren, Winston-Salem, NC

MATH

What Do You Like?

Favorite candies are the inspiration for this class survey. To begin, write on the board a tally chart like the one shown. Then ask each child to draw on a blank card a picture of her favorite candy. (Or ask each student to bring in a candy wrapper and glue it to a card.) Collect the cards and display one card near the tally chart. In turn, invite each student to draw a tally under the column of her choice, providing guidance as needed. After the tally chart is complete, have youngsters help total the tally marks in each column. Discuss the results and repeat the activity with a different candy card. ***Tally chart***

Do you like it?

Yes | No

Marsh-mal-low.

LITERACY

Pass the Candy

This fun circle-time rhyme is a real treat! To begin, pass a candy box around the circle and lead youngsters in the chant shown. At the end of the chant, have students stop passing the box and then name a candy (see the list). Direct the child holding the box to slowly repeat the candy name as his classmates clap the number of syllables. After the child holding the box announces the number of syllables, continue passing and chanting for additional rounds. ***Syllables***

Candy's yummy; candy's sweet.
Candy is a treat to eat!
Count the word parts that you hear.
Name this candy loud and clear.

Candy Names	
gum	gumdrop
mint	lollipop
fudge	marshmallow
taffy	licorice
toffee	caramel

Sweet Shop

Students pretend to fill candy orders at this center! To prepare, make candy orders by writing on separate blank cards each number word from one to ten. Place the cards at a center along with an empty heart-shaped candy box (or a large heart cutout) and a supply of large pom-poms (candy). A child reads the number word on a candy order and places the matching number of candies in the box. After checking his work, he removes the candies from the box and repeats the activity with another candy order. **For an easier version,** program the cards with the number word and the numeral. *Number words*

five

Editor's Tip:
For added fun, invite one child at the center to act as the store clerk and another to act as a customer. Also set out store-themed items such as a cash register, an apron, and shopping bags.

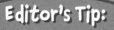

1¢
5¢
10¢
25¢

MATH

Coins for Candy

To prepare for this partner game, have each child cut out a copy of the lotto gameboard and coin cards from page 298. Assign each youngster a partner; then have the students mix their coin cards together and stack them facedown. To take a turn, a child draws a card and places it faceup on the matching value on her board. If the corresponding space is already covered, she puts the card at the bottom of the deck and her turn ends. Play continues until each child covers all four spaces on her board. *Coins and their values*

LITERACY

Frame It!

With this idea, students are sure to learn their high-frequency words by heart! Make a heart pointer by forming a pipe cleaner into a heart shape and attaching it to the end of an unsharpened pencil or dowel rod. Copy the poem shown onto chart paper. After repeated readings of the poem, name a high-frequency word from the text and invite a child to use the heart pointer to frame the word. Continue with more words as time allows. **For an added challenge,** have each youngster write the featured words on a sheet of paper titled "Words I Know by Heart." *High-frequency words*

Ten candy hearts on Valentine's Day.

Ten candy hearts to give away.

I gave one to my mom and one to my dad.

My dog ate two—that was bad!

I gave one to my teacher and three to my friends.

But that's not where the story ends.

How many hearts are left? Just two!

One for me and one for you!

Lotto Board and Coin Cards

Use with "Coins for Candy" on page 297.

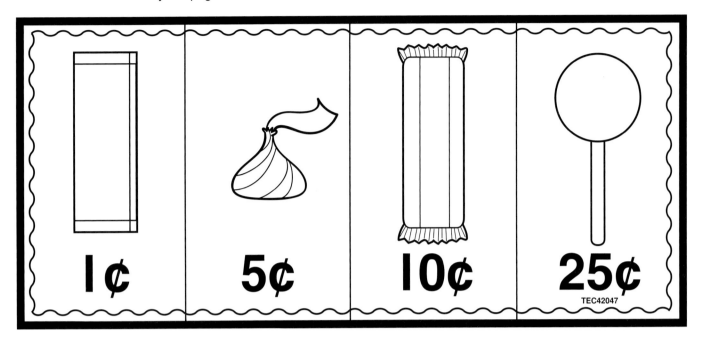

1¢	**5¢**	**10¢**	**25¢**

TEC42047

Name _____

So Much Candy!

Listen for directions.

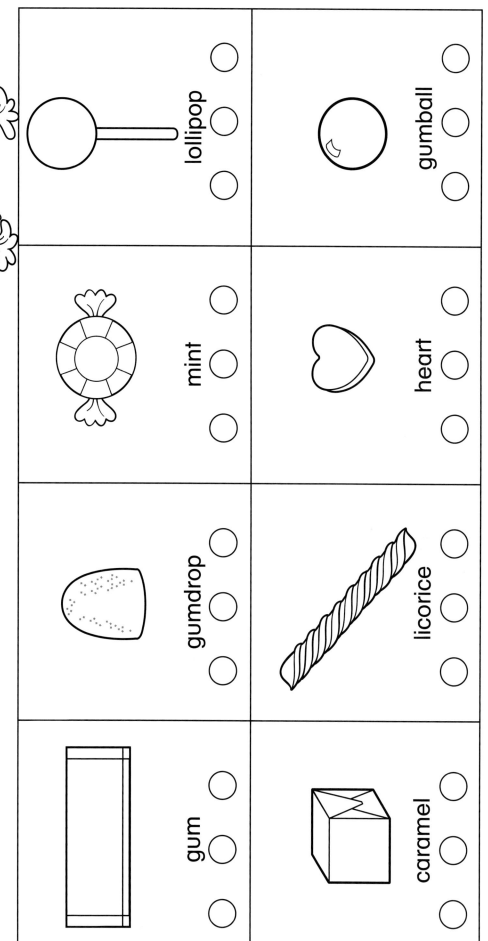

lollipop

mint

gumdrop

gum

gumball

heart

licorice

caramel

©The Mailbox® • TEC42047 • Feb./Mar. 2010

Note to the teacher: Give each child a copy of this page. Then name each candy in turn. Have each child color a ◯ for each syllable.

Seasonal Skill Practice
Showers and Flowers

When it rains literacy, math, and science, your youngsters are sure to bloom!

From Root to Flower

Teach students this song to help them remember the parts of a plant and the order in which they grow. While singing the song, post a copy of the cards from page 302. If desired, give each child a copy of the cards to manipulate while singing. *Parts of a plant*

(sung to the tune of "Head and Shoulders")

Roots, stem, leaves, and flowers make a plant.
Roots, stem, leaves, and flowers make a plant.
This is the order in which a plant grows.
Roots, stem, leaves, and flowers make a plant!

Jenn Daub
St. John the Baptist Catholic School
Longmont, CO

Raindrops and Roses

Rain showers make beautiful roses grow at this center. Program a sheet of paper with the sentence shown; then copy it to make a class supply. At a center, place the papers, blue and red washable ink pads, and a green marker. A child makes blue raindrop prints and red rose prints (using the green marker to draw stems) on her paper. When she is satisfied with her work, she counts the flowers and raindrops and then completes the sentence. *Comparing sets*

Angie Kutzer
Garrett Elementary
Mebane, NC

There are more ☐ than ☐ .

To the Top!

Before introducing this partner game, guide students to understand that in order for most seeds to grow into plants, they need water, soil, air, and light. Brainstorm with youngsters different ways that a seed meets its needs, such as getting light from the sun or a lamp and getting water from rain or a hose.

To prepare for the game, give each twosome a copy of page 303 and two game markers. After the partners cut out the cards and gameboards and stack the cards facedown, have each partner take a gameboard. To play, each player places his marker on his gameboard's seed. The first player takes a card and, if the card shows something that helps a seed grow into a plant, he moves his game marker up one space along the stem. If it is an item that a seed does not need, he sets the card aside and his turn is over. Players reshuffle the cards as needed. Alternate play continues until one child reaches the flower. *Basic needs of a plant*

Angie Kutzer, Garrett Elementary, Mebane, NC

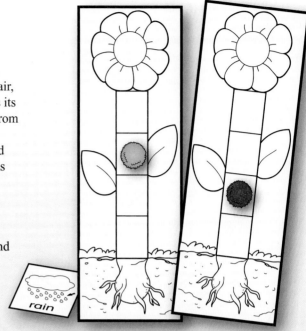

rain

MATH

Flower Arrangements

To prepare for this center, program cards with different addition problems. Place at a center the cards, a vase cutout, flower blossoms (large pom-poms or flower cutouts) in two different colors, and paper. A student places a card on the vase and then places flowers above the vase to model the addition problem. After writing the number sentence on a sheet of paper, she removes the flowers and card and plays again. *Addition*

Angie Kutzer

Editor's Tip:
Set out green pipe cleaners for youngsters to use as flower stems.

LITERACY

The Shower Shuffle

Youngsters pretend to be raindrops in this whole-group activity. To prepare, program a class supply of raindrop cutouts (patterns on page 302) with words from three different word families. (Repeat words as needed.) Draw three clouds on the board and label each one with one of the chosen word families. To begin, give each youngster a raindrop and have students gather together to form a rain cloud. Then clap your hands to represent a rain shower. As you clap, students disperse and each child lines up behind the cloud with the matching word family. After each student reads her word, collect and then redistribute the raindrops to prepare for another shower! **For independent practice,** place the raindrops and labeled cloud cutouts at a center. *Word families*

Angie Kutzer

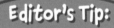

Plant Part Cards
Use with "From Root to Flower" on page 300.

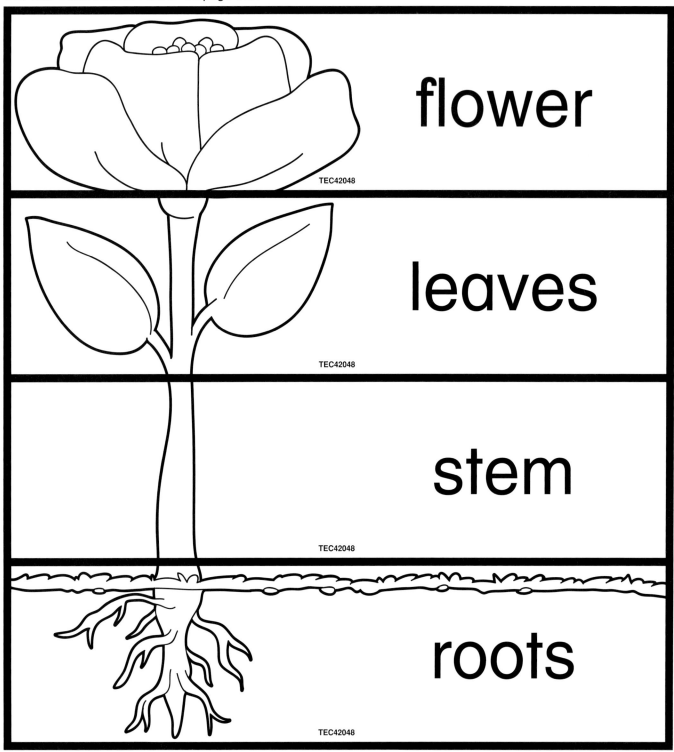

flower

TEC42048

leaves

TEC42048

stem

TEC42048

roots

TEC42048

Raindrop Patterns
Use with "The Shower Shuffle" on page 301.

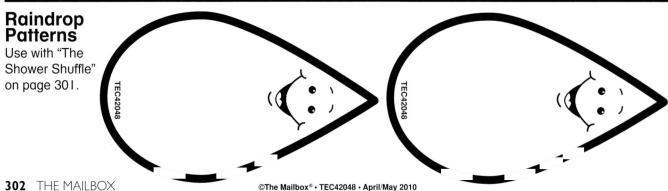

TEC42048

TEC42048

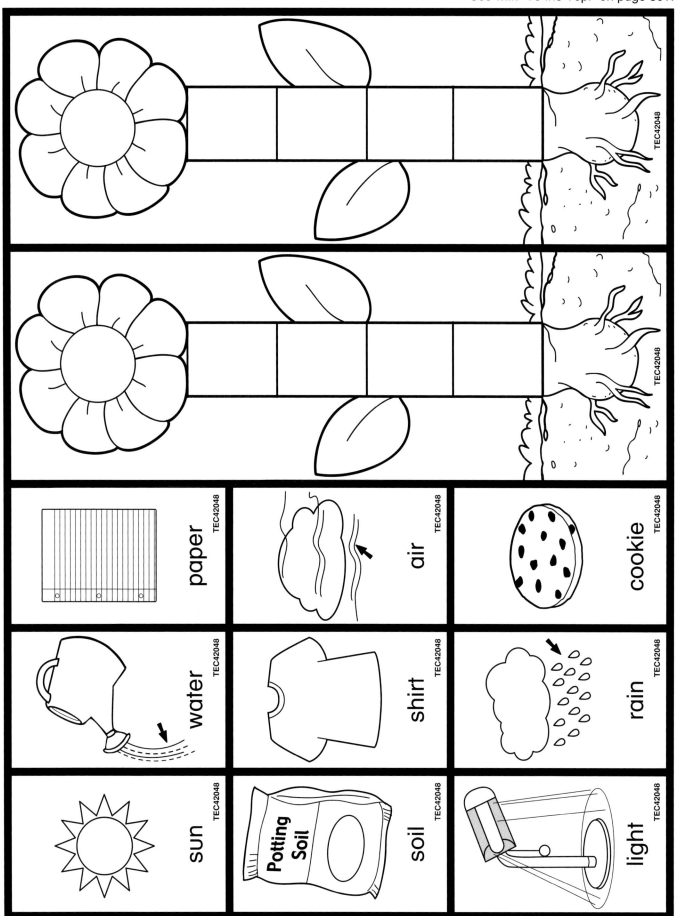

paper

air

cookie

water

shirt

rain

sun

soil

light

Name_____   Word families: -ip, -op

Drip, Drop!

✏️ Write **ip** or **op** to make each word.

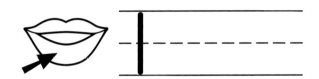 l _ _ _ _

 d _ _ _ _

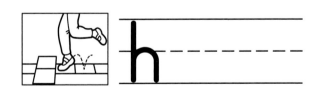 h _ _ _ _

r _ _ _ _

ch _ _ _ _

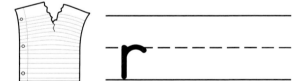 p _ _ _ _

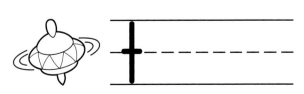 t _ _ _ _

 ch _ _ _ _

Seasonal Skill Practice
The Beach

Make a splash with this cool collection of ocean-side activities.

ideas contributed by Jennie Jensen, Clarence, IA

SCIENCE

Ocean Motion

Your kindergartners will be eager to participate in several verses of this action-packed song! Discuss the different ocean animals in the song shown and the way they move in the water. Next, guide youngsters to practice an associated action to match each suggested song verse. Then lead students in singing the first two verses, encouraging them to perform each established action. For each subsequent verse, replace the underlined text with the suggestions shown. ***Activating prior knowledge, animal behavior***

(sung to the tune of "The Mulberry Bush")

There are lots of animals,
Animals, animals.
There are lots of animals
Moving in the ocean!

This is the way the [blue crab crawls],
[Blue crab crawls], [blue crab crawls].
This is the way the [blue crab crawls],
[Crawling] in the ocean.

Continue with the following:
starfish moves, moving
dolphin jumps, jumping
orca dives, diving
stingray flaps, flapping
seahorse sways, swaying
white shark chomps, chomping
jellyfish swims, swimming

LITERACY AND MATH

Colorful Crabs

Youngsters read color words to solve these crab-related addition problems. Give each child a copy of page 307. Have her color each crab card on the bottom of the page to match its color word; then instruct her to cut out the cards.

To form the first addition sentence on the page, a youngster sorts the crab cards to find the red crabs and the blue crabs. Then she writes the total number of each color of crab under the matching crab and solves the problem. She repeats the process for each remaining problem. ***Reading color words, addition with manipulatives***

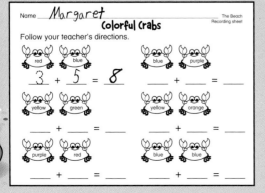

Name: Margaret

Colorful Crabs

The Beach
Recording sheet

Follow your teacher's directions.

red + blue = $3 + 5 = 8$

blue + purple = ___

yellow + green = ___

yellow + orange = ___

purple + red = ___

blue + blue = ___

Beach Bag Words

To prepare for this small-group activity, tape a word family ending card of your choice on a beach towel (or a beach towel cutout). Put several letter cards, most of which form real words when coupled with the rime, in a beach bag. Place the bag on the towel. To begin, invite a child to remove a card from the bag. Have her place the letter card in front of the rime to form a word. Then instruct her to read the word and tell whether it is a real word or a nonsense word. After confirming her answer, have her set the card aside. Continue with each remaining card. *Word families*

Sip is a real word!

There are three shells on the beach. Two more shells wash up on the shore. How many shells are on the beach altogether?

Solve It by the Seashore

Have each child draw and color a beach scene on a sheet of paper to make a math mat. Give each student ten large shell-pasta pieces (seashells). Then tell a math-related story that specifies the number of shells that washed up on the shore (addition) or the number of shells that washed away (subtraction). Have each youngster model the story on her math mat and then count the total number of shells on the shore. Continue with different stories as time allows. *Story problems with manipulatives*

Shells and Pails

Select one or more of these center-time activities for an end-of-the-year review.

Rhyming: On a copy of page 308, cut apart the bottom two rows of cards. Place the cards at a center. A student sorts to match each rhyming pair. **For a more advanced version,** include cards that do not rhyme (distracters) and have students place the distracters in a sand pail.

Vowel discrimination: Select a vowel, such as *a*. Then write "ă" and "not ă" on separate cards and tape each card to an individual pail. Cut out a copy of the cards on page 308. Set out the /ă/ picture cards, a few more cards, and the two pails. A student sorts the cards into the corresponding pails.

Vowel identification: Label two to five pails each with a different short vowel. Place the corresponding cards from a copy of page 308 at the center. (Set any remaining cards aside.) A student sorts each card into the matching pail.

Spelling CVC words: Set out a desired number of picture cards from a copy of page 308. Write the corresponding letters needed to spell each word on individual cards. A student names the picture on each card and uses the letter cards to spell the word.

Colorful Crabs

Follow your teacher's directions.

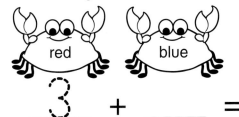 

$\underset{3}{\rule{2cm}{0.4pt}}$ + _____ = _____   _____ + _____ = _____

_____ + _____ = _____   _____ + _____ = _____

_____ + _____ = _____   _____ + _____ = _____

©The Mailbox® • TEC42049 • June/July 2010

red	yellow	green	yellow	blue
blue	orange	yellow	green	red
yellow	blue	purple	blue	orange
blue	green	yellow	red	yellow

Note to the teacher: Use with "Colorful Crabs" on page 305.

Shell Picture Cards

Use with "Shells and Pails" on page 306.

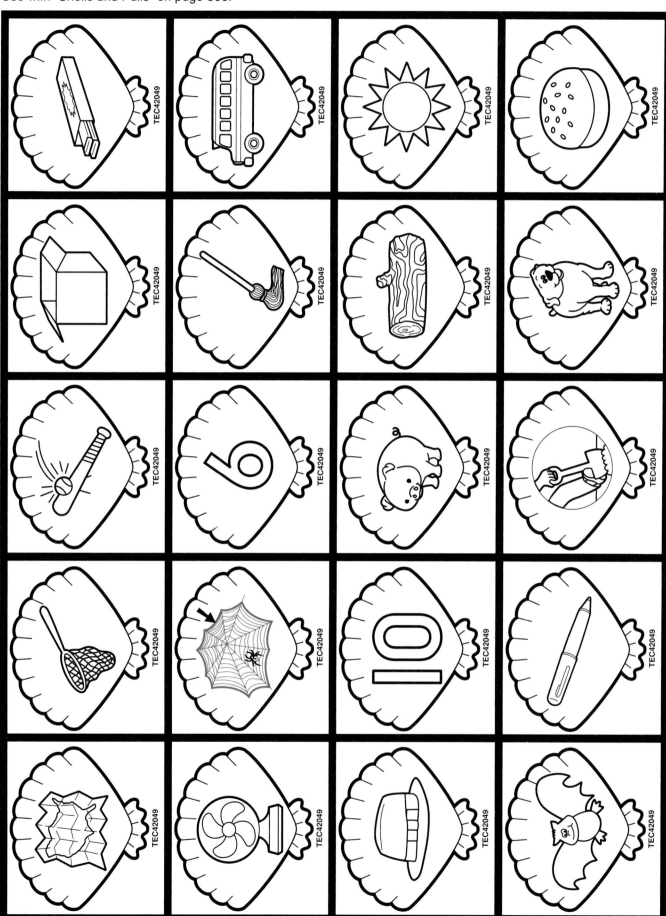

Name _____

Fun in the Sun

 Cut.

Glue to make **-un** words.

©The Mailbox® • TEC42049 • June/July 2010

f	b	r	s
un	un	un	un

☆ Give a Cheer for the End of the Year ☆

Students are sure to applaud these year-end ideas.

☆ Sign Here! ☆

Making these individual **autograph books** is a perfect way for students to collect their classmates' signatures. For each child, staple four pages between two construction paper covers. Then give each child a booklet and a copy of page 312. Have her personalize, color, and cut out the booklet cover and glue it to the front construction paper cover of her booklet. Then have her color and cut out the page headings and use a glue stick to glue each one to a separate page. Set aside a designated time for students to autograph their classmates' booklets.

Amy Lashlee, Hampton Oaks Elementary, Stafford, VA

☆ Scrap Box Creatures ☆

Use up your excess art supplies and scrap paper with this end-of-the-year **art project**! Place extra materials—such as paper, feathers, fabric, yarn, jumbo beads, and large buttons—in a large box. Then invite each child to choose desired materials from the box to make a silly creature. When each child's project is complete, invite youngsters to show and describe their projects to the class. **For an added challenge,** invite students to write stories or descriptions about their creatures.

Mary Ann Gildroy, Roundup, MT

☆ Beach Bucket Souvenirs ☆

Your kindergartners will really dig this **gift idea!** Personalize a plastic beach pail for each child. Inside the pails place items such as plastic shovels, sweet treats, or crayons. If desired, invite students to autograph their classmates' buckets with permanent markers. Youngsters will be eager to use these keepsakes throughout the summer!

adapted from an idea by Tracey Mikos
Sacred Heart School
New Smyrna Beach, FL

☆ Classy Keepsakes ☆

Encourage positive behavior right until the last day of school with this **management idea.** Put on display items such as class-made books and projects. When you see a youngster exhibiting especially good behavior, have him write his name on a "ticket" and place it in a designated box. At the end of each day, draw one or two names from the container and invite the winning student(s) to choose a book or project to take home as a memento.

Angie Kutzer
Garrett Elementary
Mebane, NC

☆ Spotlight on Teachers! ☆

This **display idea** helps students get to know the teachers they may have next year. Near the end of the school year, feature a different first-grade teacher each week as the Star of the Week. Ask the teacher to complete a short questionnaire detailing his favorite things. Then share it with the class and display it with a photo of him on a poster like the one shown. At a convenient time, invite the teacher to visit the classroom. During this time, have him share additional information with youngsters, answer their questions, and read his favorite story aloud.

Jodi Darter, Cabool Elementary, Cabool, MO

☆ Bye-Bye, Kindergarten! ☆

Wrap up the end of the school year by leading youngsters in singing this catchy **farewell song.**

(sung to the tune of "Baa, Baa, Black Sheep")

Bye-bye, classroom; now the year is through.
First grade, first grade, moving on to you!
I know how to count and write ABCs.
I'll do well in first grade—just you wait and see!
Bye-bye, classroom; now the year is through.
First grade, first grade, moving on to you!

Kim Minafo, Apex, NC

Booklet Cover and Page Headings
Use with "Sign Here!" on page 310.

_____'s

name

Kindergarten Autographs

20_____ –20_____

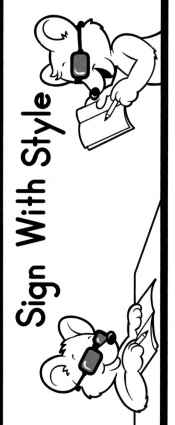

Sign With Style

Friends Are Fabulous!

Stunning Signatures

Awesome Autographs!